Liminality in
Fantastic Fiction

Liminality in Fantastic Fiction
A Poststructuralist Approach

SANDOR KLAPCSIK

McFarland & Company, Inc., Publishers
Jefferson, North Carolina, and London

LIBRARY OF CONGRESS CATALOGUING-IN-PUBLICATION DATA

Klapcsik, Sandor
    Liminality in fantastic fiction : a poststructuralist approach / Sandor Klapcsik.
       p.   cm.
    Includes bibliographical references and index.

    ISBN 978-0-7864-6473-9
    softcover : acid free paper ∞

    1. Fantasy fiction — History and criticism. 2. Liminality in literature. 3. Poststructuralism. I. Title.
PN3435.K59 2012
809.3'876 — dc23   2011037861

BRITISH LIBRARY CATALOGUING DATA ARE AVAILABLE

© 2012 Sandor Klapcsik. All rights reserved

No part of this book may be reproduced or transmitted in any form or by any means, electronic or mechanical, including photocopying or recording, or by any information storage and retrieval system, without permission in writing from the publisher.

Cover image ©2012 Brand X Pictures

Manufactured in the United States of America

McFarland & Company, Inc., Publishers
  Box 611, Jefferson, North Carolina 28640
    www.mcfarlandpub.com

Contents

Preface	1
Introduction: The Significance of Liminality in Popular Fiction	7
1. Liminality and the Fantastic in Agatha Christie's Detective Stories	31
2. Liminal Fantasy in Neil Gaiman's Fiction	54
3. Stanislaw Lem: Liminality and the Revenge of the Mirror on Alien Planets	84
4. Philip K. Dick: Urbanity, Liminality, Multiplicity	121
Conclusion: Converging and Diverging Manifestations of Liminality and Multiplicity	163
Notes	173
Bibliography	181
Index	197

Preface

It seems almost like an axiom that postmodernism brings about new spatial, temporal, and social paradigms, in which distinct categories and solid borderlines are highly questioned. As Paul Smethurst observes in *The Postmodern Chronotope*, "Postmodernism can be conceived as a shift in the indicators of space and time" (2), a shift that brings about a situation in which "simple operations in the phenomenal world that require differentiation, between for example, past and present, inside and outside, real and representational, have become problematic" (1). This spatiotemporal ambiguity is fostered by, or at least coincides with, cultural processes under which the limits between high art and low art, author and reader, reality and simulated world, factual and fictional history, realism and the fantastic, erode. The present work centers upon this perceptual and cultural virtualization, "de-differentiation" (Smethurst 72–74), cognitive and social uncertainty, by connecting it with various theoretical understandings and practices of liminality.

Liminality has been approached by various theories, such as Victor Turner's cultural anthropology, Derridean deconstruction, Lacanian psychoanalysis, Foucauldian and Deleuzian philosophy, feminism, postcolonialism, Baudrillardian and Marxist social theories, media studies, narratology, phenomenology, and cultural studies. It would be a highly problematic task to combine these — in certain ways incompatible — theories to produce a general model of liminality; yet, I firmly believe that they can be utilized to reconstitute the notion, especially if one uses them only as "a box of tools" or "toolkit"— the way Michel Foucault and Gilles Deleuze intended their arguments to be used (Foucault and Deleuze 208; Foucault, "Confinement" 197 and "Power" 143–145; O'Farrell 50–60). Thus, I draw on these theories, focusing on poststructuralist philosophies, deconstruction, psychoanalysis, and narratology, to provide an ontological and epistemological foundation for understanding and analyzing the practices of liminality.

As J. Hillis Miller stresses, "The place we inhabit, wherever we are, is always this in-between zone, place of host and parasite, neither inside nor outside" (154). The contemporary interest in liminality also coincides with the rise of postmodern geography, postmodernity becoming "the epoch of space" (Foucault, "Of Other" 22), which emphasizes the interrelatedness, the "triple dialectic," of space, time, and social being (Soja 12).

My assertion is that liminality is as much present and influential in fiction and philosophy as in architecture, urban planning and social life. It is detectable in the entirety of Henri Lefebvre's famous triad: "spatial practice," "representations of space" and "representational spaces" (38–39). My main focus is on representational spaces, the liminal chronotope in detective fiction, science fiction and fantasy as well as literary studies and philosophy, even though occasionally the anthropological (Chapter 1 and 2) and social-architectural (Chapter 4) implications of liminality are also discussed in my textual analyses.

In Turner's anthropological theory, the liminal and liminoid phase is a temporary intermediary period in the life of the individual, that of the tribe and modern society. In my work, liminality gains a broader meaning and becomes a spatial model or metaphor that refers to a wide range of spatial, temporal, perceptual, narratological, and social phenomena. It coincides with the (hypothetical) erosion of boundaries in our postmodernist mediasphere: the fading boundaries between high culture and low culture, real and virtual, human and mechanical, the self and the Other, the Object and Subject of representation.

Liminality also pivots on theories of the fantastic, especially those approaches that foreground the limits and transgressions of the genre as well as the frequent, ever-increasing phenomenon of genre crossing (Todorov, *The Fantastic* 41–44; Jackson 3–4, 26–37; Fenkl iii-viii; Mendlesohn, *Rhetorics* 182–245; Malmgren, *Worlds Apart* 139–168; Clute, "Canary Fever" 226–27). In textual criticism, liminality evokes ambiguous, multiplied narrative perspectives and the reader's oscillation between them by way of irony, metafiction, oblique intertextuality (hypertextuality, pastiche), and metalepsis. "On the map of the narrative, as on the map of the world, boundaries are everywhere," as Marie-Laure Ryan says ("Stacks" 873), but in postmodern texts the boundary crossing becomes complex, covert, and disorderly. Embeddings and textual allusions most often entail ambiguity and double coding and so the reader finds blurred "windows" instead of apparent "gates" between the narrative levels (Kafalenos 11–15). Thus, the fictional worlds and events "remain in a kind of limbo" (McHale, *Constructing* 117).

Recent narrative and spatial models concomitantly emphasize liminality: as Michel de Certeau observes in his work on spatial practices, "In the story, the frontier functions as a third element. It is an 'in-between'—a 'space between' ... [a] middle place, composed of interactions and inter-views ... a narrative symbol of exchanges and encounters" (127).

In poststructuralist theories and deconstruction, liminality and postcolonial hybridity consist in an "undecidable oscillation" between binary oppositions (Miller 155), which questions stable identities, hierarchies, and antitheses that have been dominant in human reasoning for centuries or millennia. In Lacanian and feminist psychoanalysis, a similar oscillation is found in the mirroring process and the fort-da play of the infantile subject, which questions the established boundaries between the self and its imago, between (castrated) male and female images, leading to "the birth of the long love affair/despair between image and self-image" (Mulvey 202).

In social theories, liminal and "fluid" urban spaces mediate between nature and production, the local and global market, private and public sphere (Lefebvre 83–88) when they "stand 'betwixt and between' institutions, especially the sacred sphere of culture and the secular world of commerce" (Zukin 41). In postmodern architecture, liminality is simultaneously progressive and nostalgic (Boym 80), embodying a "temporal to-and-fro" movement (Foster 513); "labyrinthine, rambling, without a definite goal, a liminal or in-between space that mediates between pairs of antinomies," creating "a new urban grammar" of overlaps, zigzagging, and "oscillating waves" (Jencks 91, 213).

Based on these approaches, I will define liminality for my own readings and research in the next chapter. I will interpret the term as a *constant oscillation*, crossing back and forth, between social, textual, and cultural positions. I also identify it with the space of continuous transference, an *infinite process* formed by *transgressions* across evanescent, porous, evasive borderlines. Furthermore, I explore liminality amid the multiplicity of domains and timelines, in the "garden of forking paths," in multiply embedded narratives, and rhizomes.

I utilize this interpretation of liminality to analyze the multiplication of perspectives and decentered, heterogeneous, and pluralized spatial and temporal formations in literary and cultural criticism as well as in postmodernist fiction — in particular, when "mainstream" novels, detective fiction, fantasy, horror, and science fiction interact with each other.

This query integrates several more specific questions, for example, how is liminality conceived in terms of structuralist and poststructuralist interpretations of space, time, mobility, narrative, and social relations? How are liminal space, time, social phenomena, reversed and in-between hierarchies interrelated, and how are they manifested in 20th century and contemporary fiction? How does liminality buttress, undermine and deconstruct dual oppositions? What are the differences and similarities between the rational, supposedly structured worlds of detective fiction and the frequently irrational, fluid, magical, uncontrollably multiplied worlds of fantasy and science fiction? How are in-between zones influenced by modern and postmodern paradigms? How are thematic and narrative liminality as well as genre crossings interrelated? How does liminality affect the pluralization of perspectives and that of worlds? Which forms of liminality and multiplicity can we detect in texts that precede the cultural turn of postmodernism? How is liminal and multiplied space related to the itinerant subject's movements across alternate realities?

What creates the most complex conundrum for this work is the following: *how to understand liminality if we have managed to free ourselves from dual structures and we conceptualize and live on the multiplicity of spatial, temporal, and social plateaus?* More specifically, in this cultural condition, how is liminality manifested in the literature of the modern and postmodern era, rational and fantastic fiction, mainstream and popular genres?

Several critics, such as Brian McHale, Fredric Jameson, and Scott Bukatman, take it as their starting point that one of the most fruitful ways to characterize postmodern fiction and literary themes, contemporary social and cultural phenomena, is by drawing on and exploring fantastic genres such as science fiction, horror, and fantasy. Cultural, ethnic, or gender hybridity is frequently symbolized by monsters and cyborgs, ontological heterogeneity is manifested by extraterrestrial and alternate worlds, weakened historicity by alternate histories. Thus, to investigate the above questions, I analyze contemporary fantasy (Neil Gaiman) and somewhat "classical" as well as postmodern science fiction (Stanislaw Lem and Philip K. Dick) in my book. My claim is that liminality provides a key to opening up their texts — or, conversely, their texts crucially contribute to our contemporary understanding of liminality.

Following McHale, it could easily be argued that several, mainly ontological, aspects of the liminal and multiple worlds came into focus in the second half of the 20th century. The fiction of Jorge Luis Borges, Julio Cortazar, Robert Coover, Paul Auster, Kurt Vonnegut, E. L. Doctorow, Angela Carter, Martin Amis, John Fowles, Umberto Eco, Italo Calvino, and many others, explicitly illustrates the contemporary and postmodern ontological interest in liminal and multiple zones.

Nevertheless, I also emphasize and I am extremely interested in the roots of liminality in literature prior to postmodernity. In a way similar to other textual and cultural qualities that are put forward as distinctively postmodern, liminality can be traced back to the literary and artistic scene centuries before. Laurence Sterne's *Tristram Shandy* (1759–1767), Gothic fiction, Mary Shelley's *Frankenstein, or The Modern Prometheus* (1818), Washington Irving's "Rip Van Winkle" (1819), a large number of E. T. A. Hoffmann's, Nikolai V. Gogol's, and Edgar Allan Poe's short stories, Sheridan Le Fanu's fiction, Fyodor Dostoyevsky's *The Possessed* (1872), Oscar Wilde's *The Picture of Dorian Grey* (1890), Charlotte Perkins Gilman's "The Yellow Wallpaper" (1892), H. G. Wells's works such as "The Plattner Story" (1896), "The Crystal Egg" (1897), and "The Door in the Wall" (1906), Henry James's *The Turn of the Screw* (1898), Hope Mirrlees's *Lud-in-the-Mist* (1926), Franz Kafka's writings, Mikhail Bulgakov's *The Master and Margarita* (1967), and numerous other mainstream and genre works, already experimented with or prefigured liminality.

In many of these texts, the narration and multiple embeddings are undermined and the horror of liminality is thematically foregrounded. Ghosts and other supernatural characters, fantastic events and places infiltrate the textual world; yet, they usually only *threaten* the reality of the text and do not alter its ontology fundamentally, unlike later in postmodernism. As the protagonist of James's *The Turn of the Screw* points out, the fantastic and liminal characters are "seen only across, as it were, and beyond — in strange places and on high places, the top of towers, the roof of houses, the outside of windows, the further edge of pools; but there is a deep design, on either side, to shorten the distance and overcome the obstacle" (54). The distance is definitely shortened and the obstacles are highly downplayed in postmodernism: liminality and alternate worlds become more apparent and tangible in recent fiction.

I chose to concentrate on one particular trend and genre in literature which prefigures the postmodern understanding and practice of liminality. This trend is detective fiction, whose rationality, order, and expectable narrative structure in many ways form the opposite of postmodern and fantastic narratives. Nevertheless, the rules, frames, borders, and restrictions of mystery fiction are not as strict and stable as they seem to be. I read Agatha Christie's oeuvre as a paradigmatic example that displays several signs of liminal spaces, periods, genres, narratives, and characters. (Even though liminality often remains hidden, implicit, "seen only across," in her fiction.) Furthermore, I identify and explore the influence of detective fiction in the works of Gaiman, Lem, and Dick, which thus become, to a certain extent, "metaphysical" detective stories in my interpretation.

This work is an hors d'oeuvre — it intends to serve as an introduction to liminality in postmodern culture and fantastic fiction. Only certain foremost trends in fantasy and science fiction are described, and neither of these genres can be fully covered. Several other trends and genres — spy fiction, horror, cyberpunk — are only mentioned on a few pages, although they could be discussed from this aspect in detail. I hope, however, that by choosing and analyzing paradigmatic examples and authors, I will be able to draw attention to the significance of liminality in contemporary culture and society.

I would like to thank the University of Debrecen, without which it would have been impossible to commence this research, the Fulbright Commission of Hungary for my fellowship at the University of Minnesota, which helped me continue the work after my studies in Debrecen, and the Research Centre for Contemporary Culture at the University of Jyväskylä in Finland, which helped me finish the project. I am personally indebted to Erzsébet Berta, Andy Sawyer, Michael Levy, Donald E. Morse, Gary K. Wolfe, Jack Zipes, Matt Hills, Brian McHale, and above all Erkki Vainikkala as well as our colleagues and friends at Jyväskylä, for helping me at times with various pieces of advice on my research topics.

Introduction: The Significance of Liminality in Popular Fiction

> We all like to congregate ... at boundary conditions.... Where land meets water. Where earth meets air. Where space meets time. We like to be on one side, and look at the other. (Douglas Adams)

> The intertwinement of social spaces is also a law. Considered in isolation, such spaces are mere abstractions.... Visible boundaries, such as walls or enclosures in general, give rise for their part to an appearance of separation between spaces where in fact what exists is an ambiguous continuity. (Henri Lefebvre)

Definitions and Theories: Divergent and Convergent Interpretations of Liminality

According to *Merriam-Webster's Dictionary*, the adjective "liminal" has three meanings: it may refer to a "sensory threshold," something "barely perceptible," or to a transitional "intermediate state, phase, or condition." The word goes back to "limen," which means threshold in Latin. In psychology, limen means a *limit* below which a stimulus ceases to be perceptible. Thus, these definitions indicate that liminality is strictly related to perception or the lack of it, and to limits as well as to the breach of limits, transgression.

The notion of liminality, as it is most often understood in literary criticism and cultural studies today, dates back to Turner's anthropological theory, his comparative symbology. Turner, in his essay "Liminal to Liminoid, in Play, Flow, Ritual," draws on Arnold van Gennep's definition of the "rites of passage," in which three separate phases are distinguished: separation, liminality, and re-incorporation. The notion of liminality thus would be a period of social transition, either that of the tribal subject or that of the community itself, when "the ritual subjects pass through a period of ambiguity, a sort of social limbo" (24). This process is often reflected in "spatial symbolism," as the transition in status is accompanied by spatial transference, which results in "a geographical movement from one place to another. This may take the form of a mere opening of doors or the literal crossing of a threshold which separates two distinct areas" (25).

Thus, liminality indicates a shift from point A to point B, from a primary to a more matured status: from the dwelling of the uninitiated novice to that of the initiated, full-fledged member of the group.

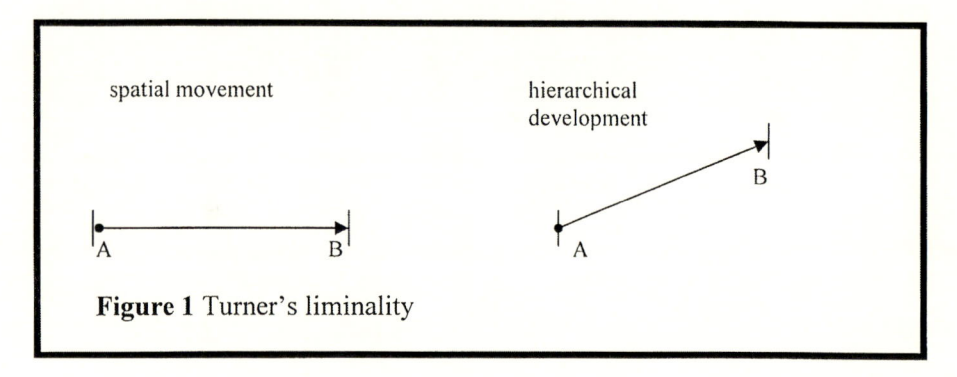

Figure 1 Turner's liminality

Turner also emphasizes the significance of *play* during liminality. He argues that one of the crucial differences between tribal and industrialist societies is the application of playful activities: while modern industrial society has produced a clear division between work and play, in "the liminal phases and states of tribal and agrarian cultures ... work and play are hardly distinguishable in many cases" ("Liminal" 34). His play indicates a social activity that involves loosened, undermined hierarchies, innovations, anti-structure, eccentric social behavior, and temporary reversals: the tribal subjects "have authority to introduce, under certain culturally determined conditions, elements of novelty from time to time into the socially inherited deposit of ritual customs. Liminality, the seclusion period, is a phase peculiarly conducive to such 'ludic' invention" ("Liminal" 31–32).[1]

It is also important to realize that Turner's other related work, *The Ritual Process*, finds liminality and "communitas" — social formations inspired by liminality — not only in tribal, but also in contemporary societies (110–13). These "liminoid" manifestations are tangible in literature and other art forms: they appear in the beat movement, in sport, the theater, the lecture room, since "almost anywhere people can be subverted from their duties and rights into an atmosphere of communitas" ("Liminal" 45). Arpad Szakolczai further extends Turner's sociological concept, inventing the term "permanent liminality" to describe both religious and communist societies, monasteries and the stereotypical image of the "American" society, under the modern condition (210–15)

Mikhail Bakhtin's carnival, described in his *Rabelais and His World*, to a certain degree resonates with Turner's liminality. The medieval carnival functioned as an intermediary phase of ambivalence, a playful period of reversed hierarchies and "temporary liberation" from the social order: "Carnival was the true feast of time, the feast of becoming, change, and renewal" (10). The carnival is also related to the grotesque, open, ambiguous body, the body "in transformation, an as yet unfinished metamorphosis, of death and birth, growth and becoming" (24). Focusing on inverted social hierarchies, Peter Stallybrass and Allon White also stress that "Bakhtin's work significantly parallels that of Victor Turner ... which puts carnival into a much wider perspective " (17).

Although I find these approaches to liminality significant and I will recurrently draw on them, they are somehow not complete, as liminality should be reinterpreted and diversified in accordance with the cultural change of postmodernism. Contemporary literature and culture, including popular fiction, frequently articulate postmodern views on liminality. Such theories question the possibility of linear movements, since linear processes can easily indicate the presence of a dualism, correlating with a hierarchized binary opposition. Poststructuralist theories intend to deconstruct these oppositions, or rather, to reveal the inherently deconstructive nature of these oppositions. Thinkers do so because, as Jacques Derrida argues, "in a classical philosophical opposition we are not dealing with the peaceful coexistence of a *vis-à-vis*, but rather with a violent hierarchy. One of the two terms controls the other (axiologically, logically, etc.), holds the superior position" (*Positions* 41; emphasis in original). Thus, the deconstruction of linear movements, binary oppositions, and hierarchies, the ambivalence of liminality, often rests on chronological and causal reversals and goes on towards the absolute questioning of precession and succession.

Reversals play crucial roles in various theories of rhetorical deconstruction, especially in the writings of Friedrich Nietzsche, Paul de Man, and Derrida. Chronological reversal indicates the possibility of stepping out of linear time flow. It is not only a theoretical maneuver, but also a frequently utilized technique in literature. As Smethurst argues, postmodernist and science fiction novels foreground "reversible time," that is, "the ability to travel back and forth within historical time," since "Historical linearity ... is generally absent from the postmodern chronotope, except where it is used for ironic subversion" (86, 173–74). Reversed time is depicted in Lewis Carroll's Alice novels, Alejo Carpentier's short story "Viaje a la semilla" (1944), Philip K. Dick's *Ubik* (1969) and *Counter-clock World* (1967) as well as Kurt Vonnegut's *Slaughterhouse-Five* (1969). In Carroll's *Through the Looking Glass* (1871), certain characters have a defective memory of the past, but they can "recall" the events of the future.[2]

> "It's a poor sort of memory that only works backwards," the Queen remarked.
> "What sort of things do you remember best?" Alice ventured to ask.
> "Oh, things that happened the week after next," The Queen replied in a careless tone. "For instance, now," she went on sticking a large piece of plaster on her finger as she spoke, "there is the King's Messenger. He is in prison now, being punished: and the trial does not even begin till next Wednesday: and of course the crime comes last of all" [80–81].

The interchange of cause and effect is another crucial and widely recognized idea in recent culture. As Nietzsche points out in his *Twilight of the Idols*, dreams often fabricate a story to explain an outside stimulus, for example a cannon shot, which becomes an effect or a "resonance"—while it should, in fact, be interpreted as the primary event or the cause. Thus, such "temporal reversal" (179) in the mind leads to causal reversal. As Guy Cook observes, "One of the commonplaces of postmodernism is its exploitation of Nietzsche's observation that contrary to common sense, cause follows rather than precedes effect. When we sit on a pin we perceive the pin as the source afterwards; only when we perceive the pin as the source does the source, as source, exist. The idea is fertile and iconoclastic" (126). Nietzsche reverses the seemingly logical order of time and causality, which correlates with questioning the binary polarity of the "inside" and "outside" world, sensual and objective reality.

Chronological and causal reversals can be linked to postmodern language and literary theories. For example, in Stanley Fish's language model, the context is prior to the meaning and so semantics precedes language: "The meaning the act produces (a better word would be presents, as in he presents a compliment) necessarily preexists it — or, to put it in another way, in speech act theory, *meaning is prior to utterance*" (Fish 222; emphasis added). Analogously, Fish's "persuasion model" presumes that interpretation is always prior to the process in which one finds facts or arguments for a reading. A pre-interpretation, which rests on premises and bias, is necessary to form an interpretation: "The facts that one cites are available only because an interpretation (at least in its general and broad outlines) has already been assumed" (365). Thus, the text itself can only follow the interpretation; as Deleuze argues in his analysis on the Alice novels, "Sense is always presupposed as soon as *I* begin to speak; I would not be able to begin without this presupposition. In other words, I never state the sense of what I am saying.... I thus enter into the infinite regress of that which is presupposed" (Deleuze 28; emphasis in original).

Humpty Dumpty, in *Through the Looking-Glass*, describes a similar semantics and literary theory for Alice:

> "You seem very clever at explaining words, Sir," said Alice. "Would you kindly tell me the meaning of the poem called Jabberwocky?"

"Let us hear it," said Humpty Dumpty. "I can explain all the poems that ever were invented — and a good many that haven't been invented just yet" [101–02].

A possible outcome of these reversals would be solipsism, the belief in the supremacy and priority of individual perception. De Man's reading of Nietzsche, however, goes further in his *Allegories of Reading* and emphasizes the unending nature of reversals:

> The two sets of polarities, inside/outside and cause/effect, which seemed to make up a closed and coherent system (outside causes produce inside effects) has now scrambled into an arbitrary, open system in which the attributes of causality and of location can be deceptively exchanged, substituted for each other at will.... [I]t seems unlikely that one more such reversal ... would suffice to restore things to their proper order. One more "turn" or trope added to a series of earlier reversals will not stop the turn towards error [107–08, 113].

Instead of the reversed system, de Man focuses on the "arbitrary, open system," which comprises of tropes, of "the language most explicitly grounded in rhetoric" (109). The rhetorical nature of language necessitates the simultaneous affirmation and denial of philosophical and scientific statements, suspending the rule of non-contradiction. Thus, a scientific statement or philosophical argument inevitably "shifts incessantly back and forth between incompatible propositions such as A = A, A better be equal to A or else, or A cannot be equal to A, etc. This complication is characteristic of all deconstructive discourse ... after Nietzsche (and, indeed, after any 'text'), we can no longer hope ever 'to know' in peace" (125, 126). Such deconstructive, repeatedly reversed reading may occupy a liminal space: "[It] always remains suspended, regardless of how often it is repeated" (130).

Analogously, Derrida stresses that although the inversions of classical philosophical oppositions are crucial, "to remain in this phase is still to operate on the terrain of and from within the deconstructed system" (*Positions* 42); that is to say, narrowing one's activities to mere reversals would only result in recreating hierarchy and dual oppositions. Derrida's deconstruction questions "the quest for a rightful beginning, an absolute point of departure, a principal responsibility" ("Différance" 6). His "différance" requires temporal and spatial slippages: hybrid, liminal phenomena, which are both inside and outside dialectics. These "infinitesimal and radical displacement[s]" appear "in the economy of the same," simultaneously disrupting and maintaining traditional duality ("Différance" 14, 17). They form a dubious escape from logocentrism, since they "can no longer be included within philosophical (binary) opposition, but ... [at the same time] inhabit philosophical opposition, resisting and disorganizing it, but *without ever* constituting a third term, without ever leaving room for a solution in the form of speculative dialectics.... Neither/nor, that is, *simultaneously* either *or*" (*Positions* 43; emphasis in original).

Thus, Derrida frequently analyzes the problematic nature of transgression and interval, their power and impotence, necessity and futility. His supplement, for example, is both an external violation and a central, internal inevitability when it "breaks into the very thing that would have liked to do without it yet lets itself *at once* be breached, roughed up, fulfilled and replaced" (*Dissemination* 110; emphasis in original). His hymen "remains suspended *entre*, outside and inside the antre ... [that is,] rending penetration that leaves a virgin womb intact" (*Dissemination* 216; emphasis in original). Analogously, Miller's parasite signifies violation and cooperation, "similarity and difference, interiority and exteriority, something inside a domestic economy and at the same time outside it, something simultaneously this side of a boundary line, threshold, or margin, and also beyond it" (144).

Derrida even proposes the necessity of a science that would examine (and deconstruct) margins, limits and liminality. This science would be "limitrophy," which concerns "what sprouts or grows at the limit, around the limit, by maintaining the limit, but also what *feeds the limit*, generates it, raises it, and complicates it" ("The Animal" 398; emphasis in original).

Homi Bhabha's theory of "hybridity as camouflage" also posits the constant disruption and reconstruction of binary oppositions and hierarchical order via small differences or slippages of signification. Hybridity involves the constant, recurring slippage of cultural translation, "*the element of resistance* in the process of transformation" (Bhabha 224; emphasis in original). His "colonial mimicry" emphasizes a similarity between the colonizer and the colonized that is not complete: the colonized individual becomes "*a subject of a difference that is almost the same, but not quite*. Which is to say, that the discourse of mimicry is constructed around an *ambivalence*; in order to be effective, mimicry must continually produce its slippage, its excess, its difference" (86; emphasis in original).

Bhabha foregrounds the "double vision" of camouflage. Colonial mimicry, on the one hand, creates "appropriate objects of a colonialist chain of command, authorized versions of otherness." On the other hand, the partial presence of mimicry "articulates those disturbances of cultural, racial and historical difference that menace the narcissistic demand of colonial authority" (88). Thus, his colonial mimicry enables us "to get away from defining subaltern consciousness as binary, as having positive or negative dimensions" (193), while the primacy and initial position of the colonizer is also challenged.

There are unique incidents and places that reveal that the colonizer and the colonized constantly switch perspectives and positions, obtaining a partial presence and an unstable identity. During the Indian Mutiny of 1857, when chapati (unleavened Indian flatbread) was distributed for utterly unknown reasons in the country, the symptomatic conditions of fear, rumor and panic created an "infectious ambivalence" (202). In such critical moments, a discourse emerges that "spreads beyond the knowledge of ethnic or cultural binarisms and becomes a new, hybrid space of cultural difference ... in a form of circulation in-between the colonizer and the colonized" (204, 206). The incident turns into a liminal state and moment, as it creates a "borderline experience" that "breaks down the stereotomy of inside/outside ... [and] resists the binary opposition of racial and cultural groups" (207). Bhabha emphasizes that the *urban space*, especially the multicultural districts where immigrants live, may also become a location that fosters such borderline experience for its inhabitants (223–29).

One can connect Bhabha's hybridity with Turner's liminality in the sense that in both theories the hierarchical oppositions are turned upside down, resulting in "reversals, inversions, disguises" (Turner, "Liminal" 54). Liminality is an unstructured, chaotic state, a "blend ... of lowliness and sacredness" (Turner, *The Ritual* 96). Yet Bhabha's theory differs from Turner's, because it is not based on a rite of passage from one state to another. The colonizer does not fully turn into the colonized, nor the other way around.

Although postmodern liminality still implies an in-between state and the transgression of borderlines, it ceases to refer to a temporary situation in a finite and teleological process. As Bhabha explains, "This liminal moment of identification ... requires a movement and maneuver, but it does not require a temporality of continuity or accumulation" (185). Instead of progress and teleology, liminality evokes an endless, oscillating movement, aimless, rambling flow, "a space extended infinitely without apparent edge" (Jencks 87).

Michel Foucault's theories, especially his "Of Other Spaces," create another link between ethnographic and postmodern interpretations of liminality. On the one hand, Foucault dates back his heterotopia to "primitive societies," in which important events, such as the sexual initiation and initiation into adulthood, always take place in "crisis heterotopias," in "privileged or sacred or forbidden places." Analogously, in modern societies the "young woman's deflowering could take place 'nowhere'" or "elsewhere," but never at home (24).

On the other hand, it is important to realize that Foucault extends his concept with his "heterotopias of deviation," arguing that there are other spaces "that seem to be pure and simple openings, but that generally hide curious exclusions. Everyone can enter into these heterotopic sites, but in fact that is only an illusion: we think we enter where we are, by the very fact that we enter, excluded" (26). This account of heterotopia resonates with Derrida's approach to transgression and limit, who emphasizes the pluralized, protean, abyssal, labyrinthine, illusory nature of limits. Derrida says that "the frontier no longer forms a single indivisible line but more than one internally divided line, once, as a result, it can no longer be traced, objectified, or counted as single and indivisible" ("The Animal" 399). Or, as Foucault's other famous essay "A Preface to Transgression" indicates (34), it is precisely the act of transgression that gives meaning and visible form to the evanescent limit. Limit and transgression depend on each other, create and obliterate each other constantly and simultaneously.

Other critics go even further and argue, as Elizabeth Grosz does, that borders must not be regarded as limits "to be transgressed," but "to be traversed," since "there is already an infection by one side of the border of the other, there is a becoming otherwise of each of the terms thus bounded" (131). Michel de Certeau's arguments on spatial and textual liminality, on "the paradox of the frontier" also highlight that "Within the frontiers, the alien is already there ... as though delimitation itself were the bridge that opens the inside to its other" (127, 129). The boundary, therefore, becomes "a permeable membrane connecting inside and outside" (Miller 145).

Thus, with the help of poststructuralist theories, I find three distinct characteristics of liminality. First, I hypothesize a *constant oscillation, crossing back and forth between social and cultural positions*; this might involve the recurring exchange of attributes between the opposite poles. Second, I imagine liminality as the *space of continuous transference, of a never-ending narrative,* forming *an infinite process towards an unreachable end.*[3] Third, liminality is created by transgressions, or traversals, across *evanescent, porous, indefinite, ambiguous, evasive borderlines.*[4] Besides Turner's liminality, my book will recurrently draw on this poststructuralist re-interpretation of liminality.

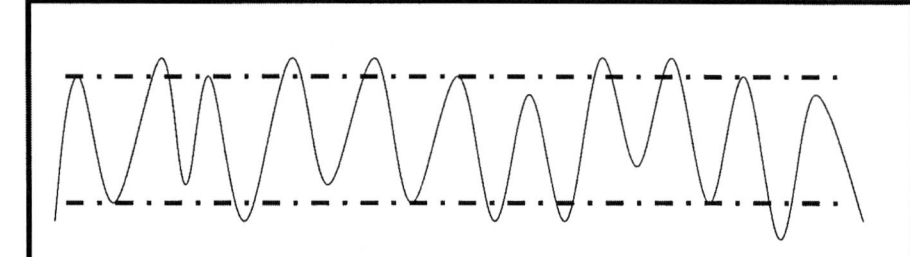

Figure 2 Liminality inspired by poststructuralism

Poststructuralist thinking also indicates that instead of duality, we should discover the multiplicity of spaces and timelines. Critics intend to eliminate dual structures in both space and time: diverse, multiplied spatial and temporal experience, pluralized histories, cities within the city, labyrinthine and fluid architecture characterize postmodernism. Liminality, therefore, should also be discovered and analyzed amid the multiplicity of domains and timelines, instead of between dual oppositions.

I believe that this new form of liminality still waits to be constructed and thoroughly analyzed in criticism and philosophy. The multiplied timelines and spaces, however, and the transgressions between them have been analyzed in detail by many critics, for example, narratological criticism and the possible worlds approach. Such theories often use spatial metaphors to describe complex, pluralized textual structures — it is enough to refer here to Thomas Pavel's and Lubomir Dolezel's possible world theories, McHale's postmodern poetics, and Marie-Laure Ryan's classification of plot and storyline structures (*Avatars* 100–07).

Multiplied timelines and spatial models as well as complexified plots can take a wide range of formations. I tentatively suggest here that certain models in particular can shape the basis for a new, postmodern understanding of liminality.

1.a: Liminality should be detected between embedded worlds, worlds that imitate stacks, onion layers, "nesting or embedding, as in a set of Chinese boxes or Russian babushka dolls" (McHale, *Postmodernist* 112). As McHale argues, in postmodernist fiction the formal and fictional transgressions often blur the narrative boundaries with strange loops or metalepses, when embedded characters and images traverse between the narrative layers, infiltrating the frame story and violating the hierarchy of realities (*Postmodernist* 119–24). Borges's "The Circular Ruins" (1941) can be an exemplary text here, as the story ends with a transgressive moment when a character of an embedded world suddenly realizes the embeddedness of his realm and establishes contact with the frame world. In Josef Rusnak's film *The 13th Floor* (1999), the pro-

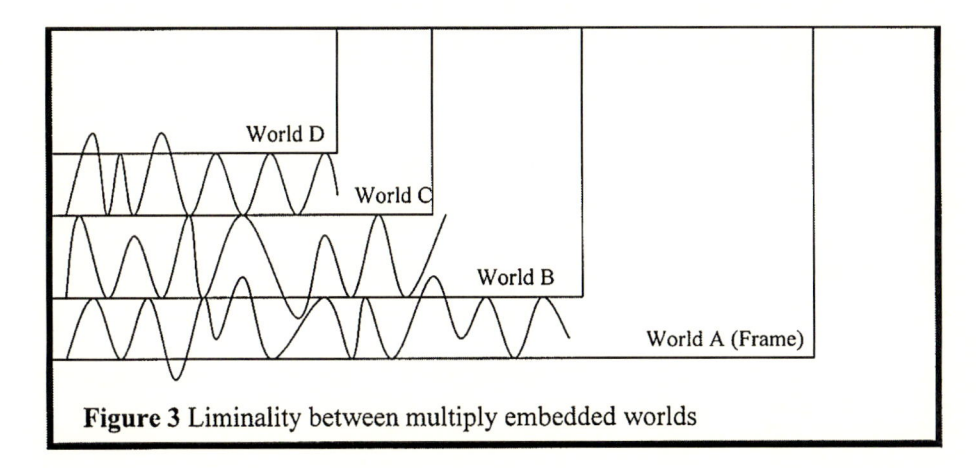

Figure 3 Liminality between multiply embedded worlds

tagonist, a character of a hierarchically "inferior" level, establishes contact and reaches the level of the "superior" world, in a way similar to other cyberpunk avatars, who often try to escape from their simulated realm.

1.b: McHale outlines a modified version of the above model and the possibility of a subtype in this category, when the embedding involves several realms but only two layers: several "microworlds" or "zones" are juxtaposed, "occupying the same ontological plane and arranged along the same horizontal axis" (*Constructing* 251). Foucault also recognizes this version in his "heterotopias of deviation" that are "capable of juxtaposing in a single real place several spaces, several sites that are in themselves incompatible." This sort of space comprises "a whole series of places that are foreign to one another" (25). The juxtaposition may be spatial or temporal; the theater, for example, brings onto the stage one world after another in temporal succession. Another primary example can be Dick's "I Hope I Shall Arrive Soon" (1980), in which Victor Kemmings goes from one simulated world to the other, and the worlds that he encounters are permeated by each other: certain memory traits (his early experience with death, the surname Shelton) migrate from one zone to another.

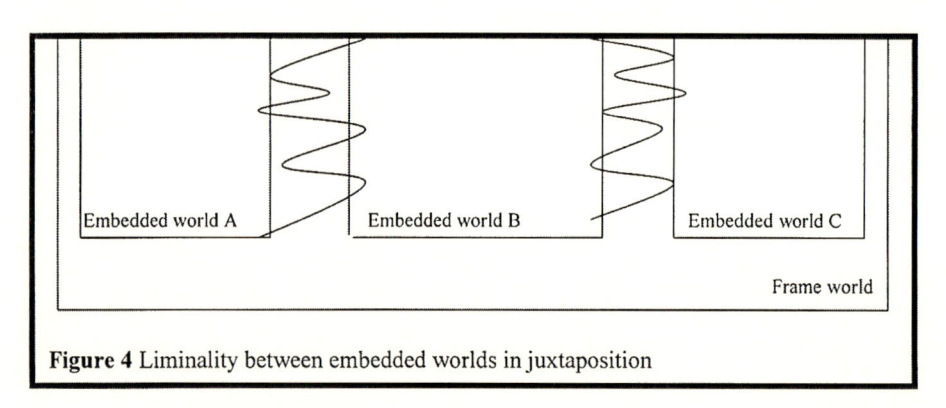

Figure 4 Liminality between embedded worlds in juxtaposition

2: Another form of multiplicity, which is even more important to my research, can be engendered by the entanglement of alternate timelines, the stories of forking paths. It is somewhat in opposition with the previous, framing-embedding models (Ryan, "Stacks" 876), the layered, "lamellar or laminar" space (Deleuze and Guattari, *A Thousand* 361).[5] In Douglas Adams's *Mostly Harmless* (1992), Dick's *The Three Stigmata of Palmer Eldritch* (1964) and Borges's "The Garden of Forking Paths" (1941), mazes emerge instead of or across parallel universes. All of these mazes are three or even four dimensional; they are as much temporal as they are spatial formations:

There are limitless futures stretching out in every direction from this moment — and from this moment and from this. Billions of them, bifurcating every instant! Every possible position of every possible electron balloons out into billions of probabilities! Billions and billions of shining, gleaming futures! ... Billions and billions of markets! [Adams, *Mostly* 49].

Furthermore, the bifurcating plateaus are just as much subjective, fictional, and hallucinatory as they are objective and real spaces. As McHale argues, in certain (postmodern) works the textual universe transforms into an entangled subjective universe, into "an 'impure' garden of forking paths ... [because a] number of the alternative 'routes' ... are realized only in the protagonist's fantasies, in his subworld" (*Postmodernist* 107). The term "paraspace" should be used here, a term created by Samuel Delany and Scott Bukatman, which designates worlds other than reality such as those of dreams, the future, hallucinations, and so on: "an alternate space, sometimes largely mental, but always materially manifested" (Bukatman, *Terminal* 157).

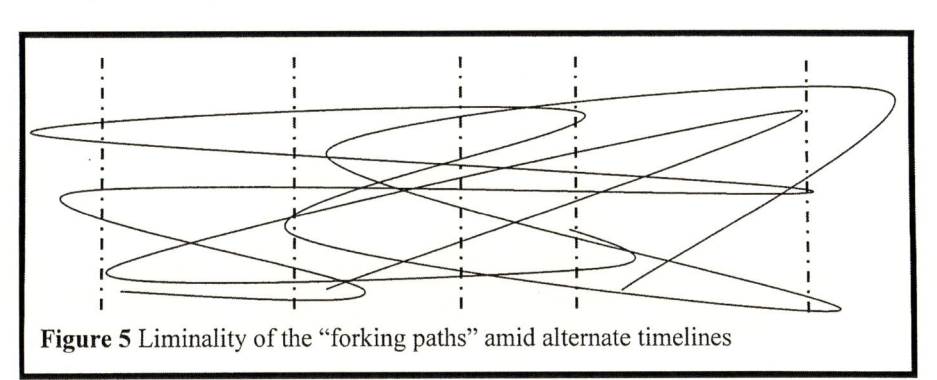

Figure 5 Liminality of the "forking paths" amid alternate timelines

Deleuze and Guattari's rhizome, which they describe in their *A Thousand Plateaus*, is to some extent analogous to the above described labyrinth of forking paths. A rhizome is a complex labyrinthine organism and a postmodern variety of book writing, in which connections and heterogeneity are crucial: "Any point of a rhizome can be connected to anything other, and must be" (7). The rhizomatic organism may form a subterranean "holey" space, the space of wormholes, in which shortcuts "create the fantastic forms corresponding to these breakthroughs ... [t]ranspierce the mountains instead of scaling them, bore holes in space instead of keeping it smooth, turn the earth into swiss cheese" (413). Holey space is "a kind of rhizome, with its gaps, detours, subterranean passages, stems, openings, traits, holes, etc." (415). The rhizome is made of plateaus, liminal terrains (21), multiplicities "connected to other multiplicities by superficial underground stems in such a way as to form or extend a rhizome" (22).

The rhizomatic organism is linked to a rhizomatic movement, which has no beginning or end—"it is always in the middle, between things, interbeing, *intermezzo*" (25; emphasis in original). This model, evoking Bhabha's liminality, implies a movement within territories and antitheses but eliminates development, accumulation, starting points, endings, and teleology: "Where are you coming from? What are you heading for? These are totally useless questions" (25).

Paradoxes, pure "becoming," the elimination of the principle of non-contradiction turn out to be crucial for Deleuze and Guattari, as crucial as it is for Nietzsche, de Man and Derrida: "The fabric of the rhizome is the conjunction, 'and ... and ... and'" (*Thousand* 25; see also Deleuze 1–11). The teleological movement between A and B becomes problematic or meaningless; the critics envisage another way of traveling and moving, which implies knowing "how to move between things ... [in order to] do away with foundations, nullify endings and beginnings" (*Thousand* 25; emphasis in original).

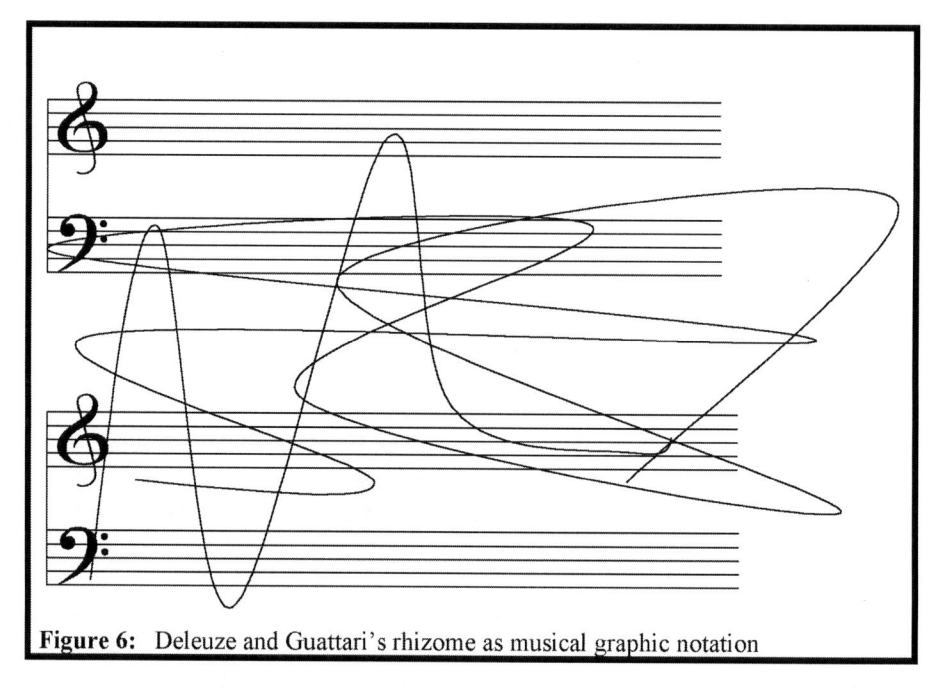

Figure 6: Deleuze and Guattari's rhizome as musical graphic notation

The rhizomatic structure is associated with various forms of mobile existence, *traveling* life: that of the itinerant blacksmith, the transhumant, the merchant, the immigrant, the wandering schizo, and most of all, that of the *nomad*. The wanderings of the nomads, the movements of tribes are liminal in a postmodern sense because they permanently inhabit a space between two fixed points and it is their movement that defines and constitutes boundaries, not the other way around. As Deleuze and Guattari argue:

> The nomad has a territory; he follows customary paths; he goes from one point to another; he is not ignorant of points (water points, dwelling points, assembly points, etc.). But the question is what in nomad life is a principle ... To begin with, *although the points determine paths, they are strictly subordinated to the paths they determine*, the reverse of what happens with the sedentary.... A path is always between two points, but the *in-between* has taken on all the consistency and enjoys both an autonomy and a direction of its own. The life of the nomad is the *intermezzo*. Even the elements or his dwelling are conceived in terms of the trajectory that is forever mobilizing them [*A Thousand* 380; emphasis added].

Thus, the nomad somewhat follows but is simultaneously contrasted with the urban migrant, Bhabha's immigrant, "for the migrant goes principally from one point to another, even if the second point is uncertain, unforeseen, or not well localized" (Deleuze and Guattari, *A Thousand* 380). A precursor of the nomad may be Walter Benjamin's flaneur, the strolling, itinerant character of labyrinthine cities, who lives in the liminal space of the arcades, in a hybrid realm, "a cross between a street and an *interieur* [of a house]" (*Charles Baudelaire* 37; emphasis in original). Another related figure can be detected in de Certeau's "walker," whose "tricky and stubborn procedures" are simultaneously within and outside the discipline of systematic city planning: "The long poem of walking manipulates spatial organizations, no matter how panoptic they may be: it is neither foreign to them ... nor in conformity with them ... [but it] creates shadows and ambiguities within them" (96, 101).

Liminality in Detective Fiction, Fantasy and Science Fiction

So far I have summarized the main theoretical approaches to liminality and outlined my own understanding of the concept. But on which textual levels, in what sort of literature and what thematic and formal structures can liminality be detected?

In this book, I will analyze liminality in science fiction and fantasy, particularly in the oeuvre of three authors: the fiction of Neil Gaiman, Stanislaw Lem, and Philip K. Dick. As a preliminary study, I will also examine Agatha Christie's detective fiction to find examples of liminality in a supposedly rational and univocal textual tradition. These writers produced well-known, keynote texts of these genres, fictional works that provide telling examples of liminality. I argue that at least four major forms of liminality can be detected in their texts. In the further chapters, I will often discuss these manifestations of liminality simultaneously and so it is crucial to clarify them here one by one, outlining somewhat distinct categories.

First, we should keep in mind what could be named as *cultural* or *institutional liminality* in so far as the texts that I analyze hover on the brinks of mainstream and popular literature: their target audience is a blend between readers of mainstream and genre literature. Gaiman, for example, is a fantasy writer whose novels are categorized as bestsellers. On the other hand, he is an essential member of the New Wave Fabulists, a movement that appeared in the literary magazine *Conjunctions* (2002). Lem is perhaps the most famous non–English speaking science fiction author, who in fact frequently debunks the genre. He characterizes most of the English language science fiction as trash, a "hopeless case" with a few exceptions (by which he means mainly Dick), and he rather intends to follow the absurd writings of Franz Kafka and the philosophical works of Jorge Luis Borges (Lem, *Microworlds* 34–42; 72–75; 233–38). Perhaps consequently, he was positively reviewed by Theodore Solotaroff in the *New York Times Book Review* in 1976 and by John Updike in *The New Yorker* in 1979. All in all, Lem's fiction, at least *Solaris* (1961), is well-known amongst readers and critics of both genre and mainstream literature. The same is true of Dick, whose fiction was analyzed by Fredric Jameson in his widely acclaimed *Postmodernism, or, the Cultural Logic of Late Capitalism* (279–96). Furthermore, a selection of Dick's novels was published in the series *The Library of America*, marking a milestone event that was celebrated by Frank Rose in the online version of *Wired* as the moment when "the most outré science fiction writer of the 20th century has finally entered the canon."

Second, I will recurrently discuss *generic liminality*, since I find it highly important that these authors are on the edges of various (sub-)genres such as fantasy, horror, detective fiction, and science fiction. Gaiman's texts, for example, blend the genre norms of horror, detective fiction, fairy tale and fantasy. Lem mixes detective fiction, spy stories, Kafkaesque modernism, Swiftian satire, cybernetic fairy tale and traditional science fiction: he "takes the reader through the mosaic of styles and genres that would have buried a lesser artist" (Swirski, *From Lowbrow* 153). Dick's science fiction novels seem more consistent regarding their genre than Lem's and Gaiman's works; at first glance he appears less playful with genre conventions. But even he mixes the psychological and philosophical insights of the New Wave movement occasionally with detective stories, postmodernist fiction, spy stories, (proto-)cyberpunk themes, alternate histories, mainstream realism, and so on. His fiction belongs to a category that Bukatman describes as "terminal identity fiction," a mixed genre that confronts the ontological problematics of cyberspace and paraspace, and includes cyberpunk fiction and films, experimental or neo-avantgarde science fiction, postmodern literature, and postmodern media and social theories

(*Terminal* 9–12). Thus, Dickian fiction can be interpreted as "the current model of this science fiction that is no longer one.... Obviously the short stories of Philip K. Dick 'gravitate' in this space, if one can use that word (but that is precisely what one can't really do any more, because this new universe is 'anti-gravitational,' or if it still gravitates, it is around the *hole* of the real, around the *hole* of imaginary)," as Baudrillard argues (*Simulacra* 125; emphasis in original).

Third, I identify and extensively explore cases of *narrative liminality*, when the reader oscillates among various perspectives, focal points, styles, and intertextual registers. In Dick's fiction, the narrative perspective is occasionally alienated as the storytelling evokes the perspective of a schizophrenic, that of a drug user, or that of a cyborg-machine. Gaiman's fiction often prompts the reader to face a hesitation, an inability to choose between the competing narrative perspectives and language registers, thus evoking Linda Hutcheon's theory of irony. Hutcheon finds irony in texts that feature dual or multiplied meanings and perspectives that are perceived and kept in mind simultaneously by the reader. She highlights in *Irony's Edge* (60) a rapid oscillation between narrative perspectives, an ironic oscillation that evokes Farah Mendlesohn's liminal fantasies, texts where the restrained or "blasé" voice of storytelling becomes echoed by the reader's growing wonder and estrangement (Mendlesohn, "Toward a Taxonomy" 180). This ironic oscillation in the reading process is a foremost element of the contemporary, poststructuralist and postmodern, interpretations of liminality.

Fourth and perhaps foremost, there is a general tendency of *thematic liminality* in these texts, which blurs the boundaries of the self and the Other, organic and artificial, human and mechanical, and most of all, between the real world and the fantastic-virtual. The portal between the ordinary and the magic realms, between reality and the cyber-world is a crucial liminal space in fantasy, science fiction and cyberpunk. In many cases, the question whether the protagonist has gone through the portal, on which side the character is, remains ambiguous and so the whole fantastic or virtual place becomes a liminal space (Todorov, *The Fantastic* 41–44; Tomas 39–41; Swanstrom 19–26; Miller 154). As Mendlesohn puts it, this "*irresolution* of the fantastic becomes the locus of the 'fantasy'" in liminal texts (*Rhetorics* xxiii; emphasis in original). My analysis reveals that fluid, ever-changing, heterogeneous, ambivalent spaces and time structures characterize Gaiman's, Lem's, and Dick's fictional places. Their chronotopes exemplify liminality by evoking Foucault's heterotopia, McHale's ontological zones, Jean Baudrillard's simulacra, Deleuze and Guattari's rhizomes, and Hutcheon's historiographic metafiction.

After this brief overview, let me outline a more detailed analysis of these four manifestations of liminality, meanwhile explaining the cultural context of their dominance in contemporary literature.

Many critics, such as Jameson in his well-known essay "Postmodernism and Consumer Society," associate the rise of interactions between popular and high culture with postmodernism (14). Jameson argues here that modernism was elitist and defiant towards society when it disrupted the governing cultural discourse and formed "a provocative challenge to the reigning reality- and performance-principles" (27). Postmodernism, however, was born in an utterly different age; the early 1960s. Its peak in the 1970s and 1980s coincides with the era of popular fiction, advertisements, music videos, punk rock, and science fiction, when there are hardly any fragments of culture that would be shocking for us: "There is very little in either the form or the content of contemporary art that contemporary society finds intolerable and scandalous. The most offensive forms of this art — punk rock, say, or what is called sexually explicit material — are all taken in stride by society, and they are commercially successful, unlike the productions of the older high modernism" (27).

The history of science fiction seems to confirm that the decline of distinction between mainstream and popular literature dates back to the 1960s and the 1970s. In this era, the New Wave authors (for example, Dick, J. G. Ballard, Samuel Delany, Ursula K. Le Guin) intended to focus on quality instead of quantity: "The mask of pulp fantasy was slipping" (Aldiss 330). The generation intended to dehumanize the formally humanized alien characters and cultures. Also, their fiction represented "a movement away from the stars and towards Earth," focusing on the human psyche (Aldiss 331). Following the traditions of Alfred Bester's prose, the New Wave writers often applied experimental narrative techniques. The movement also marked a milestone in the process of the institutionalization of the genre: as the urge arose to create and read esthetically elevated literature, critics soon started to distinguish "sci-fi," the trashy Hollywood influenced pulp from science fiction or SF, that is, the proper, canonized books of the genre.

McHale, however, warns us that the New Wave authors were utilizing slightly "outdated" literary sources in so far as they were influenced mainly by high-modernist literature (*Constructing* 228). He argues that the two modes of literature became synchronic only after the cyberpunk movement in the 1980s. Cyberpunk brings forth a simultaneous form of coexistence between mainstream and genre fiction. By this time, the formal and thematic influences have become omnipresent and the sparse interaction has turned into interactive cooperation: "Cyberpunk SF can thus be seen, in this systematic perspective, as *SF which derives certain of its elements from postmodernist mainstream fiction which itself has, in its turn, already been 'science-fictionized' to some greater or lesser degree*" (*Constructing* 229; emphasis in original).

It is undoubtedly true that the most important experience of cyberpunk, the influence of technologized societies and the information age, fascinated both genre and mainstream criticism, both high culture and popular literature at this time. In postmodernism, new communication models, architecture, space and time experience saturated all levels of the cultural landscape. As early as the 1960s, Marshall McLuhan declares his well-known axiom that "the medium is the message," while Guy Debord analyzes "the society of the spectacle." Later on, the media critic Paul Virilio describes the "end of geography" (9), while Manuel Castells's defines his "space of flows" (205–30). Jameson constructs his postmodern esthetics, in which cyberpunk is described as "the supreme literary expression if not of postmodernism, then of late capitalism itself" (*Postmodernism* 419). Meanwhile, Baudrillard portrays and condemns our cultural-communicative obscenity and simulacrum-society.

Larry McCaffery's cyberpunk anthology, *Storming the Reality Studio* (1991), is explicitly grounded in these theories when it comprises of science fiction and theoretical pieces, including excerpts by Baudrillard, Derrida, Jameson and Jean François Lyotard. The history of popular culture and the theory of high culture, at least for a moment, became openly and irrevocably intertwined.[6]

Cyberpunk was always a hybrid (sub-)genre, comprising film noir, anime, hard science fiction, hard-boiled detective fiction, avant-garde, underground punk culture, and so on. Post-cyberpunk, that is, the second and third generation of cyberpunk (Neal Stephenson, Greg Egan, Cory Doctorow, Charles Stross) is supplemented with psychology, social sensibility and social criticism: a reinterpreted (post–)humanism. As Lawrence Person indicates, contemporary post-cyberpunk often manifests itself as a specific textual tendency, a "flavor" instead of a unified and influential movement (see also A. Butler, *Cyberpunk* 57). Even in the works of Stross and Doctorow, "the alpha cyberpunks" (Kelly and Kessel 389) of today, the post-cyberpunk overtone is intertwined with urban fantasy (Doctorow's *Someone Comes to Town, Someone Leaves Town* [2005]), or Lovecraftian horror and British spy novel (Stross's *The Atrocity Archives* [2004]). The Shadowrun role playing games and the inspired book series also portray a world that is a blend, due to the co-presence of fantasy and cyberpunk themes.

The post-cyberpunk phenomenon recapitulates Carl Freedman's assertion in his *Critical Theory and Science Fiction* that (sub-)genres function only as stylistic marks: "A genre is not a classification but an element or, better still, a tendency that ... is active to a greater or lesser degree within a literary text that is itself understood as a complexly structured totality" (20). Swirski confirms that genres "don't function like empirical classes, but, rather, as invitations to a literary game ... [producing] the convergence of reciprocal expectations" (*From Lowbrow* 82). Similar critical arguments could be brought up endlessly (A. Butler, "Between" 208, 213–14; Bakhtin, "Discourse" 321; Derrida, "The Law" 62, 65) from German Romanticism to Russian Formalism and Deconstruction, as David Duff's *Modern Genre Theory* candidly explains (4–17).

Contemporary science fiction and fantasy movements, the "new, 21st century paradigm" (Wolfe and Beamer 20) in popular fiction such as Interstitial Writing, New Wave Fabulism, New Weird, and the Slipstream overtly exemplify genre crossings.[7] They illustrate Clute's axiom in his "Canary Fever" that "[t]he genres are too old, and have interjaculated all too promiscuously in recent years, to give us, any longer, rules to obey — much less rules worth breaking" (226). In *Interfictions* (2007), the first anthology of Interstitial Writing, Heinz Insu Fenkl emphasizes Turner's liminality and Bhabha's hybridity (iii) when he places Interstitial Writers in the interstices of high culture and pop-culture, fantasy and postmodern fairy tales, horror and science fiction.

In his Introduction to *Interfictions 2* (2009), Henry Jenkins dates back interstitial art to the era of the Studio System in Hollywood, from the 1920s to the 1950s (xii). He also refers to Tzvetan Todorov's fantasy theory. Todorov, in his analysis on mainly 18th and 19th century authors, emphasizes the reader's *hesitation* between two interpretations of the fictional events: between the uncanny, when the reader decides that "the laws of reality remain intact," and the marvelous, when "new laws of nature must be entertained" (*The Fantastic* 41). Todorov's fantastic literature is a longstanding, ambiguous and "evanescent genre" (42), a borderline case, the liminal barrier itself: "The fantastic in its pure state is represented here by the median line separating the fantastic-uncanny from the fantastic-marvelous. This line corresponds perfectly to the nature of the fantastic, a frontier between two adjacent realms" (44).[8]

Consequently, I think it important to emphasize that the *genre crossings* in my work *do not form a special case* in literature. Quite the contrary: these texts exemplify the age-old, all-encompassing urge towards the erosion of (sub-)genre boundaries in (popular) fiction: texts are, and always were, hybrid. Such an approach to genre questions the existence of a rupture in literary history such as postmodernism, which would mark a specific moment, a temporal limit between "pure" texts and mixed genres (Derrida, "The Law" 61).

My interpretation of genre distinctions will be outlined in the introduction of Chapter 2. Drawing on Philippe Lejeune's autobiographical pact, I will argue that texts usually include specific markers, distinctive genre traits for the reader, but both the text and the reader subvert these traits at some point or another. Genre pacts, rules or "laws" integrally involve problematic cases, breaches, transgression, "engendering" and "degenerescence," "a principle of contamination, a law of impurity" (Derrida, "The Law" 59, 74).

Genre interactions may lead to another form of liminality, which rests on transgressions between epistemology and ontology, between modernism and postmodernism. McHale argues that the cultural shift from modernism to postmodernism is reflected in certain genres of popular literature: while modernism "governed by an epistemological dominant" is represented in detective fiction, the "poetics of postmodernist fiction" and its "ontological dominant" are expressed in science fiction and cyberpunk in so far as "ontologically-oriented fiction (postmodernism, SF) is preoccupied with questions such as: what is a world? How is a world constituted? How do different worlds, and different kinds of worlds, differ, and what happens when one passes from one world to another?" (*Constructing* 247).

Although this approach may look overly clear-cut at its face value, there are several possible ways to find transgressions between the two cultural and fictional paradigms. I just bring up two of them here. First, McHale refines his sharp distinction by defining his term "limit-modernity," a notion that "manage[s] to incorporate the notion of *cas-limite*, of teetering on the brink" (*Postmodernist* 237; emphasis in original). In limit-modernist texts, "[*b*]*oth* epistemological *and* ontological questions seem to be raised ... but which focus of attention *dominates* depends upon how we look at the text" (*Postmodernist* 12; emphasis in original).

Second, transgression is also possible in the form of "anti-detective story" or "metaphysical detective fiction." These stories "evoke the impulse 'detect' ... in order to violently frustrate this impulse by refusing to solve the crime" (Spanos 25). The texts draw on epistemological questions, but they avoid giving answers, eschew a narrative closure and so they often bring these questions to an ontological level. In the stories of (proto-)postmodernist authors such as Jorge Luis Borges, Vladimir Nabokov, Umberto Eco, Lem, and so on, the text "displays ontological concerns within an epistemological genre" (Merivale and Sweeney 8), thus displaying an overt link between McHale's dominants. (Then again, McHale is aware of the significance of this literary trend and he analyzes it in his *Constructing Postmodernism* [149–51, 163–67]).

It would lead too far to thoroughly examine the question of modernity and postmodernity, epistemology and ontology, since there are countless disseminal approaches to and definitions of these cultural paradigms and philosophical notions. What matters here is the permeating influence of detective fiction, the recycling of its fragmented norms and the re-interpretation of its clichés in contemporary fantasy, science fiction, postmodernist and parodic literature.

To explain this overarching influence, I first analyze traditional detective fiction, the oeuvre of Agatha Christie, to reveal that classical authors are much more subversive than we usually think. Even Christie's supposedly "traditional" murder mysteries repeatedly provide prototypical cases of liminal space and multiplying ontology.

Furthermore, Christie's detective, in a way similar to many other well-known detectives, is usually a liminal figure who teeters simultaneously within and outside society, retaining both highly individual and stereotypical characteristics. The sleuth evokes Benjamin's descriptions of the flaneur, who is a highly complex and controversial figure: both idle and active, a scientist and an artist, a member of the social elite or that of the crowd, but he also "dissociates himself from them. He becomes deeply involved with them, only to relegate them to oblivion with a single glance of contempt" (*Charles Baudelaire* 128). This controversial character often finds him- or herself in highly controversial, liminal, semi-fantastic and simulated places, such as those in Christie's *At Bertram's Hotel* (1965), *Murder on the Orient Express* (1934), *The Thirteen Problems* (1932), *Ordeal by Innocence* (1958) and *Crooked House* (1949) — this is what I intend to prove in Chapter 1.

In Chapter 2, I examine Neil Gaiman's writings, whose intertextual allusions frequently refer to detective fiction conventions. His fiction demonstrates that historical and theoretical approaches can uncover ample examples of overlapping between fantasy and murder mysteries (see Pierce 204 and Panek 6). The uncanny and fantastic horror of Gothic tales, for example, was never completely at odds with the conventions of detective fiction. Edgar Allan Poe continued this tradition, adding proto-science fiction to the repertoire (Moskowitz 47–60; Todorov, "The Limits" 93), and Arthur Conan Doyle did not only invent the figure of the detective Sherlock Holmes, but he also wrote fantastic tales, horror and science fiction stories such as *The Lost World* (1912), "The Poison Belt" (1913), and "When the World Screamed" (1928).

Further, I will also outline Gaiman's narrative markers of introducing a possible world, that is, a magic realm. Gaiman's worlds are often based on unstable ontology, evoking Todorov's definition of the fantastic, his "playing with the boundary between the natural and the supernatural" (Todorov, "The Limits" 95). Gaiman's *thematic* hesitation between reality and the fantastic is mirrored on the *formal level* of the text: the narrative voice and focalization is often doubled, demonstrating Farah Mendlesohn's notion of liminal fantasy. Thus, Gaiman's stories are liminal not only because of the dubious nature of the fantastic realm, but also because the reader hesitates to choose from and oscillates between the alternative narrative perspectives. His texts, analogously to the writings of mainstream postmodern authors and his fellow New Wave Fabulists, demonstrate the contemporary urge to pluralize our critical perspectives, questioning the possibilities of an objective vision and a universal language. This is a postmodern stance, which Lyotard links to the moment when "grand narratives" lose their credibility and locally determined "little narratives" become the quintessential forms of scientific and cultural discourses (37, 60–61).

Stanislaw Lem's fiction, which I discuss in Chapter 3, manifests an overt link between traditional detective stories, metaphysical detective fiction, and ontological science fiction. As Carl Malmgren's analysis points out, Lem's "speculative" science fiction oeuvre is inseparable from traditional — and his own — detective fiction topoi, usually featuring a scientist-detective protagonist who tries to solve a mystery of commonplace or uncanny origin (*Worlds Apart* 41). The mystery leads these characters to philosophical and existential anxieties and so Lem creates novels "whose thematic dominant is epistemology *in extremis*" (*Worlds Apart* 43; emphasis in original). McHale's analysis of Faulkner, Samuel Beckett, and Alain Robbe-Grillet can characterize Lem's oeuvre as well, since such fiction "dramatizes the shift of dominant from problems of *knowing* to problems of *modes of being*— from an epistemological dominant to an ontological one ... and perhaps crosses the boundary between modernist and postmodernist writing" (*Postmodernist* 10; emphasis in original).[9]

It is virtually a truism that science fiction — in addition to fantasy and horror — describes the relationship of the self and the Other (Wolfe, *The Known* xiv), and so the genre can illustrate Jacques Lacan's psychoanalysis (Freedman, *Critical Theory* 106–111; Jackson 88–91). Lacan's theory, especially his notion of the mirror stage, questions the possibility of clear distinctions between the self and the Other, totality and rupture, original and reflected image. Lacan stresses that although the mirror image seemingly provides a flawless totality, a perfect system for the infant's ego, it is an utterly *imaginary totality*: "This form situates the agency of the ego, before its social determination, in a fictional direction ... in a mirage" (Lacan, "The Mirror" 2).[10]

Several other poststructuralist and postmodern approaches subvert the distinctions between duplication and originality, image and reality. Various theories by Laura Mulvey, Judith Butler, Luce Irigaray, Homi Bhabha, Foucault, and Baudrillard, suggest that mirroring is never simple and neutral but highly ambiguous and impregnated by social prejudices, resulting in both the death and the re-birth of the Subject. The mirroring process becomes conscious and overt in postmodernism and turns into a subversive act: the reflection is frequently accomplished with a difference, refraction, rupturing surprise — with the *revenge* of the mirror. Thus, self-formation and self-alienation, totality and fragmentation, the self and the Other, absence and presence, interior and exterior, reality and reflected image are irrevocably interwoven in the mirror, leading to a psychologically and socially constructed liminal space.

My analysis finds illustrations and parodies of these theories in Lem's fiction: while *Solaris*, *Return from the Stars* (1961), *The Investigation* (1959), and *The Chain of Chance* (1976) discuss these issues in a complex manner and with tragic overtones, other times — in *The Star Diaries* (1971) and *The Cyberiad* (1967) — Lem describes mirroring with self-deprecating irony.

The problematics of representation, uncanny repetition, labyrinths, and mirroring, which are crucial in Lem's oeuvre, become equally important in Dick's fiction. But when Dick discusses these issues he always brings them to various ontological levels, foregrounding the presence of divergent timelines and alternate universes.

Dick's stories demonstrate Deleuze's and Baudrillard's theories on simulacra, revealing that we need to go beyond and deconstruct mirroring, mapping, and other traditional forms of representation and duplication. Cyberspace brings forth new forms of space and representation; as Baudrillard observes, "Today the scene and the mirror no longer exist; instead, there is a screen and network" ("The Ecstasy" 126). Thus, I will analyze Dick's virtual realities and alternate universes by juxtaposing his fiction to postmodern and cyberpunk fiction, which emphasizes ontological questions and "bring[s] into view the 'worldness' of the category 'world' itself" (McHale, *Constructing* 248).

At first glance, cyberpunk seems to be grounded in a dual space structure: the texts rely on the duality of reality and cyberspace, human and mechanical, corporeal and virtual, "this side" and "beyond." Nevertheless, many novels and films of cyberpunk exceed such dual spatial structures. Multiply-embedded worlds are manifested in *The 13th Floor*, evoking McHale's Chinese box ontology. David Cronenberg's films *Videodrome* (1983) and *eXistenZ* (1999) display multiple embeddings and later engender a labyrinthine rhizome for the viewer, who finds himself "trapped in a web of representations which infect and transform reality" (Bukatman, *Terminal* 98). In other cases, a certain transcendence, traces of the fantastic infiltrate the cyberspace, opening up the duality for further plateaus. For example, in Gibson's *Count Zero* (1986) and *Mona Lisa Overdrive* (1988), voodoo spirits, "loas," mythical creatures mediate between the cyberworld and reality, creating "a subversive effect upon the rational, geometric perfection of cyberspace" (Bukatman, *Terminal* 214). Analogously, in the second and third films of *The Matrix Trilogy*, ghosts, vampires and werewolves inhabit the computer generated realms, "disrupting the seamless presentation of the world of the matrix" (Constable 244).

Dick's oeuvre confirms that cyberspace might trigger multiple, not only dual, universes. His novels, however, come to this conclusion from the opposite direction; it is a basic premise of his fiction that the universe is based on multiplicity and alternate timelines, thus forming rhizomatic models — and some of these alternate realities happen to derive from computer generated realms.

In Chapter 4, therefore, I analyze the ontological problematics, the multiplied and liminal zones in Dick's fiction. I intend to demonstrate the interrelatedness of liminality and multiplicity by analyzing architecture, urbanity, various forms of traveling, cyberspace and paraspace, time and historicity, technological instruments, and narration in Dick's alternate histories, psychological and proto-cyberpunk fiction. I will examine *Time Out of Joint* (1959), *The Man in the High Castle* (1962), *Ubik*, *Do Androids Dream of Electric Sheep?* (1968), *A Scanner Darkly* (1977), *Martian Time-Slip* (1964), *We Can Build You* (1972), and several short stories by Dick.

My textual analyses will utilize the varieties of liminality that I identified in the theoretical discourses of Derrida, Bhabha, Foucault, de Certeau, Deleuze and Guattari, and others. In this way hopefully I will be able to give a brief summary of how liminality is reinterpreted in postmodernism, demonstrating that in the fictional zones of metaphysical detective fiction, fantasy, science fiction and "terminal identity fiction," liminality requires unconventional forms and brings forth innovative meanings.

CHAPTER 1

Liminality and the Fantastic in Agatha Christie's Detective Stories

The Sleep of Reason Produces Monsters. (Painting, Francisco Goya)

Connotation is the way into the polysemy of the classic text, to that limited plural on which the classic text is based. (Roland Barthes)

In this chapter I characterize liminal places and characters in Agatha Christie's oeuvre to describe how one of the most notable authors of traditional whodunits can simultaneously maintain and modify the traditional formulas of detective fiction. I intend to demonstrate here that — as Chapter 2 will confirm — detective fiction and fantasy are in many respects intertwined, in so far as they present the motif of liminality in different but somewhat complementary ways. My analysis of "rationalistic" detective fiction, therefore, serves as an introduction to the structure of overtly fantastic, "irrational" genres, which will be discussed starting from Chapter 2.

Rationality and Its Limitations

The theoretical backgrounds of detective fiction, the possibilities of puzzle-solving that can successfully investigate the Universe, can be traced back to Enlightenment rationalism (Sawyer 174). As Thomas S. Kuhn argues, rationalistic "normal science" considers puzzle solving as its main task, when scientists do experiments to "add to the scope and precision" of a particular paradigm, but they do not largely differ from it (36). Thus, the key feature of the "normal" scientist and the puzzle-solving researcher is conservatism, since it becomes extremely palpable "how little they aim to produce major novelties, conceptual or phenomenal" (35).

Analogously, widely accepted interpretations of detective fiction emphasize that the fictional detective should be extremely law-abiding and rational. A major premise of the genre is the sleuth's "rational scrutiny" (Belsey 283). The mental process of the detective is similar to that of an apt reader or researcher: the flaneur-detective "claims that reality may be read simply by looking at its commonly accessible surface in the proper way" (Brand 231). The detective recreates the formulaic language of rationalism, "a language conceived as a transparent system of signs" (Bürger 50; see also Shklovsky 108). Thanks to the sleuth who finds the single valid interpretation of events, society and language maintains its unity and order.

The esthetic of rationalization can be detected in the formal aspects of detective fiction, as well. Critics often point out that a major characteristic of detective fiction is to solidify and conserve the rules, the narrative structure and the genre conventions, instead of modifying or revolutionizing them. As Todorov argues, "Detective fiction has its norms; to 'develop' them is also to disappoint them: to 'improve upon' detective fiction is to write 'literature,' not detective fiction" ("The Typology" 43).

Yet, in spite of the formulaic structure, simple language, and the transparent and imperceptible style, the genre is interpreted by Todorov as a showcase of literature. The most traditional form of detective fiction, the whodunit, clearly displays the narratological

Figure 7. *The Sleep of Reason Produces Monsters* (Francisco Goya).

model of formalist and structuralist literary schools. The fable (or fabula) and the sjuzet (or plot) are the equivalents of the story of the crime and that of the investigation. The story of the crime is the simple chronological order of events, that is, the theoretical reconstruction of "what has happened in real life"; analogously to the fabula, it outlines the sequence of events as they happen in everyday life (Todorov, "The Typology" 45). On the other hand, the story of the investigation is similar to the plot, the disrupted chronology, in which the narrator presents and the reader becomes familiarized with the order of events.

Thus, the genre becomes the playground of formalist and structuralist thinkers: such "[p]opular tales ... and traditional narratives in general stick closer to the pole of repetition. This is why they constitute the preferred kingdom for structuralism" (Ricoeur 25). With some additional malice, I. I. Revzin argues in a similar way: "Before applying structuralist methods to the study of great literature ... these methods should be worked out on simpler objects, such as literature with mass appeal" (385).

Consequently, the traditional whodunit becomes both a straightforward and a multilayered genre, a simple and self-conscious or self-reflective narrative, featuring a rigid structure that nevertheless calls for complex structural analysis.[1]

Of course, the detective writers themselves soon realized the formulaic nature of their genre. Certain writers openly embraced the rigid structures and strict rules: in the "Golden Age" of detective fiction, roughly between the two World Wars, the success and uniformity of whodunits escalated due to the control of the Detection Club, Ronald Knox's "Ten Commandments," and S. S. Van Dine's "Twenty Rules." Self-reflexive references in these stories often attack the predecessors on basis of the order-chaos dichotomy, arguing that the criticized novels are too messy, not as rational, orderly and intellectual as the conventions require (Hutcheon, *Narcissistic* 72).

Meanwhile, American writers in the 1920s and 1930s such as Dashiell Hammett and Raymond Chandler established the hard-boiled school, which intended to modify or even reverse the conventions of the genre. These authors formed a palpable reaction against the stable rules and orderly space of detective fiction when they utilized chaotic, "decentered" scenes and tangled storylines, depicting the corrupt, ever-changing, contingent world of the American city (see, for example, Malmgren, *Anatomy* 74, 137).

It is important to notice, however, that several critics foreground the minor mistakes and purposeful deviations of *traditional* mystery fiction, namely, even such classical authors as Edgar Allan Poe, Arthur Conan Doyle, Dorothy Sayers, and Agatha Christie. As Julian Symons argues, "The book that has no interest whatever except the solution of a puzzle, does not exist, and if it did exist it would be unreadable" (12). Poe has not only established the genre but already diversified it.² At least occasionally, following the rules becomes highly difficult for Conan Doyle's Sherlock Holmes: he lets the culprit go at the end of "The Blue Carbuncle" (1892), and burgles a house and refuses to investigate in "The Adventure of Charles Augustus Milverton" (1904). As semioticians observe, his pure reason, the rationalistic basis of his investigation, is not completely untainted and immaculate (Sebeok and Umiker-Sebeok 18–30; Ginzburg 267; Truzzi 69–70), which brings his character close to fantastic interpretations and science fiction adaptations. (A short overview of the Holmes saga will follow in Chapter 3.)

Christie's fiction provides perhaps even more clearly prime examples of narrative and thematic deviations. To analyze Christie's subversions, I first need to explore the genre conventions by drawing on Bakhtin's abstract chronotope and Roland Barthes's textual codes in his *S/Z*. Thus, I will find ever-present dual oppositions in detective fiction, such as the dichotomy between home and alien world, order and chaos, society and antisocial elements, countryside and the city. It is my assumption that such examples of "inexpiable" antithesis, recapitulating Barthes's symbolic code, always integrally imply transgression, "excess" and "supplement" by constructing an "intermediate place" (*s/z* 21, 27).

Although the thematic, formal, and institutional rationality of the genre exalts the first part of the above dichotomies, favoring order over chaos and society over antisocial rebellion, Christie's latent subversions question the strict oppositions, temporarily undermining—or often just pretending to undermine—the cultural dichotomies of detective stories. Thus, liminal spaces and characters saturate Christie's texts, which simultaneously imply and deny the possibilities of class transgression, multiple universes, and the pervasion of the fantastic.

The Abstract Chronotope and Its Transformations

The spatial dichotomy of detective fiction allegedly avoids the fantastic-reality opposition as the genre seems to rigorously ban the fantastic: "Everything must be explained rationally; the fantastic is not admitted," argues Todorov in his "The Typology of Detective Fiction" (49), based on one of the "Twenty Rules" of S. S. Van Dine.³

What is more, the whodunit, the most analytical type of murder mysteries, even seems to conceal or efface the structural problems and semantic connotations of fictional space and time. The stories evoke the chronotope that Mikhail Bakhtin describes in his analysis of the highly formulaic adventure stories. The abstract "adventure-time" of certain ancient Greek and baroque texts completely neglects the biographical or historical flow of time, as time "changes nothing in the life of the heroes, and introduces nothing into their life" (Bakhtin, "Forms of Time" 90).

In these romances and adventure novels, chronology lacks causal relations and everything happens randomly: most fictional events are subject to chance. In traditional detective fiction, reversely, causality has a crucial role and the role of chance is refuted, as the genre is based on analytical thinking and the methods of induction and deduction. The resulting chronotope, however, is quite similar in both (and several other) formula fiction genres, since the texts pivot around a static, abstract space-time structure. The characters do not age and their psyche does not change; even if they obtain a new formal status, that is, if they get promoted, married or relocated, it does not effect their actions. As Todorov observes, the characters "do not act, they learn. Nothing can happen to them" ("The Typology" 44).

Time, therefore, becomes "empty" in these novels, deviating from the patterns of a biography. Although the serialized nature of crime fiction, the recurrence of the same detective cannot avoid outlining the traces of a biographical chronology, the stories still form a digression from the normal course of life. The physical and mental development of the central character is frequently minor and unpersuasive: most often biographical errors saturate the novels. Christie's stories provide telling examples of this phenomenon. As Marion Shaw and Sabine Vanacker observe, "By the time of her last published appearance ... Jane Marple would be well over 100. But of course, in the world of Marple novels, although there is often a recognition that change does take place, Miss Marple herself changes very little, so that in *Nemesis* she familiarly appears as a fussy, slightly rheumaticky, elderly lady, hardly less frail than she had been forty years before" (45). Poirot's biography is also problematic: in his last appearance he should be about 120 years old, but he changes little in the novels. As Gillian Gill argues, "In essence the Poirot of the novels written in the late sixties is extraordinarily the same man as the Poirot of 1917" (50).

The typical detective is just as much sharp and effective after the age of sixty when retired as at the beginning of his career: the grey hair of Holmes or Poirot's grey moustache is just a disguise that indicates senility but, in fact, hides their still sharp genius. Thus, the great sleuth of detective stories, such as Poirot, "is in fact best seen as an efficient narrative unit rather than as a person" (Gill 53). Or, as Robert Barnard argues, the detective "has function rather than character" (105).

The sketchy portrayal of historical events is another example of the "abstract" or empty chronology in detective fiction. Christie's first novel, for example, *The Mysterious Affair at Styles* (1920) is set during World War I, but the events of the war hardly have an effect upon the storyline.

In a way similar to time, "the space of this chronotope is 'abstract' in the sense that the adventures could occur anywhere" (Holquist 110). Or, as Bakhtin argues, "what happens in Babylon could just as well happen in Egypt or Byzantium and vice versa" ("Forms of Time" 100). In Christie's novels, murders can take place on a train, plain, in a European or exotic city, on the Nile, and so on, but the clues always lead to a small group of suspects, evoking the setting of a desolate English country house. Consequently, spatial descriptions often remain sketchy: as Barnard points out, Christie's "villages are totally interchangeable, they are generalized and flat. Similarly London has no feel of London, Mesopotamia has no feel of Mesopotamia. We are in an eternal no-man's-land" (14). Characters, locations and historical backgrounds become artificial and mostly irrelevant for the reader, who is primarily looking for mysteries, clues, deductions, and other elements of the analytical process. Christie's fictional detective writer Ariadne Oliver reflects on the insignificance and variability of her settings, and the crucial role of the puzzle, in *Cards on the Table* (1936):

> "Women," said Mrs. Oliver, "are capable of infinite variation. I should never commit the same type of murder twice running."
> "Don't you ever write the same plot twice running?" asked Battle.
> "*The Lotus Murder*," murmured Poirot. "*The Clue of the Candle Wax*."
> Mrs. Oliver turned on him, her eyes beaming appreciation.
> 'That's clever of you — that's really very clever of you. Because, of course, those two are exactly the same plot — but nobody else has seen it. One is stolen papers at an informal weekend party of the Cabinet, and the other's a murder in Borneo in a rubber planter's bungalow."
> "But the essential point on which the story turns is the same," said Poirot [54].

Although the crime scene is a crucial and occasionally a meticulously described location, it gains its significance indirectly. The typical crime scene, the locked room — manifested in one of the earliest stories of the genre, Poe's "The Murders in the Rue Morgue" (1841) — is crucial only insofar as it provides obstacles and clues in the process of solving the puzzle. The setting in this type of story loses its importance when the detective finds the secret passage that the murderer used and solves the "locked room mystery."

The closed space is foregrounded by Christie when she utilizes a murder scene that allows the presence of only a few characters and so the detective has to find the murderer within a family or a small group of suspects. This is what happens, for example, in her *Cards on the Table*, in which Poirot finds the culprit by asking the suspects to describe the room where the murder happened:

> I next made a second test. I got everyone in turn to tell me just what they remembered of the room. From that I got some very valuable information. First of all, by far the most likely person to have noticed the dagger was Dr. Roberts. He was natural observer of trifles of all kinds — what is called an observant man. Of the bridge hands, however, he remembered practically nothing at all [*Cards* 187].

Even in this case, however, the location becomes relevant in an indirect way, as the characters' descriptions about the room specify their psyche, perception, recollection, interests, and so on. Instead of the place, it is the recollection and *description* of the place that becomes crucial and provides psychological clues for the detective.

Thus, one could venture the assumption that the geographic or spatial elements — interweaving two analysis by Roland Barthes, the "topographic" "lexia" ("The Structural" 233; *S/Z* 13–14) — of whodunits are essentially formed by Barthes's hermeneutic code, as they generate markers "by which an enigma can be distinguished, suggested, formulated, held in suspense, and finally disclosed" (*S/Z* 19).[4]

The function of the crime scene is to create retardation, false resolutions while — drawing on Gill's term — the Actively Detecting Reader is attempting to solve the enigma. The reader attempts to find crucial and authentic clues in the room, but false clues and erroneous interpretations distract their attention. As Viktor Shklovsky argues about the genre, "Chekhov says that if a story tells us that there is a gun on the wall, then subsequently that gun ought to shoot.... In a mystery novel, however, the gun that hangs on the wall does not fire. Another gun shoots instead" (109–110).

It is important to realize, however, that Barthes's semic code also operates in the abstract world of detective fiction. The spatial expressions provide metonymical, "additional connotation" for readers who want to find sociological, feminist, classist or racist references. As Barthes observes, the setting of realist fiction frequently "forms a pertinent signifier: the wealth of the ... family" (*S/Z* 17, 18). Analogously, the typical whodunit depicts identical, uniform upper-middle-class surroundings and so creates a reassuring environment for the middle class. As Kathy Mezei argues, the country house represents the hierarchical structure and power relations of traditional society, serving "as symbols and settings of the community ... [which is] hierarchical in structure, with a head, a heart and hands — father, mother, children and servants" (105).

Barthes's symbolic code is also displayed when "on the symbolic level, an immense province appears, the province of the antithesis" (*S/Z* 17). The difference between an alien world and a familiar space, for example, forms a crucial spatial opposition in literary texts. In the chronotope of Greek romance, due to the random, unpredictable flow of events, the world "is an *alien world*: everything in it is indefinite, unknown, foreign" (Bakhtin, "Forms of Time" 101; emphasis in original).

This complete alienness is absent in detective fiction. The detective finds nothing that eludes his attempts of exploration and familiarization — this is what distinguishes him from the hero of hard-boiled detective fiction and postmodern anti-detective fiction. The traditional detective embarks upon a quest for a rational explanation, and the whole universe appears basically rational for him from the beginning — even though it often looks mysterious and supernatural in the eyes of other characters. The detective, therefore, is at home in the fictional world throughout the story.

The detective's social position — nationality, age, rank, economical and marital status — slightly contradicts, but eventually confirms this epistemological coziness. Miss Marple initially appears as a marginal, somewhat despised spinster in *The Thirteen Problems*, but she immediately becomes a crucial member of the rural society as only she can solve the mysteries. As Shaw and Vanacker point out, "Not only is the criminal one of us ... but the detective is one of us too ... Miss Marple is a kind of social conscience, dormant most of the time but always there, watchful and easily aroused" (3). Marginality gains the power of judgment and inside observation; as Mezei argues, the spinsters of detective fiction "exercise power through their position at the edge" (106).

Poirot can be a foreigner, but he acts in the circles of British aristocracy and bourgeoisie with an efficiency of an insider. In the early novels, especially in *The Mysterious Affair at Styles*, Poirot is described as a "cartoon character," a "social oddity" (Gill 53), but he soon becomes a gentleman, "a distinguished foreigner of refined tastes," since his "impeccable black clothes and patent-leather shoes are proper, his formal manner correct, his foreign accent and mannerisms charming" (Gill 142).

Miss Marple's and Poirot's age and unmarried status, the latter's foreignness become disguises: they seem naïve, senile, ignorant, marginal characters, but their remarkable social position helps them solve the case and so they become acute inside observers of the society. Analogously, Miss Marple's fellow detective in *4.50 from Paddington*, Lucy Eyelesbarrow, is not only a former scholar, but also a character who willingly spends certain periods of her life as a maid, while other times she is an upper-class traveler.

Such marginal but fluctuating, intermediary, liminal characters demonstrate Dana Brand's argument that the detective, like Walter Benjamin's flaneur, "distances himself from what he observes in order to achieve his panoramic perspective" (237). Or, as Shaw and Vanacker put it, "Relieved of sexuality and undistracted by close emotional [and social] bonds, such a figure cannot but see things clearly and act impartially as an agent of moral law" (4). The lack of emotional bonds and asexuality become most apparent in the detective-Watson figure of Christie's Harley Quin stories, Mr. Satterthwaite, a feminine character who is a great observer, listener, and assistant of lovers, but he is "half a woman" (Christie, "The Man" 176), who never participated in love affairs (Christie, "Harlequin's Lane" 396).

Another spatial dichotomy that detective fiction recapitulates is the order-chaos distinction, which correlates with the opposition of countryside and the city. Conventional stereotypes and many thoughtful criticisms associate crime with urban poverty and the flaneur-detective with the chaotic city (Brand 226–37). Shklovsky argues accordingly: "Conan Doyle rarely gives us a landscape, and, when he does, it is usually to remind us that nature is good while man [and the city] is evil" (115). Franco Moretti, however, points out that Conan Doyle's *fictional* crime, the murder as an abstract enigma or "adventure" needs to be situated in unlikely places, such as the exquisite districts of London or the "peaceful" countryside (*Atlas* 137–38).

The Golden Age writers and Christie shifted the focus on the countryside even more openly. Their murder mysteries are mostly set in the English country house so that the peace, simplicity, lucidity, and order of innocent rural life could form a sharp contrast with the brutality and opaqueness of murder. As Symons argues, "The most satisfying detective stories are those set in idyllic and preferably rural conditions," because in this environment the corpse appears shockingly out of place (15). The orderly space of innocence is disrupted temporally by the murderer, but the detective recreates stability and order when he or she eliminates the culprit.

Yet, even such a "traditional" writer as Christie occasionally diverges from the formulas: her chronotopes evoke more diverse connotations and her narrative technique often becomes playful and devious. This can be explained by the fact that a major contradiction of the genre is formed by the unavoidable co-presence of novelty and schematic conservatism. As Moretti observes, the text "must tell ever-new stories because it moves within the culture of the novel, which always demands new content; and at the same time it must reproduce a scheme which is always the same" ("Clues" 141).

Narrative Games and Naïve Psychology

Christie's oeuvre becomes highly intricate and contradictory as she both follows and subverts the traditional model of murder mysteries. On the one hand, reading clues is a crucial element in several (but not all) of her stories, occasionally creating perfect riddles for the reader and so "[b]ook-length studies of Christie acknowledge her skill as a maker of puzzles" (Merrill 87).[5] The

Todorovian dual narrative structure of the whodunit is usually neatly maintained "in her technically brilliant plots" (Knight 89). Todorov, in fact, cites a Christie novel as an example for "the purely geometric architecture" of the genre ("The Typology" 45). Carl Malmgren, in his typology of murder fiction, associates Christie's writings with the "relatively pure examples of ... classic mysteries," which feature "a centered world [which] is at once orderly, stable, resistant to change, and relatively free of contingency" (*Anatomy* 8, 14).

Thus it is hardly surprising that Poirot occasionally argues candidly for the significance of objective truth and justice:

"The truth, I have always thought, is curious and beautiful."
"Sometimes," said Colonel Carbury, "it's damned unpleasant."
"No, no." Poirot was earnest. "You take there the personal view. Take instead the abstract, the detached point of vision. Then the absolute logic of events is fascinating and orderly" [*Appointment with Death* 252].

On the other hand, as several critics have observed, "Some of Christie's puzzles can seem a teasing game with her readers, such as *Ten Little Niggers* (1939) ... [in which] the (apparent) first victim is the killer; in reverse, in *Murder on the Orient Express* (1934) all the suspects acted together" (Knight 91). Both novels elude the genre conventions because the great detective does not punish crime: Poirot justifies the murder in the latter, while the triumphant detective is almost entirely missing in the former story. Christie, in fact, quite often omitted the central detective figure; "in her autobiography she says her favourites were two basically detective-free novels *Crooked House* (1949) and *Ordeal by Innocence*" (Knight 90–91). Malmgren cites Christie's *Endless Night* (1967) as an example of "crime fiction," a "deviant" subgenre of murder fiction, and he describes it as a novel that rewrites traditional mystery stories; he also draws on the relative randomness and arbitrariness of murder in her *Murder in Three Acts* (1934).

The formal perfection of Christie's novels is supplemented by formal transgressions, "narrative games" (Merrill 88), misleading narrative focalization (Mezei 107–08), and metafictional references. Christie's own name as that of a successful story writer is mentioned in *The Body in the Library* (88), and the fictional detective writer Mrs. Oliver has a novel entitled *The Body in the Library* (*Cards* 15). Further, Christie hides the culprit behind the character of the narrator in *The Murder of Roger Ackroyd* (1926). (A short analysis of this novel will follow in Chapter 2.) As Barnard points out, the success of *The Murder of Roger Ackroyd* motivated Christie to carry on with her subversive games:

From time to time during her career, then, Christie brought off a series of outrageous coups that kept alive the reputation she gained with Ackroyd. When the time for a solution came round the most unaccountable rabbits were produced from her hat: the murderer was the investigating policeman, he was a child, he was one who we thought already dead, he was all the suspects together, he was Poirot, and so on ... because she dared to think the unthinkable there is no trick in the trickster's book, it seems, that she hasn't thought of first [47].

Transgressions between fictional levels, between the story of the investigation and that of the crime, result in metafictional and metaleptic games in Christie's fiction. Her highly successful play *The Mousetrap* (1950), for example, becomes similar to Julio Cortazar's "Continuity of Parks" (1956), in which the reader of a detective story is murdered while reading. In Christie's play, the listener of a radio program is murdered in a way similar to and approximately at the same time as the radio presenter describes the psychological reasons behind a frightening scene, evoking a horror or detective story:

> VOICE ON THE RADIO. ... to understand what I may term as the mechanics of fear, you have to study the precise effect produced on the human mind. Imagine, for instance, that you are alone in a room. It is late in the afternoon. A door opens softly behind you...
> (The door down R opens. The tune of "Three Blind Mice" is heard whistled. Mrs. Boyle turns with a start) [320; 1.2].

The Mousetrap, therefore, resembles other metaleptic, self-reflexive plays and films, for example, Wes Craven's *Scream* (1996), a postmodern horror film in which the character Randy (Jamie Kennedy) almost gets killed under very similar circumstances: the frightening events that happen to him seem to "copy" the horror film that he watches. (See Hills, *The Pleasure* 193.)

Analogously, the protagonist in *Murder, She Said* (1961), George Pollock's film adaptation of Christie's *4.50 from Paddington* (1957), witnesses a murder through the compartment window of a train right after she has been reading the crime story *Death Has Windows* and fallen asleep. (In the novel, only the conductor suggests a similar possibility [8–9]). The crime she witnesses can be interpreted not just as a dream or an odd coincidence, but as the horrifying materialization of the book that she was reading, a metaleptic device or mise-en-abyme with which an embedded story infiltrates the level of the frame (Devas 259–60).

Christie creates a notable *thematic* divergence from her predecessors when she describes a detective who utilizes not only clues, but also relies on a certain experience or know-how, which cannot be reduced to pure rationality. As Gill observes, although Christie's first novel *The Mysterious Affair at Styles* features numerous material clues in the manner of Poe and Conan Doyle, "[m]ore often than not, obvious, classic, material clues in Christie's novels are red herrings" (40), since, especially in the later novels, "Poirot will be much less concerned with material clues than with understanding the overall logic of crime"

(39). Further, Miss Marple often finds the culprit by associating the characters of the case with village dwellers of her St. Mary Mead. Thus, her method is basically empirical and rhetorical: as Gary Day argues, "Miss Marple's habit of seeing events in terms of village incidents is not dissimilar to the totalising power of metaphor" (90).

Additionally, the knowledge of rural life and household duties, the wisdom of the housewife needs to be obtained and deployed by the detective. Miss Marple's dénouement in "Ingots of Gold," for example, openly stresses the importance of horticulture: "'Gardeners don't work on Whit Monday. Everybody knows that.' ... 'When you are a householder, dear, and have a garden of your own, you will know these little things'" (44).

Accordingly, the active woman investigator, storyteller, and reader come to the foreground: "'Gentlemen,' said Miss Marple calmly, 'never see through these things'" ("The Four Suspects" 124). This female knowledge and detection, however, is owned not only by female characters, since "[b]efore Miss Marple is invented Poirot already represents a heightened version of female domestic knowledge as a weapon against fictional disorder" (Knight 91). Moreover, not all female characters acquire this knowledge: a woman and artist in *The Thirteen Problems,* Joyce Lempriere, for example, frequently fails to provide the right solution to the puzzles. The detective writer Mrs. Ariadne Oliver is usually a step behind Poirot in *Cards on the Table* (although accidentally she does come up with the right solution at the very beginning of the mystery). Thus, utilizing and subverting both traditional gender clichés and certain feminist formulas, "Christie upsets the stereotypes she makes use of" (Shaw and Vanacker 33).

Besides the domestic knowledge, revealing one's hidden characteristics and knowing their personality are also crucial means to find the murderer. Both Poirot and Miss Marple emphasize that everyone possesses a central core, a hidden but crucial part of their personality which is identified as "nature" or "type" and which primarily defines one's actions. As Miss Marple reveals: "It's just that living in a village as I do, one gets to know so much about human nature" ("Strange Jest" 32).

The "nature" of the suspect's personality determines whether the suspect committed the type of crime in question: a culprit always commits "essentially the same type of crime" (*Cards* 54).[6] Deciphering the clues and examining the facts has to be implemented by an emotional, empathic process, a psychological study. As Poirot observes, "I had to examine the evidence for *myself.* To examine the facts and to satisfy myself that the psychology of the case accorded itself with them" (*Five Little Pigs* 308; emphasis in original).

Thus, the detective's reading and investigating process is not just a semiotic phenomenon, but also a psychological method that implies Norman Holland's reader response theory. Holland posits "a 'primary identity,' itself irreversible but capable of infinite variation" (121), which is similar to Christie's "type" and "nature," as it is stable, constant, and entirely defines one's personality and life. Holland argues that the reading process, the interpretation of texts is dependant on such an identity: "We can explain such differences in interpretation by examining differences in the personalities of the interpreters. More precisely, *interpretation is a function of identity*" (123; emphasis in original).

The job of the detective is to find the inner core of the personality and correlate it with the inner core of the murder. In spite of being an extremely simplified idea of the human psyche,[7] Christie's theory somewhat questions the epistemologically safe universe of analytical thinking. The psychological assumptions in her stories lead to an upsetting anxiety, a nightmare that evokes the lack of trust in middle-class society. Christie's characters have to presume that the criminal, the evil, may be hiding behind politeness, beauty, and innocence in everyone's case:

> You ask yourself questions and you begin to doubt. You feel that somebody you love and know well might be — a stranger.... That's what happens in a nightmare. You're somewhere in the middle of friends and then you suddenly look at their faces and they're not your friends any longer — they're different people — just pretending. Perhaps you can't trust anybody — perhaps everybody's a stranger [*The Mousetrap* 335; 2].

When Christie's novels describe the criminal as "one of us," they become highly disturbing, since they indicate that reality cannot be read simply by looking at its surface. The rational approach to puzzle-solving and to the Other is replaced by an epistemological anxiety in so far as the characters need to realize that, as Shaw and Vanacker point out, "we can never entirely identify with the Other; absolute trust, a perfect mutual understanding is impossible" (21).

Liminal Places, Periods and Social Structures

Cultural traditions and hierarchic oppositions become somewhat ambiguous in Christie's fiction, especially via secret liaisons and murders. For example, a respectful "conservative banker who apparently stands behind and is the principal prop of the government of Britain" (Barnard 63) becomes a murderer in *One, Two, Buckle My Shoe* (1940). The symbol of old Britain, a highly respected and traditional hotel, turns out to be not only a nostalgic simulacrum (that is quite obvious from the beginning), but also a total scam, the concealed headquarters of a robbery team in *At Bertram's Hotel*. A countryside inn or a fashionable restaurant in London may become a portal to the fantastic, the headquarters of the divine figure Harley Quin or Harlequin in *The Mysterious Mr. Quin* (1930). No one is as innocent and no place is as safe as they look and so even the English countryside, "Mayhem Parva," loses the aura of innocence: "St. Mary Mead is, in its miniature way, as much a seat of evil ... as the busiest town" (Shaw and Vanacker 61).

Numerous controversial characters and liminal places saturate Christie's books, for example, the train in her *4.50 from Paddington* and *Murder on the Orient Express*. In spite of dividing the passengers into first, second and third class compartments or carriages, the crowded commuter train easily shuffles the different social classes: as Miss Marple observes in *4.50 from Paddington*, "There is something so anonymous about a train ... a train is full of strangers coming and going" (44, 45). The long international train journey in *Murder on the Orient Express* temporarily brings together "people, of all classes, of all nationalities, of all ages.... They sleep and eat under one roof, they cannot get away from each other" (38). The collapse of social hierarchies is enhanced by a minor catastrophic incident and the resulting panic, a snowdrift that blocks the train indefinitely, bringing the characters even closer to each other: "Any barriers there might have been between the passengers had now quite broken down. All were united by a common misfortune" (56).

As Christie's characters wear masks to hide their real nature, the stories evoke Bakhtin's carnival. Bakhtin argues that the middle-age carnival is a descendant of mythic rites, a festivity that "marked the suspension of all hierarchical rank, privileges, norms and prohibitions" (*Rabelais* 10). Turner characterizes liminality analogously: liminality forms a playful "weird domain" in space and time, in which "ordinary regularities of kinship ... are set aside, where the bizarre becomes normal, and where ... [the participants] are induced to think, and think hard, about cultural experiences they had hitherto taken for granted" ("Liminal" 27, 42).

This carnivalesque liminal stage is portrayed in several of Christie's works that foreground the period between the murder and dénouement and describe it as a liminal phase in the life of a family. As it is frequently the head of the family, "a tyrannical figure and husband whose death is eagerly desired by the family" who is the victim, the crime is followed by the relatives' "jostling for positions of power" (Mezei 105, 106).

The narrator in *Crooked House* stresses that due to the murder of the head of the Leonides family "The old order changeth" (109). The new order, however, cannot commence before the guilty party is found. The indicted culprit does not even have to be the actual murderer, just somebody who is a suitable scapegoat for the family. Thus, the liminal period of the investigation evokes another ritual, "sacrificial rite" (Moretti, "Clues" 137), the rite of the scapegoat, when "a man-hunter locates a *pharmakos* and gets rid of him" (Frye 46; emphasis in original).

In *Crooked House*, everybody would prefer the young second wife, the stepmother Brenda, to become the pharmakos, the murderer. A member of the family openly reveals that the incident "won't matter — as long as the right person killed him" (18). The narrator/detective/Watson-figure also experiences the effects of sacrificial rite: "The Crooked House was having its effects upon me also. I, too, wanted to find, not the true solution, but the solution that suited me best" (190).[8] A servant, a foreigner, an insane stepmother or stepchild would be the ideal culprit who would suit the family the most, making it possible for them to start a new order of spotless innocence. In *Crooked House*, the family's wish does not come true and the dénouement is hardly reassuring when a juvenile family member turns out to be the murderer. In other novels — *Ordeal by Innocence*, *Appointment with Death* (1938), *4.50 from Paddington*, and so on — the family can start the new era without losing their innocence, since the culprit turns out to be an outsider. But no matter what it takes, finding any kind of murderer is still better than lacking the solution.

Ordeal by Innocence, a novel "Short on detection, but fairly dense in social observation" (Barnard 193), also foregrounds the unstructured stage in the history of a bourgeois family, in this case the family of Leo Argyle and his stepchildren. The characters live in tranquility after the arrest, indictment and death of the son "Jacko," who was found guilty of the murder of the tyrannical stepmother. However, two years later an unexpected outsider named Arthur Calgary turns up, reveals the alibi for Jack Argyle and proves his innocence. His arrival and news is accepted with little delight in the family. As the family solicitor puts it:

> "Jack Argyle was the perfect answer to the unpleasant fact of murder in the family. He had been a problem child, a delinquent boy, a man of violent temper. Excuses could be and were made for him within the family circle. They could mourn for him, have sympathy with him, declare to themselves, to each other, and to the world that it was not *really* his fault, that psychologists could explain it all! Yes, very, very convenient."
> "And now—" Calgary stopped.
> "And now," said Mr. Marshall, "it is different, of course. Quite different. Almost alarming perhaps" [39; emphasis in original].

Calgary obliterates the stable relationships of the family that were formed after the supposed murderer — the perfect scapegoat, the mentally unstable stepson — had been found guilty, and so he creates the situation of "anti-structure," the "dissolution of normative social structure, with its role-sets, statuses, jural rights and duties" (Turner, "Liminal" 28). Until the new murderer is found, the family needs to go through a second, extremely unpleasant liminal period. (Their first liminal period took place between the murder and the indictment of the supposed murderer.) They have to live apart from the society, evoking van Gennep's period of seclusion, which is a state prior to liminality, another requirement of the "passage" (Turner, "Liminal" 24).

The secluded nature of the murder scene, the isolation of the English country house is a topos in detective fiction, but it is foregrounded in great detail on the first pages of *Ordeal by Innocence*. The novel describes the opposition between the modern, well-structured family mansion representing the middle-class desire for order and conformity, and the mysterious, gloomy, desolate, island-like environment. The latter evokes the mysticism of the Underworld, resembles fairy tale settings and deviates from regular order:

> The boat grounded on the beach. He had crossed the Rubicon....
> For the view was magnificent. The river here curved sharply round the point almost turning back on itself. Wooded hills rose opposite; up-stream to the left was a further bend of the river with meadows and orchards in the distance.
> Calgary looked for a moment up and down the river. One should have build a castle here, he thought, an impossible, ridiculous, fairy tale castle! The sort of castle that might be made of gingerbread or of frosted sugar. Instead there was good taste, restraint, moderation, plenty of money and absolutely no imagination [10, 11].

During the second liminal stage brought about by Calgary, the family's former harmony and structure is suspended and its hierarchy is turned upside down. The Father becomes "remote" (149) and inaccessible, two couples split up (Leo Argyle and Gwenda Vaughan separate temporarily, while the relationship of Hester Argyle and Dr. Craig dissolves permanently), and a new relationship (between Michael and Tina Argyle) is formed.

The family's liminal period resembles the Bakhtinian carnival because the characters wear masks and they live under the lack of social order, but it differentiates from the carnival when the situation lacks the laughter and the joyful celebration of the masses. The character Hester Argyle, for example, describes the situation as the following:

> "I don't know," she wailed. "I just don't know. I'm — it's an awful thing to say — but I'm frightened of everybody. It's *as though behind each face there was another face*. A — sinister sort of face that I don't know. *I don't feel sure that Father's Father*, and Kirsten keeps saying that I shouldn't trust anybody — not even her. And I look at Mary and I feel I don't know anything about her. And Gwenda — I've always liked Gwenda. But now I'm not sure about Gwenda anymore. *I see her as somebody different*, ruthless and — and revengeful. I don't know what anybody's like. There is an awful feeling of *unhappiness*" [148; emphasis added].

The distressing, painful, enforced and obligatory nature of the Argyle family's liminal period corresponds with Turner's liminal stage. Turner argues in his essay "Liminal to Liminoid" that during liminal periods "even the normally orderly, meek and 'law-abiding' people would be *obliged* to be disorderly in key rituals, regardless of their temperament and character." Thus, liminal and liminoid events may evoke anxiety in the subject: "Liminality may be the scene of disease, despair, death ... alienation, *angst* ... the verge of suicide" (43, 46; emphasis in original). The chaotic intermission, the transitory period without patriarchal rule and hierarchy repels and frightens the family members in Christie's novel, who would otherwise intentionally and gladly follow community rules and maintain the established social structure and family relations.

The behavior of such characters in *Ordeal by Innocence* foregrounds a major contradiction in detective fiction: the genre presumes and portrays desire for a stable social structure and hierarchical order, but the murder and the following investigation necessitates and embodies a liminal stage, a disturbing intermission in the rule of rationality and that of financial or feudal hierarchy. As Hazel Beasley Pierce argues, "Before conventional order reasserts itself, events tend to assume a perverse life of their own ... [as] the unexpected becomes the expected; the unknown becomes the real. The unexplained or seemingly inexplicable is the norm" (6).

Thus, for a short period even the supernatural becomes believable, and even a butler can be suspected of the murder of a wealthy and noble victim. Eventually, of course, social stability returns and the reader usually finds out that it was neither a ghost nor the butler who had murdered the master of the house. Marvin Carlson warningly stresses that in spite of Christie's thematic and narrative subversions "she remains firmly within the moral and ontological world of traditional detective fiction" (435). Mezei also underlines the recurrence of order in Christie's fiction: "Although positions of power have been temporarily altered or undermined ... the veils of tradition and authority once more descend over the households" (116).

Although Christie's novels rarely question the social and financial status quo openly, she deploys a few lower-middle-class (Michael and Tina Argyle) and working class (Maureen Clegg) characters in *Ordeal by Innocence*, in which a foreign employee of the family named Kirsten Lindstrom murders the extremely wealthy Mrs. Argyle. In her short story "The Tuesday Night Club," the young maid Gladys Lynch becomes the culprit, who has a secret liaison with the master of the house, "who had got Gladys Lynch into trouble, as the saying goes" (18). In other words, while it is almost a truism that "The servants in Christie's novels are usually stupid and amiable" (Shaw and Vanacker 20) and so rarely commit murder, there are intersections between social levels especially in the form of liaisons. As Gill points out, "In the fifteen Christie novels in which murder is committed by a man-woman team, it is interesting to notice that either the male or the female conspirator can come from a lower social class" (193). Christie's murders are unpredictable as the reader never knows whether her characters have transgressed social layers and violated social taboos, or the traditional middle-class order is emphasized and maintained throughout the text.

Fantastic and Multiple Spaces

As Revzin points out, the elements of the supernatural and those of the Gothic horror become tangible in Christie's oeuvre when she utilizes "such ancient devices as the introduction of twins, the substitution of a corpse, and so on" (387). Doppelgangers confuse the characters, ghosts and eldritch atmosphere haunt the houses, dead bodies look alive and living characters pretend to be dead. (See the Gothic elements in the stories of *The Thirteen Problems*, among others, in "A Christmas Tragedy," "The Bloodstained Pavement," and "The Idol House of Astarte.") The murder victim is visualized as a ghost in *Ordeal by Innocence* (102) and in *Endless Night*, and sends a divine messenger from the afterlife in "The Man from the Sea." The motif of the simulated space and that of the Double, which are crucial elements in horror and science fiction, gain significant roles in *At Bertram's Hotel*.

Fantastic elements in detective fiction have been tangible since the very beginning of the genre. The Gothic tradition can be interpreted as a reaction against the classic esthetic ideals and rationality of neo-classicism: "Never defeated completely by reason, imagination reinstated sensationalism in [the Gothic] literature ... promising a battlefield for the rational and irrational" (Pierce 204). A subgroup of Gothic stories resembles even more closely detective fiction, as they "explained all the weird goings-on in the story by rational means." (Panek 6). As Pierce observes, Ann Radcliffe's *The Mysteries of Udolpho*, a novel written in this fashion, was published in the same year (1794) as William Godwin's *The Adventures of Caleb Williams*, a novel foreshadowing or establishing detective fiction (205). Thus, the conventions of the Gothic and those of detective fiction go back to the same historical origins: they have a contradictory "love-hate relationship" with each other (Panek 6) as it is manifested, for example, in Edgar Allan Poe's stories. Other keynote texts also underline this slightly controversial genre-symbiosis, such as Conan Doyle's supernatural tales, proto-science fiction, and *The Hound of the Baskervilles* (1902).

Robert Merrill emphasizes the mysterious elements of the Marple stories, drawing a comparison between the investigation of the Poirot and that of the Miss Marple cases. He argues that the Belgian detective usually arrives at the beginning of the story or right after the murder. Thus, these novels utilize the convention that the reader should be capable of following the investigation: "the Poirot novels require that Christie play as fair as possible with the clues" (Merrill 95). The Marple stories, however, are not quite balanced and "fair." Miss Marple often comes up with a deus ex machina solution and so the reader can participate in the analytical game of the investigation only with great difficulties. As Merrill puts it, "The Miss Marple books are, in fact, almost impossible to 'solve,' for the game played stresses mystification rather than deduction" (96). Barnard also observes that "the way Miss Marple arrives at the identity of the murderer in *4.50 from Paddington* is never made clear, and might as easily be by divine revelation as by any process of ratiocination" (52). The deus ex machina solution and the "divine revelation" become most tangible in *The Mysterious Mr. Quin*, in which a godlike character, the harlequin-figure Mr. Quin helps the detective Mr. Satterthwaite to solve the puzzles: "a figure invisible except when he chose, not quite human, yet concerned with the affairs of human beings and particularly of lovers. He is also the advocate for the dead" (Christie, Foreword).

Christie's *The Thirteen Problems* can be read as a prime example of Merrill's analysis. The stories of the collection feature Miss Marple as the detective (for the first time in Christie's oeuvre), but they also follow the club-story conventions of horror and fantastic stories. The Tuesday Night Club intends to tell mysteries which have remained unsolved either due to the cleverness of the culprit, or because of the influence of (seemingly) unexplainable, supernatural events. In the "The Idol House of Astarte," a mystery that "resembles a Gothic horror story" (Shaw and Vanacker 62), the analytical, logical explanation does not explain every detail and the dénouement remains unsatisfactory. Miss Marple has to admit that "Of course there is only one way that poor Sir Richard could have been stabbed, but I do wish I knew what caused him to stumble in the first place" (31). The final sentences of the narrator, a clergyman who by occupation should not believe in pagan gods and forces, also disclose doubts about Miss Marple's rational account: "I do not think that explanation quite covers the facts. I still think there was an evil influence in the grove, an influence that directed Elliot Hayden's action" (32).

In "The Blue Geranium," nobody knows the solution of the "ghost-story" before it is told in the club and Miss Marple gives a rational explanation. The narrator begins his story stressing that "I've never believed much in the supernatural. But this..." (80). The question arises: what would happen to the story, its narrator and its fictional world, without Miss Marple? Would they remain in the realm of the fantastic forever? Christie, in fact, wrote several supernatural stories, such as those in *The Hound of Death and Other Stories* (1933) and "In a Glass Darkly" (1959), where the final, rational explanation is entirely absent. Her *The Mysterious Mr. Quin* is a prime example of mixing supernatural horror, detective stories, and mythic fantasy.

As Linda Hutcheon argues in her *Narcissistic Narrative*, detective fiction is a highly self-reflective genre, as the stories frequently comprise references to their predecessors and conventions: "the reader of a murder mystery comes to *expect* the presence of a detective-story writer within the story ... [and] a conversation about how such events as are then under discussion occur in detective stories, but never in real life (that is, in that novel)" (31; emphasis in original; see also Shklovsky 114).[9] As Day observes, *The Thirteen Problems* also becomes "conscious of itself as a work of fiction ... by various references to detective stories" (88). A story in the collection, "The Bloodstained Pavement," however, alludes (albeit ironically) to the ghost story conventions: "'I protest,' said Sir Henry. 'This is not a problem — this is a ghost story. Miss Lempriere is evidently a medium'" (50).

Thus, I disagree with Day when he argues that "The stories in *The Thirteen Problems* reassure the reader that life, despite its chaos and uncertainty, is really a very ordered affair" (81). In my reading, the hardly rational, randomly conducted investigations of Miss Marple do not compensate for the ambiguous, mysterious atmosphere in the short story collection.

Another fissure on the surface of the rational world and a possible node between detective fiction and the fantastic genres is described by Shaw and Vanacker. The two critics analyze Dorothy L. Sayers's *Five Red Herrings* (1931), a novel that describes six suspects who could commit the murder. Consequently, as the critics argue,

> there is a fear of *all* versions being equally true — or untrue. The fissure at the heart of logic, the fact that logic can lead to many truths in a world of multiple meanings, is quickly covered up by the success of the sleuth but not before the writer and reader of detective fiction have enjoyed a *frisson* at the possibility that logic may not be able to make sense of the complexities of existence [17; emphasis in original].

In other words, the description of mutually exclusive but simultaneously maintained solutions creates alternate timelines, which for a short period seem equally justifiable. Panek interprets Sayers's novel in a similar fashion, arguing that the "readers know that the last solution is the best, not because it is right or true, but because it comes last. The multiple solution story, consequently, stands not as an example of an unshakable logical edifice, but as a monument to the cleverness of the writer" (133).

Thus, one could venture the opinion that readers enjoy not only the final moments of such a detective novel, the recurrence of order in the dénouement, but also the majority of the book, the fissure of logic, when the universe is unstable enough to create doubts about the supremacy of univocal rationalism.

Christie's stories frequently portray similar cases. The detective-fiction writer Mrs. Oliver, for example, argues in *Cards on the Table* that "I can never think of even one plot at a time. I always think of at least five, and then it's agony to decide between them" (81). In *Murder on the Orient Express*, Christie probably could not choose, as all suspects turn out to be murderers. The introduction of *Cards on the Table* forewarns the reader that unlike traditional detective stories, in which the least likely person is the murderer and the other suspects are innocents, Christie's novel — at least initially — seems to feature *four* murderers. The question is not who the murderer is, but who has committed another crime *recently*.

> There are only four starters and any one of them, *given the right circumstances*, might have committed the crime. That knocks out forcibly the element of surprise. Nevertheless there should be, I think, an equal interest attached to four persons, each of whom has committed murder and is capable of committing further murders. They are four widely divergent types; the motive that drives each one of them to crime is peculiar to that person, and each one would employ a different method. The deduction must, therefore, be entirely *psychological*, but it is none the less interesting for that, because when all is said and done it is the *mind* of the murderer that is of supreme interest [5; emphasis in original].

Of course, only the foreword and the initial context of the novel offer multiplicity — eventually, the supremacy of one valid solution and one proper culprit is regained, and the rational world prevails. The universe of polysemy and multiple dimensions is rationalized with the help of psychology and the conclusion eliminates the former space-time disseminations.

Conclusions and Caveats

I intended to demonstrate in this chapter that detective fiction frequently foregrounds a liminal figure, the character of the detective, who oscillates between the margins and the central core of the society. He or she is a member of the social elite or that of the crowd but somehow stands out, evoking Benjamin's flaneur-detective, who is part of the crowd but demands elbow room and remains a unique, separate individuality (Benjamin, *Charles Baudelaire* 54, 69).

Further, Christie's detective fiction provides ample examples of overt and covert, playful and serious genre subversions. The slim possibility of the fantastic and the temporary presence of mutually exclusive timelines evoke the conventions of fantastic genres and put rationality to trial. Her transgressions of thematic and narrative conventions evoke dubious and temporary identities, somewhat flexible social structures, simulated and liminal places, and unstable class hierarchies. Her characters hide behind masks and her settings frequently turn out to be not so peaceful, resistant to change, orderly and stable as they at first glance seem to be. Thus, I somewhat question Malmgren's arguments that sharply contrast the masqueraded characters and decentered, "fluid" places of hard-boiled detective fiction with the uninteresting flat characters and stable, centered places of (Christie's) mystery fiction (*Anatomy* 8, 13–19). Although the hard-boiled school more candidly foregrounds chaos and contingency, conventional mystery fiction also features simulated, masqueraded, disorderly and fantastic places.

Especially in those Christie novels where the head of the family is murdered (such as *Crooked House* and *Ordeal by Innocence*), the investigation process coincides with a carnivalesque liminal period. The new order cannot commence straight away: the characters have to go through a mourning period, a temporary era in which faces are masked and positions are relatively flexible, since the family members try to regain and redefine their own and other's roles, positions and duties. This complex psychological and social process is described in a somewhat simplified manner in detective fiction: the place at the top of the social and financial pyramid needs to be filled, but it has to be gained by an "innocent" character. Thus, the murderer—in fact any murderer, a suitable murderer or scapegoat—has to be found by the detective.

My analysis of Christie's stories stresses that the more writers and readers become familiar with the rules, topoi, and patterns of the genre, the more they will be able to create and detect minor alterations in the patterns. An aficionado of the genre has sharp eyes that observe even the slightest modification in the analytic formulas. The forbidden and innovative element evokes either disapproval or a secret pleasure in the reader, but it does not leave one unaffected. Thus, in my understanding, Christie did not revolutionize traditional detective fiction but utilized, extended and played with its relatively flexible rules, which had always allowed certain forms of narrative plays and thematic subversions.

A final word of caution, however: in conventional murder mysteries and Christie's fiction, despite the scarce appearances of the fantastic, rationality passes the test in most cases. Analogously, after the characters go through the ordeal, the ritual of liminality and that of the pharmakos, eventually they can regain a stable identity. Hence, a new social order is created and conventional cultural dualities are more or less reinstated. As Shaw and Vanacker observe, "When everybody's identity has been established without a shadow of doubt, it becomes easy to identify the motive for murder and hence the killer. After this, a more secure world than ever before is created because the truth about everyone has been ascertained and any unease and doubt has been located and expelled in the figure of the murderer" (21). After the new order has been instated, a stabilized social life can commence in Christie's novels, in a way similar to traditional comedies. What Northrop Frye says about comedies may equally well apply to Christie's stories: "The appearance of this new society is frequently signalized by some kind of party or festive ritual," and so "Weddings are most common" at the end of the play or story (163).

Detective fiction, in a way similar to Frye's comedy, is centered around "the theme of ... the integration of the society," the (re)birth of society, a state that "the audience has recognized all along to be the proper and desirable state of affairs" (43, 164). Thus, the genre manifests Turner's arguments in his "Liminal to Liminoid" that emphasize the *temporary* and *re-constitutive* nature of liminality: the liminal phases "invert but do not usually subvert the *status quo*, the structural form, of society; reversal underlines to the members of the community that chaos is the alternative to cosmos, so they'd better stick to cosmos, i.e., the traditional order of culture" (41; emphasis in original). In other words, the evoked and then eliminated doubts possibly even reinforce the traditionally hierarchized world order: the provisional uncertainties liberate the reader from the monotony and dullness that derive from the oneness, rigidity, and predictability of the fictional universe of detective fiction.

CHAPTER 2

Liminal Fantasy in Neil Gaiman's Fiction

> A story's a good way of gettin' someone on your side. (Gaiman: *American Gods*)
>
> Stories are like spiders, with all they long legs, and stories are like spiderwebs, which man gets himself all tangled up in but which look so pretty when you see them under a leaf in the morning dew, and in the elegant way that they connect to one another, each to each. (Gaiman: *Anansi Boys*)
>
> What the map cuts out, the story cuts across. (Michel de Certeau)

Narrative Pacts in Gaiman's Fiction

The fantastic elements and multiple universes in Christie's oeuvre point to a covert resemblance between detective fiction and fantastic genres such as horror, fantasy and science fiction. In the following chapters, I intend to further clarify the possibilities of such genre bending.

A thorough analysis of Neil Gaiman's stories may reveal that the distinction between the highly rationalistic whodunits and the fairy-tale-like, mythical, "irrational" fantastic texts can become ambiguous, relative, and nearly contingent. As Bakhtin argues, the novel is a dialogical form of literature that often incorporates various genres, which possess their own "verbal and semantic forms for assimilating various aspects of reality" ("Discourse" 321). Although Bakhtin characterizes the *novel* with the heteroglot language, I find diverse representational aspects in several *short stories* by Gaiman, which are realized and kept in mind by the reader.

In several texts that I analyze in my book, the thematic, stylistic and narrative diversity frequently results in transgressions between, or oscillations across, genres. Such transgressions or oscillations can be explained by theories of narrativity and reader response criticism. Wolfgang Iser's theory of "contract" between author and reader as well as Philippe Lejeune's analysis of the "autobiographical pact" assume that during the reading process, pacts or contracts are formed in the reader's mind. The texts draw on well-known formal methods and thematic elements, "conventions shared by author and reader" (Iser, *The Fictive* 11).

When a contract is formed, this may result in the illusion that a text unmistakably belongs to a particular genre. For example, a text falls into either a mundane and rationalistic, or a fantastic genre, as it evokes either "the detective fiction pact" or "the fantastic pact" between author and reader. The seemingly abstract chronotope of detective fiction, the presence of an intelligent mastermind and the clearly-structured, simple narration would evoke the former pact. By contrast, the fantastic chronotope, the slightly archaic language, the "introduction of a fantasy actant" such as a witch, ghost, fairy or unicorn (Malmgren, *Worlds Apart* 141), and — at least in numerous contemporary fantasies, such as the works of the New Wave Fabulists — a subtle and unreliable narration would lead to the fantastic pact.

Yet in most cases the situation is not that simple: the pact falls under suspicion right after it has been formed. There are at least two ways to undermine the contract. First, from the reader's side: as Lejeune stresses, most readers intend to detect mistakes, "look for breaches of contract" (14), even in those cases when the pact offered by the author seems clear and unquestionable. As I indicated in the previous chapter, a fan of detective fiction, especially that of Agatha Christie, constantly searches for deviations in the conventional pattern, which occasionally bring forth the deployment of fantastic elements. Second, some texts are overtly edging on the borderline, temporarily offering two or more contracts, and so they urge the reader to hesitate or choose without clear guidance. Prime examples of these ambiguous, liminal cases can be found in Gaiman's "Murder Mysteries" (1992) and "A Study in Emerald" (2003) — short stories that recall both the fantasy and the murder mystery traditions and so question the traditional distinction between the two genres.

But genre overlapping, that is, *generic liminality*, is not the only instance of liminality in Gaiman's fiction. His ironic stories evoke *narrative liminality* when the pluralized perspectives deny the reader the possibility of nominating, let alone maintaining, a privileged point-of-view. These texts also result in *thematic liminality* in so far as the texts hover on the edge of reality and that of the fantastic.

To analyze these liminal phenomena, I utilize diverse approaches to the fantastic and various theories of narrativity. As for the former, I find useful suggestions in J. R. R. Tolkien's, Brian Attebery's, Nancy H. Traill's, John

Clute's, and Tzvetan Todorov's fantasy theories, but none of these fully accounts for Gaiman's stance. As for the latter, I utilize Linda Hutcheon's analysis of irony and parody, Mieke Bal's studies of vision, and Iser's theory of reading in order to explain that Gaiman's fantasies are ironic due to their doubled narrative perspectives, the multiplication and estrangement of voice and focalization. To bring these two approaches, the narrative and the fantastic, into some sort of coherence, I draw on Farah Mendlesohn's taxonomy, adapting—and perhaps slightly refining—her concept of liminal fantasy.

My narrative analysis focuses essentially on Gaiman's short stories, because these brief and intricate texts encapsulate and epitomize the narrative games and formal subversions of the author. His novels usually feature a more straightforward narration, and draw on traditional, less subversive fantasy conventions. Yet, as my mottoes have indicated, the novels often *thematize* the problems of narration and visibility due to the metafictional disclosure of narrative voice and focalization. *Anansi Boys* (2005), for example, reveals that if a narrator, hero, or god owns and dominates the archive of fairy stories, which happens recurrently, then inevitably a slanted point-of-view will emerge and dominate in the community's cultural consciousness. Furthermore, his *Neverwhere* (1996) and *The Graveyard Book* (2008) demonstrate contemporary Foucauldian theories, emphasizing that visualizing, narrating, and rendering visible are always controlled by psychological, cognitive, historical, and social factors. These texts promote our engagement in pluralized perspectives, subjectivized narratives, and estranged fantasy. Thus, I argue that liminality can be observed as a crucial, both thematic and formal, technique in Gaiman's fiction.

Fantasy Theories and Narrative Perspectives

Brian Attebery considers the genre of fantasy "a fuzzy set ... defined not by boundaries but by a center," whose "boundaries ... shade off imperceptibly" (12). He suggests that the hub of the genre is J. R. R. Tolkien's *Lord of the Rings* (1954–1955): "[Tolkien's book] was not the first modern fantasy ... may not be the best fantasy ... [b]ut Tolkien is most typical, not just because of the imaginative scope and commitment with which he invested his tale but also, and chiefly, because of the immense popularity that resulted" (14).

Tolkien, in his essay "On Fairy-Stories," characterizes fantasy with a descriptive inventory of a landscape in the realm of Faerie (9), emphasizing that the fantastic world should be kept intact and stay apart from reality. He argues that "[t]he moment disbelief arises, the spell is broken; the magic or rather art, has failed" (37). Tolkien's fantastic realm is a place to "escape" from everyday reality, a romantic utopia — as Jack Zipes interprets it (*Breaking the Magic* 147–49) — which suspends the rules of reality. Faerie, the setting of his ideal fairy tales or fantasy stories, is a land filled with magic creatures and enchanted humans, and it is governed by supernatural rules.[1]

In spite of Tolkien's crucial influence and enormous popularity, the fantasy that we read today has changed, or at least, expanded. Our postmodern culture is eager to read and analyze contemporary rewritings of fairy tales and fantasy parodies: readers enjoy not only the traditional "portal-quest" fantasies but also fantasies of the sort that Mendlesohn describes as "intrusion fantasies," which imply that the fantasy world or at least its alien creatures can intrude into and interfere with our everyday life; "immersive fantasy," where there is only the magical universe, which "allows us no escape" ("Toward a Taxonomy" 171, 175); and "the liminal fantasy," a subgenre that "in defiance of the conventional understanding of the fantastic as straight-faced ... [is based on] the ironic mode" (*Rhetorics* xxiv).

In Mendlesohn's portal-quest fantasies — that is, in the great classics, C. S. Lewis's *The Lion, The Witch and the Wardrobe* (1950) and Tolkien's *Lord of the Rings* — the protagonist leaves behind a mundane life to experience "direct contact with the fantastic" (xx).[2] The story in portal-quest fantasy pivots on a descriptive inventory of a landscape in the realm of Faerie. Tolkien's fantastic realm is a secondary world which suspends the rules of our everyday reality; his "subcreation" results in images "which are indeed not to be found in our primary world at all, or are generally believed not to be found there" (Tolkien 48). The subgenre, therefore, describes a direct confrontation and opposition between reality and the fantastic realm.

Liminal fantasy, however, hides the threshold, suggesting that the boundaries between fantasy and reality are elusive or insignificant, evoking humorous and surreal overtones. As Mendlesohn argues, "When the fantastic appears, it should be intrusive, disruptive of expectation, but instead while the events themselves might be noteworthy and they may cause chaos, their magical origins barely raise an eyebrow" (*Rhetorics* 179). The fantastic is no longer interpreted as a realm different and distant from consensus reality: reality and the fantastic world overlap in a playful or "blasé" manner, indicating the run-of-the-mill, unremarkable nature of fantastic events.

Mendlesohn's definition of liminal fantasy at one point (*Rhetorics* 182) refers to McHale's arguments on the "banality" of the fantastic in several modernist and postmodernist texts, from Franz Kafka to magic realism (*Postmodernist* 76–77). But Mendlesohn, instead of stressing the connections with canonized literary traditions, emphasizes the crucial role of the category in the popular fantasy genre: "Liminal fantasy ... may prove to be the purest form of the fantastic" ("Conjunctions" 238), as it "distill[s] the essence of the fantastic" (*Rhetorics* xxiv).

Tolkien highlights that the fantastic story should exclude doubts about the magical nature of the text: illusion, dreams, parody, or at least parodying the fantastic are banned: "[Magic] cannot be laughed at or explained away" (11). These principles are in sharp contrast with Mendlesohn's liminal fantasies — which "create a moment of doubt, sometimes in the protagonist, but also in the reader" (*Rhetorics* 182) — and with Gaiman's oeuvre, as he often uses dreams and parody, comparing storytelling to magicians' illusions with mirrors (Gaiman, "An Introduction" 3; Dowd 105). Gaiman emphasizes "the balancing and twining of the mundane and the miraculous" (Foreword 8), following the tradition of Edgar Allan Poe, and evoking Tzvetan Todorov's definition of the fantastic: "a hesitation common to reader and character, who must decide whether or not what they perceive derives from 'reality' as it exists in the common opinion" (*The Fantastic* 41). These kinds of texts are described by Clute with the term "equipoise," which "is not a term normally applicable to [traditional] fantasy, which may be described as comprising stories set in worlds which are impossible but which the story believes ... [b]ut it certainly applies to works ... which are built upon sustained narrative negotiations of uncertainty, without coming to any necessary decision as to what is real" ("Beyond the Pale" 424).

In Mendlesohn's portal-quest fantasies, the narrative perspective often remains one-sided: "We ride alongside the protagonist, hearing only what she hears, seeing only what she sees ... with a guided tour of the landscapes" (*Rhetorics* xix). In liminal fantasies, however, the pretense of the narrator that nothing unique is happening doubles the narrative perspective, as the restrained, naïve voice of narration becomes echoed by the reader's growing wonder and estrangement; as Mendlesohn argues, "We sit in the subconscious of the point-of-view character, quietly screaming 'but something is wrong'" ("Toward a Taxonomy" 180).

This doubled approach toward the fantastic is a crucial trait of liminal fantasies: "The insistence that what is fantastic [and astonishing] to the protagonist is at variance to what is fantastic to the reader" (Mendlesohn, *Rhetorics* 186). In Mendlesohn's examples, it is usually the reader who finds the events breathtaking or dire, while the main character and the narrator remain "blasé." But it can happen the other way around, as well, for example in Henry James's *The Turn of the Screw*, where the narrator-protagonist is convinced of the fantastic and horrifying nature of the events, while the reader remains doubtful or skeptical about the presence of the fantastic. (James's classic has been interpreted convincingly as a liminal story by Richard Dilworth Rust.)

Mendlesohn's analysis of liminal fantasy draws on Wayne C. Booth, who argues that recognizing "stable irony" in parodies necessitates "a reconstructing of implied authors and implied readers" (Booth 133; Mendlesohn, *Rhetorics*

184). Thus, analyzing the perspective of the narrator, implied author, implied reader, and detecting "inferences about intentions" (Booth 133) may become useful to capture irony in liminal fantasy and Gaiman's texts. Parodies create perspectives that they simultaneously deny: they outline and reject the perspective of "silly readers of conventional fiction" (Booth 131). Booth's theory of irony also becomes useful when it emphasizes the significance of intertextuality, that of "spotting allusions.... When critics do so they are, in a sense, 'reading between the lines,' discovering an author who 'means' something other than he 'says,' and they are thus engaged in a process very similar to the reading of stable irony" (264).[3]

Irony and Subversions in Gaiman's Murder Mysteries

"Murder Mysteries," although just a short story, becomes a medley of (sub-)genres. It features a subtle, multilayered narrative, which first resembles intrusion fantasy and horror, then becomes portal-quest fantasy and detective fiction, until finally, due to its unreliable narrator, evokes certain characteristics of liminal fantasy.

The story starts with a first person singular narration: the narrator describes himself as a British visitor in Los Angeles, an "alien" character who is lost in "the city of angels." Besides evoking (misleading) references to an auto-biographical reading — Gaiman is a British author who lives in the United States and has Hollywood connections — the opening scene depicts an uneasy space that constructs the latency of horror, similarly to Mendlesohn's intrusion fantasies, which often feature "a protected space, one that cannot be ruptured, and a sense that such a rupture is imminent" (Mendlesohn, *Rhetorics* 117). The narrator-protagonist meets a stranger who turns out to be Raguel, the angel of revenge, who brings on the intrusion foreshadowed by the setting of eerie Los Angeles. He tells a story that takes place in heaven before the human universe was created. Because of his desire to hear the story, the protagonist (the first narrator and later the narratee) rarely intervenes or expresses his surprise, with his silence accepting the perspective of the angel, the second narrator.

The narratee's absolute acceptance of the alien viewpoint reiterates the "willing suspension of disbelief," evoking the conventions of Mendlesohn's portal-quest fantasy, in which "the authority and reliability of the narrator must be asserted" (*Rhetorics* 7; emphasis in original). Raguel's advice about how to listen to or read his fantastic story could be a guideline to the implied reader of many traditional, portal-quest fantasies: "Don't worry about it.... You got to understand, a lot of the stuff I'm telling you, I'm translating already;

putting it in a form you can understand. Otherwise I couldn't tell the story at all. You want to hear it? ... So shut up and listen" (351).

The portal-quest fantasy, as well as "Murder Mysteries," draws on the Club Story conventions (although Raguel's tale is recounted only to one person, not a group), which often introduce "Tall Tales in a way that eases our suspension of disbelief during the duration of the telling" (Clute, "Beyond the Pale" 422). But as Clute observes, contemporary fantasy writers, especially the New Wave Fabulists such as John Crowley, Kelly Link, China Miéville, Peter Straub, James Morrow, and Gene Wolfe, most often utilize "equipoise," Todorov's uncertainty, instead of the suspension of disbelief: the stories reduce the fantastic "into a world of false codes, lamings of Story" (429) ("Beyond the Pale" 420).

Mendlesohn also stresses the stunning, frequently subversive first person narration of the New Wave Fabulists: "Many of these stories are 'told.' ... the use of the first person narration in so many of these tales suggests that the authors are deliberately relying on the collusive aspect of the club story ... and then [they] fracture that structure" ("Conjunctions" 238). Again, this is exactly what happens in *The Turn of the Screw*: the frame story gives credibility by using the conventions of the club story, relying on transcripts and deathbed confessions, while several elements (for example, the incompleteness of the frame) counteract this credibility "by the undermining of the frame structure itself, something we counted on to provide control" (Rust 444).

In the stories of New Wave Fabulists, the Club Story conventions are often turned upside down as a result of experimental, metafictional, subversive narrations. Kelly Link's "Lull" (2002) and "Magic for Beginners" (2005) are prime examples of this phenomenon: transgressions between the narrative levels, "strange loops" or "metalepses" saturate the texts, when characters migrate from one narrative level to another, and the reader is repeatedly confronted with the "violation of the hierarchy of narrative levels" (McHale, *Postmodernist* 119). Mendlesohn's analysis of Link's "Lull" may prove to be illustrative here: "Which is the world and which the frameworld? ... We are not asked to join a consensual reality but instead, perhaps, to accept that all realities are embedded" ("Conjunctions" 238).

"Murder Mysteries" undermines the conventions of the portal-quest fantasy and the Club Story because of its increasing resemblances between the frame story (consensus reality) and the embedded story (the fantastic). Thus, the two levels of narration generate the structure of mise-en-abyme, as the embedded story seems to repeat the frame: the world within the fictional world "constitute[s] some salient and continuous aspect of the primary world, salient and continuous enough that we are willing to say the nested representation *reproduces* or *duplicates* the primary representation as a whole" (McHale,

Postmodernist 124; emphasis in original). The "fantastic" and the "real" story, the frame and the embedded tale become inseparable and metaleptic, spiraling together to create an uncanny, double-layered structure: murders and interrelated investigations take place on both levels, both narrators are "sexless," remembrance and amnesia is a key issue, and so on.

Gaiman's short story also diverts from the intrusion fantasy conventions, which focus on an outsider disturbing the peace, chaos interfering with the structure of order. In "Murder Mysteries," the narrator becomes a suspect, making it impossible for the reader to decide who represents order and chaos, innocence and sin, and to distinguish between reality and the fantastic. The short story becomes slightly similar to Christie's *The Murder of Roger Ackroyd*, where crucial information remains hidden from us — "the narrator 'neglects' to tell us that it is he who has committed the murder" (Todorov, *Introduction* 37) — and the final disclosure reinterprets the whole text, evoking an ironic reading of the previous chapters.

> I am rather pleased with myself as a writer. What could be neater, for instance, than the following: "*The letters were brought in at twenty minutes to nine. It was just on ten minutes to nine when I left him, the letter still unread. I hesitated with my hand on the door handle, looking back and wondering if there was anything I had left undone.*"
> All true, you see. But suppose I had put a row of stars after the first sentence! Would somebody then have wondered what exactly happened in that blank ten minutes? [Christie, *The Murder of Roger* 254].

In Christie's novel, as in Gaiman's "Murder Mysteries," there is a transgression within the narrative levels, as the narrator himself becomes involved in the murder. Hühn's analysis of detective fiction indicates that, in a metaphorical sense, the murderer writes the story for the detective: "The author of the first story [the culprit] endeavors to gain control also over the second story [the detection] by acting as its narrator" (459). But, unlike in traditional detective stories where this control and writing remains covert and metaphorical by creating clues and red herrings, it becomes overt in *The Murder of Roger Ackroyd* and "Murder Mysteries," where the culprit *literally* writes the tale of the investigation. Thus, this technique may be interpreted in two ways: first, it follows the genre conventions of the detective story, which oblige the narrator to conceal the identity of the perpetrator. After all, what would be the perfect spot to hide the culprit on if not on another narrative level? Second, it can be accounted for by the intention to subvert the genre conventions and confuse the reader, who expects a simple structure with clear-cut narrative boundaries.

The blending of horror and detective story conventions becomes also overt in Gaiman's "A Study in Emerald." In this short story, H. P. Lovecraft's motifs are mingled with thematic elements of Sherlock Holmes stories, especially those of *A Study in Scarlet* (1887), "The Adventure of the Empty House" (1894), and "A Scandal in Bohemia" (1891).

Intertextuality provides a crucial approach to interpret Gaiman's oeuvre. The abundant number of textual allusions in Gaiman's fiction has been emphasized by many critics. Bethany Alexander, for example, argues that "Neil Gaiman borrows rituals, deities, tricksters and fairy tales from under every stone, roof or teacup" (139) Yet, as Linda Hutcheon implies, postmodern texts not only quote, but also modify and play with their source texts: "Ironic inversion is a characteristic of all parody.... This ironic playing with multiple conventions, this extended repetition with critical difference, is what I mean by modern parody" (*A Theory* 6, 7). Darrell Schweitzer, analyzing Gaiman's fiction, argues in a similar fashion: "a writer can't merely stand on the shoulders of giants. He has to do something interesting while he's up there. A little tap-dance, maybe. Gaiman does at least that" (116).

Gaiman's "tap-dance" is a prime example of Gerard Genette's hypertextuality: "any relationship uniting a text B (which I shall call the hypertext) to an earlier text A (I shall, of course, call it the hypotext), upon which it is grafted in a manner that is not that of commentary" (5). According to Genette, hypertextuality has to be distinguished from intertextuality, as the latter indicates a text directly quoting from or alluding to another text, "the actual presence of one text within another" (2). The foremost characteristic of hypertextuality is that the hypertext does not (only) quote, but transforms and/or imitates the hypotext: "Text B ... [is] unable to exist, as such, without A, from which it originates ... and which it consequently evokes more or less perceptibly without necessarily speaking of it or citing it" (5).

Genette's hypertextuality may be achieved either with "direct transformation" or "imitation." Direct transformation preserves the themes and characters of the source text, but places them into another setting, genre or context, such as James Joyce's *Ulysses* (1922), a text transposing the story of *The Odyssey* to twentieth century Dublin, and burlesque travesties, which depict a noble story in a vulgar manner (Genette 5–6, 22). Analogously, Gaiman's "Snow, Glass, Apples" *transforms* Snow White's tale by placing the events of the fairy tale into a macabre vampire story, but essentially preserving the original fabula.

The aim of the imitator, on the other hand, is to repeat a style, an idiolect, a dialect, while the subject of the source text may be considerably altered, such as in mock-heroic pastiches. Gaiman's "Shoggoth's Old Peculiar" *imitates* Lovecraft's language and style, becoming a pseudo-Lovecraftian text, as it renews Lovecraft's universe. Here, Gaiman becomes an "imitator" who detects and reproduces the favorite terms, the frequently used linguistic constructions of another author, utilizing Lovecraftisms: "The suffix *-ism* is here the equivalent of the prefix *pseudo-*" (Genette 77).

"A Study in Emerald" is essentially a story of Genettian intertextuality, as it incorporates several direct quotations from Conan Doyle's oeuvre: for example, a literal quotation from his *A Study in Scarlet* is the word "Rache," a message written with blood on the wall of the crime scene. The word is a homonym both in Conan Doyle's and Gaiman's text. In Conan Doyle's novel, the term is first interpreted as an unfinished word (Rachel), then as the German word "vengeance," but finally turns out to be a red herring, a "blind," a false clue that disguises a private vengeance as a political murder. In Gaiman's "A Study in Emerald," the German word becomes a genuine clue, as the story describes a political murder. Gaiman's detective also finds an additional meaning for the word, as it is, he says, "an old term for a hunting dog" (50).

The title of the short story is another intertextual reference, as it draws on Conan Doyle's *A Study in Scarlet*. In this novel, the title is a pun, both referring to the room where the body and a large amount of blood is found, and figuratively, to the case as a preliminary artistic outline, a composition for the practice of a point of technique. It was, after all, the first proper case of the great detective. The "study" helps to generate Holmes's "ars poetica," his rules of the art of investigation: the adventure becomes "the finest study I ever came across: a study in scarlet, eh? Why shouldn't we use a little art jargon? There's the scarlet thread of murder running through the colorless skein of life, and our duty is to unravel it, and isolate it, and expose every inch of it" (Conan Doyle, *A Study* 26). With this reference, Gaiman closely follows Conan Doyle's novel, as the short story also deploys the two meanings of the word "study," although it slightly alters the context, and the color, of course:

> The body, what was left of it, was still there, on the floor. I saw it, but at first, somehow, did not see it. What I saw instead was what had sprayed and gushed from the throat and chest of the victim: in colour it ranged from bile-green to grass-green. It had soaked into the threadbare carpet and spattered the wallpaper. I imagined it for one moment the work of some hellish artist, who had decided to create a study in emerald [34–35].

Another — slightly more covert — direct quotation is the fictitious name "Sigerson." In Conan Doyle's "The Adventure of the Empty House," Sigerson is the Norwegian pseudonym that Sherlock Holmes uses while he is exiled from London and hides from his enemies, the accomplices of James Moriarty. In Gaiman's "A Study in Emerald," Sigerson is the perpetrator's Icelandic pseudonym. Besides the altered nationality, it further complicates the allusion that Gaiman's characters form an inverse relationship with those of Conan Doyle. Sherlock Holmes and Dr. Watson turn into the perpetrators, described as "the Tall Man" and "the Limping Doctor" (48). Thus, the detective must be James Moriarty, while his sidekick-narrator is most probably Sebastian Moran, the sharpshooter and culprit in Conan Doyle's "The Adventure of the Empty House." Although both the detective and the first person narrator remains unnamed throughout Gaiman's story, the text is eventually signed with the initials "S_ M_" (56), which may stand for Sebastian Moran.

Gaiman's reversed characters reveal the covert but crucial similarity between the detective and the murderer in detective fiction. As Julian Symons points out (28), although the distinctions between the law-enforcing officials and the culprits were crucial for the Golden Age writers, they had been fuzzy throughout the history of the genre, since the late 18th century, the fiction of William Godwin, François Vidocq and Edgar Poe. Christie's *The Mousetrap* is one of the many examples in detective fiction that demonstrates the interchangeability of the detective and the culprit (Carlson 433–34).[4]

Gaiman's story indicates the substitutable nature of conflicting sides and characters in detective fiction, and thus creates a text which resembles Viktor Shklovsky's hypothetical detective story. The Russian critic describes an imaginary situation, a rewriting in which "the state detective ... would be victorious ... while the private detective would no doubt be floundering in vain. In such a hypothetical story Sherlock Holmes would no doubt be working for the state while Lestrade would be engaged in private practice, but the structure of the story (the issue at hand) would not change" (110). Something similar happens in Gaiman's story: although Sherlock Homes becomes the culprit and the traditional perpetrator Moriarty turns into the ingenious detective, the structure of the story, the pattern of detective fiction is neatly maintained.

"A Study in Emerald" also utilizes and demonstrates Genette's hypertextuality, when the text *transforms* the Holmesian elements — characters (Lestrade, private detective, sidekick), settings, and so on — into a fantastic story; the fabula of a detective story is placed into a fantastic narrative. The story can also be read as a transformation of Lovecraftian fantasy-horror, as it transfers Lovecraft's supernatural characters — the Great Old Ones — from rural New England to the Victorian London of a detective story. The Victorian atmosphere is emphasized when each section of the short story is introduced by a motto, in which historical and literary figures advertise their "services": they are infamous human monsters of the era, for example, Jack the Ripper, Count Dracula, Henry Jekyll, who have become shady entrepreneur physicians. "A Study in Emerald," therefore, in a way similar to a certain trend in science fiction, outlines an *alternate history*, a Victorian society that has never existed, a mixture of Conan Doyle's and Lovecraft's universe. (An analysis of the subgenre, and Philip K. Dick's alternate histories, will follow in Chapter 4.)

The interaction between Gaiman's fantastic fiction and detective stories does not end here. In Gaiman's "Only the End of the World Again" (1994), the mystical, Lovecraftian thematic elements are narrated by a private investigator, a character who evokes the protagonist-narrator in Raymond Chandler's hard-boiled detective fiction. In the online short story "The Case of the Four and Twenty Blackbirds" (1984), Christie's nursery rhymes and the narrative voice of hard boiled detective fiction are intertwined, with a title alluding to Christie's short story "Four and Twenty Blackbirds" (1940). Further examples are Gaiman and Dave McKean's graphic novel *Violent Cases* (1987), and a photographic book that Gaiman contributed to, *Who Killed Amanda Palmer: A Collection of Photographic Evidence* (2009).

Liminal Fantasies

Gaiman's "When We Went to See the End of the World by Downie Morningside, age 11¼" (1998) can serve as a prime example of Mendlesohn's liminal fantasy, a story in which apocalyptic events are narrated by a child who rarely gets surprised by the fantastic nature of her adventures. The estranged point-of-view of the narration is due to the narrator's age: "a small child sees things in a totally different way from an adult" (Bal, *Narratology* 142). Thus, reality is just as much fantastic to the protagonist-narrator as the apocalyptic and supernatural events that she encounters. As Alexander points out, "The contrast between the bizarre images and her lack of reaction gives me the shivers. Of everything on her family's trip the element that she gives the highest word count is the potato salad" (136).[5]

Gaiman's "How to Talk to Girls at Parties" (2006) also features a first person, naïve and juvenile narrator, as the protagonist-narrator Enn, a fifteen-year-old boy considers earthly girls just as alien as girls from other planets. His friend Vic advises him to talk to girls at the party, and so, in order to keep up the conversation, Enn ignores the peculiarities of the partiers who vaguely describe interstellar journeys, cloning, nations metamorphosed into a poem, and so on. The story becomes a humorous liminal fantasy (or liminal science fiction) when the narrator constantly misinterprets his conversations with the girls, identifying the foreign-accented extraterrestrials with Americans.

Both stories feature first person narration, deploying a young, homodiegetic narrator who actively participates in the story and who becomes unreliable due to his or her age, "limited knowledge," "personal involvement," and "problematic value-scheme" (Rimmon-Kenan 100). The storytellers have a limited point-of-view and they suffer from a visual impairment that makes them partially blind to the fantastic.

As Nancy H. Traill observes, the status of the possible worlds in fantastic fiction "is determined by the degree of narrative authentication. A narrator's power to authenticate rests largely on whether it is a third-person omniscient narrator (the Er-form) or a first person, subjective (Ich-form) narrator" (11). Traill defines a category within the fantastic as "the ambiguous mode," a subtype that in some points coincides with Mendlesohn's liminal fantasy and recalls Gaiman's "When We Went to See" and "How to Talk to Girls at Parties." The ambiguous mode features "[a] narrator, or protagonist-narrator, [who] does not fully authenticate [the supernatural domain]" (Traill 13). The narrator is misguided, his or her perspective is "distorted," which leads to "an unreliable narrator and makes the narrative ambiguous" (Traill 13–14).

Gaiman's extremely ironic "Chivalry" (1992), however, goes even further with the narrative estrangement. Here, the *third-person* narrator is basically omniscient and appears to be reliable, as the storyteller does not participate in the story. The impartial narrator's voice should authenticate the fantastic realm in the text, but the focalization presents an extremely alienating perspective and questions the boundaries of the supernatural domain. The narrator tells the events by following the experiences and focusing on the thoughts of the protagonist-focalizer, the elderly Mrs. Whitaker, who lives in consensus reality Britain, and knowingly transgresses the limits of reality and encounters the fantastic — but she seemingly does not care.[6] Thus, the "imperfect vision is not necessarily accompanied by the character's *mistake*," and neither it is due to the unreliability or limited scope of the narrator, but "it may be a matter of deliberate *dissimulation*" (Todorov, *Introduction* 36; emphasis in original).

Mrs. Whitaker buys the Holy Grail in a charity shop, in the medley of "secondhand flotsam" (35), hidden by the diverse merchandise. Gaiman's description of the cheap antiques illustrates a postmodern attitude toward the fantastic and history: an existing book about the past (Moncrieff's *Romance and Legend of Chivalry* [1912]), a nondescript relic from the past (a walking stick) and a legendary object (the Holy Grail) are collected together — the latter being turned onto its side and placed in a position that is hardly recognizable. As Fredric Jameson points out, contemporary culture considers history as a mixture of pop-culture representations from various ages; history is accessible only via "a vast collection of images," nostalgic texts, and "a set of dusty spectacles" (*Postmodernism* 18). In "Chivalry," the historical object is literally dusty, part of a vast collection of nondescript objects, images and texts.

Not only the shopkeeper, but also Mrs. Whitaker shows disrespect towards the autonomy and sacredness of history when she cleans the Holy Grail, knowingly removing a "brownish red dust," the blood of Jesus Christ, from the goblet. She places the sacred item on her mantelpiece, "between a small, soulful, china basset hound and a photograph of her late husband Henry, on the beach at Frinton in 1953" (36). She creates a medley of past and present, sacred and profane, kitsch and exquisite art, and when she receives visits by Sir Galaad, who intends to obtain the Holy Grail, Mrs. Whitaker sticks to her opinion that the goblet "is just right, between the dog and the photograph of my late Henry" (39).

The unascertainable reasons behind the narrator's and protagonist's lack of surprise, the tangible disrespect towards history and the fantastic, provide an uncanny and humorous tension in the text. The pretense of the narrator that nothing unique is happening doubles the narrative perspective, as the restrained voice of narration becomes echoed by the reader's growing wonder and estrangement. "Chivalry" becomes a foremost example of Mendlesohn's liminal fantasy, in which the lack of surprise is accompanied by another lack: the lack of our understanding the reserved narration of the fantastic events. The protagonist's unexplained failure "to be amazed by supernatural happenings serves to heighten *our* amazement" (McHale, *Postmodernist* 76; emphasis in original). The narrative situation also becomes somewhat similar to Traill's "paranormal mode," in which "supernatural and natural are no longer mutually exclusive" (17).[7]

The conspicuously naïve and therefore unreliable and absurd narration and the resulting "playful irrationality" or "playful fantasy" recapitulates Paul de Man's unsettling, subverting irony ("The Concept" 180). Irony is interpreted by de Man as permanent parabasis, a trope that constantly appears and disrupts the narrative. It is a self-reflexive trope, and self reflexive metafiction — explicitly describing the storytelling process and blurring the boundaries of text and reality — is a crucial characteristic of Gaiman's fiction: "Gaiman holds up a mirror to the storytelling process" (Dowd 103).

"Chivalry" may be read as such a self-reflexive text, illustrating Iser's theory of the reading process. The lack of surprise in Gaiman's liminal fantasy indicates that the story that we are reading is not full, but it is based on gaps. Iser compares the interaction between text and reader to human communication, as both the written text and the oral communication is constituted of "no-things," lacks of knowledge, gaps. People are unfamiliar with each other's perspective, however certain clues such as conventions and stereotypes help them communicate. Analogously, in the reading process: "Whenever the reader bridges the gaps, communication begins. The gaps function as a kind of pivot on which the whole text-reader relationship revolves" (*Prospecting* 34). These gaps operate on the level of the story (for example, a chapter ends at an exciting moment), themes (some events come to the foreground, creating a "blank," which brings other events to the foreground), and perspectives ("vacancies" between the perspective of the narrator, that of the protagonist, fictitious reader, and so on).

In "Chivalry," the textual gaps are manifested by a distance between the narrator's perspective — who, similarly to the protagonist and the "fictitious reader" (Iser, *The Act of Reading* 33), finds the fantastic normal — and the actual reader's perspective, who knows that the fantastic is in contrast with the rest of the story in the realistic passages.[8] The result is the implied reader's oscillation between the two viewpoints, a cognitive process analogous to Hutcheon's theory of irony, which states that "interpreting irony, we can and do oscillate very rapidly between the said and the unsaid.... But ... it is not the two 'poles' themselves that are important; it is the idea of a kind of rapid perceptual and hermeneutic *movement between* them" (*Irony's Edge* 60; emphasis in original).

The reader's oscillation becomes a metafictional, self-reflexive act: Gaiman's liminal fantasy raises a tension within the implied reader in a tangible, overt manner. Such a tension is covertly present in the reading process of every text, because of the difference and distance between "the role prescribed by the text" and the "reader's own disposition" (Iser, *The Act of Reading* 37). "Chivalry," therefore, lays bare its own fictionalizing process and subverts its fictional, fantastic world.

Reversed Perspectives in Gaiman's Fairy Tales

A foremost characteristic of fairy tale rewritings is their unusual perspective. Yet, unlike Gaiman's liminal fantasies, these stories often just *reverse* the traditional viewpoint, replacing the seemingly omniscient and reliable narrators with overtly unreliable narrators who are involved in the plot. Unlike traditional fairy tales that pretend to have "an external or impersonal narrator whose straightforward statements carry no explicit mark of human perspective" (Bacchilega 34), the narrators in postmodern rewritings are frequently revealed to be overtly biased. The reversed and subjectivized viewpoint in these texts conforms to Linda Hutcheon's postmodern parody, which consists in "a form of imitation, but imitation characterized by ironic inversion" (*A Theory* 6).

Gaiman's online short story "I Cthulhu," although not a fairy tale adaptation, is a typical example of a reversed perspective. It deploys a first person narrator who outlines earthly history from the perspective of an alien god. Thus, the story provides a twist on Lovecraft's stories, which frequently describe encounters with alien forces from the point of view of earthly characters that experience something beyond the capacity of human understanding.[9]

The significance of fairy tales in Gaiman's oeuvre may be illustrated in the embedding of an early version of Little Red Riding Hood, "The Grandmother," in *The Sandman: The Doll's House* (1989–1990).[10] In this tale, which is earlier than the version recorded by the Brothers Grimm, the werewolf not only kills the grandmother but "poured her blood into a bottle and sliced her flesh onto a plate" (146). The wolf offers the blood and flesh to the girl, who naively accepts, eats and drinks the remnants of the grandmother. The story ends without the consolation of a happy ending, without featuring the hunter or resurrecting the heroine (see Zipes, *The Great Fairy* 744).

Gaiman's *Anansi Boys* includes folk tales about Anansi the Spider, an animal-god and trickster-hero of African and Caribbean tales. He is not just the usual hero but also the owner of these stories: "Each and all of the stories ... [would] be classed by the Akan-speaking African under the generic title 'Anansesem' (Spider stories), whether the spider appeared in the tale or not" (Rattray xiii). It is because Kwaku Ananse wins the tales from Sky-god, using his cunning tricks (Rattray 54–58). Or, as Gaiman tells the tale, "Mawu gave him the stories, back in the dawn days, took them from Tiger and gave them to Anansi, and he spins the web of them so beautifully" (*Anansi* 181). After the Anansi-stories replace the Tiger-stories, trickster-heroes and cunning human characters will dominate the human imagination instead of the hunter or the beast. As Wolfe argues, "The world is as it is ... because of how it is told and who owns the stories" (Wolfe, Rev. of *Anansi* 15). The lifestyle of humanity changes from prehistoric hunting to civilization due to Anansi's stories:

> Now, all over the world, all of the people they aren't just thinking of hunting and being hunted anymore. Now they are starting to *think* their way out of problems — sometimes thinking their way into worse problems. They still need to keep their bellies full, but now they are trying to figure out how to do it without working — and *that's* the point where people start using their heads.... Because now people are telling Anansi stories, and they're starting to think about how to get kissed, how to get something for nothing by being smarter and funnier. That's when they start to make the world [Gaiman, *Anansi* 290; emphasis in original].

Nevertheless, the righteousness of Anansi's domination is vindicated by Anansi himself, which may call into question the objectivity of the justification. If a narrator, hero, or god owns and dominates a story, inevitably a slanted point-of view will emerge and be utilized. As Chris Dowd points out, "Gaiman makes it explicitly clear that we should not trust storytellers. It isn't a matter of storytellers being unsavory people, although some of the ones in Gaiman's stories surely are. The real reason we shouldn't trust storytellers is that they are untrustworthy by nature" (110). Or, as Gaiman puts it: "In the old stories, Anansi lives just like you do or I do, in his house.... Sometimes he is good, sometimes he is bad. He is never evil. Mostly, you are on Anansi's side. This is because Anansi owns all the stories" (*Anansi* 181).

Gaiman's "Snow, Glass, Apples" may be read as a postmodern, feminist rewriting of the traditional fairy tale Snow White. As Sandra M. Gilbert and Susan Gubar point out, the female characters in fairy tales are often passive and destined to remain mute, similarly to real-life women in traditional societies who were forbidden to write or express themselves freely. Referring to the execution of the stepmother, the two critics underline in *The Madwoman in the Attic* that "women have been told, that their art, like the witch's dance in 'Little Snow White,' is an art of silence" (43). In Gaiman's version, the execution of the Stepmother is not silent: she talks, narrating the story of her innocence and characterizing Snow White as a vampire. The story is narrated by the witch, the originally monstrous character, illustrating Marleen S. Barr's argument that "With Helene Cixous's and Jane Gallop's positive definitions of 'monstrous' in mind ... feminist fabulation need no longer remain marginalized.... It is time to canonize the monstrous" (21, 22).

Although this feminist interpretation is convincing at first glance, and to some extent remains maintainable, three dilemmas somewhat question this reading after a closer inspection of the text and its context.

First, it is important to realize that the two foremost characteristics of "Snow, Glass, Apples," that is, Snow White being a monstrous vampire and telling the story from a twisted perspective, are long established topoi in fairy tale adaptations — and not only feminist ones. As early as 1926, Franz Hessel published "The Seventh Dwarf," in which Snow White's tale is narrated by a neglected dwarf, who has to share his bed with his room-mate due to Snow White's arrival and has to clean the corners of the house for her. Robert Coover's "The Dead Queen" (1973) also presents a reversed point-of-view, focusing on the charming prince as the narrator. Tanith Lee's macabre "Red as Blood" (1979) depicts both Snow White and the king's first wife as vampires. Angela Carter's "The Snow Child" (1979) portrays Snow White as a supernatural monster, a product of (male) fantasy, "no flesh and blood, no life ... [o]nly an imaginary being" (Bacchilega 38) that "bites" even after her death (Carter 92).

Second, in spite of the twisted point-of-view of "the wicked stepmother," the monstrous becomes once again to some extent marginalized in Gaiman's story. This time it is Snow White who becomes gruesome, characterized as a vampire, while her point-of-view remains covert in the story. The child Snow White is described by the Queen as an alien, monstrous creature: "I do not know what manner of a thing she is. None of us do" (325). As Dani Cavallaro argues in *The Gothic Vision*, children have often been considered as the frightening Other: one of the ideological explanations of child abandonment is "the notion that children are somehow tainted by their proximity to prenatal darkness, and, by implication, primordial chaos ... the young are essentially untrustworthy due to their connection with alternative fantasy worlds" (151). This argument reiterates Todorov's theory that there is a correspondence between the themes of the fantastic and the perspective of the young child or infant (*The Fantastic* 120). The monster-child, therefore, becomes the fantastic Other and loses its voice in Gaiman's story — unlike, for example, the monster in Anne Rice's *The Vampire Lestat* (1985), which narrates the events entirely from the vampire's perspective.

Third, the question arises: can the reader believe the Queen who demonizes Snow White, or does she just vindicate her case after the death sentence? We could say that Gaiman's other unreliable narrators and multiple perspectives question the credibility of this particular narration, as well. Furthermore, when the Queen stresses that Snow White distorts the "original," the "true" story, her accusations cast doubts on her own reliability as well: "Lies and half-truths fall like snow, covering the things that I remember, the things I saw" (328). Her unreliable nature is revealed further when the reader understands that she neglects to tell certain important events: the narrator mentions (in brackets) that the magic with the poisoned apples is not her first magical act, but she used enchantment before, in the beginning of the story to seduce the King: "I cast a glamour on the apples (as once, years before, by a bridge, I had cast a glamour on myself)" (333).

Thus, when reading "Snow, Glass, Apples," it is possible reconstruct and oscillate among at least three perspectives. The perspective of Gaiman's subjective first person narration evokes and contests the (seemingly) objective narration in Grimms' fairy tale. Furthermore, as we gradually discover the omissions and distortions of Gaiman's own storyteller, we intend to create a third perspective, which would finally provide genuine narration or a true story.

Naturally, the actual possibility of reconstructing this objective perspective and trustworthy narrative remains highly unlikely. The story ends with the Queen's execution and the image of snowflakes on Snow White's cheek, indicating that snow, that is, the "half-truths" of storytelling, will always cover and conceal the real nature of events and characters.

Thus, *Anansi Boys* and "Snow, Glass, Apples" demonstrate that visualizing, narrating, and rendering visible are historically, socially, and psychologically positioned. As Bal argues, "It is possible to try and give an 'objective' picture of the facts. But what does that involve? All comment is shunned and implicit interpretation is also avoided. Perception, however, is a psychosomatic process ... [and] depends on so many factors that striving for objectivity is pointless" (*Narratology* 142). Contemporary Foucauldian approaches frequently emphasize that we see what we are allowed to see: "There is much more regularity, much more *constraint*, in what we can see than we suppose. To see is always to think, since what is seeable is part of what 'structures thought in advance'" (Rajchman 92; emphasis in original). These theories promote our engagement in pluralized perspectives, since "unification (e. g. of 'man,' 'woman,' 'language,' or 'life') tends to promote in and of itself a usurpation of power, if only through rendering invisible other aspects, elements, or positions within the unified category" (Bal, "His Master's" 380).

Possible Worlds, Narrative Techniques and the Fantastic

Kathryn S. Hume stresses that *"Fantasy is any departure from consensus reality"* (8; emphasis in original). Although Hume celebrates the fantastic mode in literature, she maintains a dual opposition according to which fantasy is in conflict with realism, since the former has a protean, unstable, impermeable nature, while the latter is rooted in our everyday world, that is, in consensus reality. Iser intends to subvert the idea of such duality when he argues that during the fictionalizing event the narration always transgresses boundaries. The real and the imaginary (the fantastic) become intertwined: "Extratextual reality merges into the imaginary, and the imaginary merges into reality ... The fictive, then, might be called a 'transitional object,' always hovering between the real and the imaginary" (*The Fictive* 3, 20). Iser also points out that narrative transgressions can be manifested on the thematic level of texts that "provide the occasion for the hero to step over their boundaries" (*The Fictive* 9). Consequently, transgressions between fictional worlds are reflected in formal transgressions, narrative methods such as irony, metafiction, intertextual allusions, and contamination of narrative levels (metalepsis and mise-en-abyme).

The complex relationship between fantasy world and consensus reality, the resulting formal and thematic transgressions, can be analyzed with the means of possible worlds theory. Following Traill, one could say "simply, that the natural domain is a physically possible world having 'the same natural laws as does the actual world' ... The supernatural domain, in contrast, is a physically impossible world" (8, 9; see also Ekman 65).

The portrayal of physically impossible magical worlds gives way to various narrative techniques. To analyze such techniques, it is worthwhile outlining Marie-Laure Ryan's narrative theory, which points out that the consensus reality of a fictional text — which she calls the textual actual world, TAW — may allow the presence of other physically possible, physically impossible, and utterly impossible worlds in specific ways. (The latter are self-contradictory worlds where the principle of non-contradiction does not apply.)

First and foremost, the introduction of a new world may be marked and accomplished by introducing a different narrative level, that is, utilizing a new narrator. A fictional character can imagine, dream, tell or write a story of fantastic events. The transition between the physically possible and impossible worlds, between the primary and secondary world is obviously marked in this case, and the switch becomes easily distinguishable for the reader. This is what happens in "Murder Mysteries," for example, where the fantastic realm and its events are described by a supernatural character, an angel.

Second, it is also common that the appearance of a secondary world is only *indicated* by a character. In this case, the new narrative level is only partially achieved: "a fictional story is described rather than actually narrated" (Ryan, "Stacks" 875).[11] This subtype can be exemplified by Gaiman's "Shoggoth's Old Peculiar," where the consensus reality, the initial TAW opens up for Lovecraft's fantasy world temporarily when a few characters draw on Lovecraft's vocabulary and thematic conventions. The locals of a hidden British village drop a few words about their job, which is to await the awakening of Great Cthulhu, but they never actually tell a proper Lovecraftian story. Only fragmented details of a drunken stupor are ascertained by the reader and so the characters do not become proper storytellers. (One should call them perhaps "semi-narrators.")

Another — the third — alternative to introduce a new world is provided by the shift of language. In this case, "the narrative transports the reader to a new system of reality without introducing a new speaker" (Ryan, "Stacks" 874), and by introducing a new style.[17] The fictional jump to another realm is even more covertly marked than in the previous case, as instead of a special character or a semi-narrator only the narrator's style, the diffusion of voice indicates the introduction of a new world.

Analogously, in Gaiman's "Only the End of the World Again" the descriptive, everyday prose of the protagonist-narrator is occasionally interrupted by a mystical language. A prime example of the diversity of languages can be found in a letter written to the protagonist:

> There was a note under the door from my landlady. It said that I owed her two weeks' rent. It said that all the answers were in the Book of Revelations. It said that I made a lot of noise coming home in the early hours this morning, and she'd thank me to be quieter in the future. It said that when the Elder Gods rose up from the ocean, all the scum of Earth, all the nonbelievers, all the human garbage and the wastrels and deadbeats would be swept away, and the world would be cleansed by ice and deep water. It said she felt she ought to remind me that she had assigned me a shelf in the refrigerator when I arrived and she'd thank me if in the future I'd keep to it [202].

Gaiman's *Anansi Boys* is narrated by an extradiegetic, third person narrator who remains outside the storyline. Nevertheless, the novel is set in three different realms, which are narrated in three different tones. First, the story of Fat Charlie Nancy (the majority of the novel) is narrated in common language, that is, in contemporary, humorous storytelling tone, one similar to that of Douglas Adams. Second, the mystical realm where the mythical struggle between the wicked god Tiger and the trickster god Anansi takes place is described in a straightforward, authoritative tone, where humor is basically absent (83–84; 163–76). Third, Anansi as a fairy tale hero is narrated in the language of a jovial, rural, unsophisticated storyteller of folktales, slightly imitating the oral performance of fairy tales (42–45; 111–14; 182–84). Naturally, as the three storylines gradually become intertwined, the three different styles are also occasionally interwoven (347–51). The plurality of worlds is reflected on the formal level: the thematically multiplied zones manifest themselves in multiplied discourses, turning "a discursive heterotopia into an ontological heterotopia" (McHale, *Postmodernist* 164).

Thus, especially in these moments, the novel exemplifies Bakhtin's heteroglossia in the comic novel, where the "parodic stylization" draws on "all strata and forms of literary language" ("Discourse" 301). The authoritative and authorial language of the narration is frequently interrupted by other discourses: "The comic style demands of the author a lively to-and-fro movement in his relation to language" ("Discourse" 302). As McHale observes, postmodernism often revels in Bakhtinian heteroglossia, using it as "an opening wedge, a means of breaking up the unified projected world into a polyphony of worlds of discourse" (*Postmodernist* 167).

Due to the refraction and dispersion of narrative voices, the fantastic or fictional worlds in these narratives are never completely stable. They become what Dolezel calls "worlds without authentication," as the text deprives the narrator of any authentication authority, and the narrator "takes an ironic attitude ... and thus turns the narrating act into a non-binding game" (22).

Visibility and Liminal Places in *Neverwhere* and *The Graveyard Book*

As Bakhtin points out in his "Discourse in the Novel," another highly frequent and tangible way of creating diversity in a novel is to utilize conflicting characters, as "a character in a novel always has, as we have said, a zone of his own" (320). This zone is named by critics as "character-accessible subworld" (Werth 212–16) or "narrative domain" (Eco, *The Role of the Reader* 235; Hidalgo-Downing 86–90; McHale, *Postmodernist* 32). As Thomas Pavel argues, the possible worlds of a fictional work can be created by "*domains* centered around one or several main characters" (105; emphasis in original).

The characters' worlds can be distinguished with a particular focalization technique, when the events are presented by the same narrator but from the points-of-view of certain characters. In this case, the focalization reveals various ideological and cognitive systems, demonstrating that "[every] character in a novel ... has his own perception of the world that is incarnated in his action and discourse" (Bakhtin, "Discourse" 335). When diverse focalizers are utilized, various ideological and cognitive systems are portrayed — characters interpret events differently because of their diverse beliefs and points-of-view. What is more, the characters observe or ignore, they decide to see or not to see a certain phenomenon. As Bal points out, because of focalization "we are presented with a certain, far from innocent, interpretation of the elements" (*Narratology* 150).

Yet, the cognitive and perceptual differences can also be marked on the thematic level of the text, when the narrator *explains* the differences between the perspectives, creating a metafictional guide for the reader. This is what happens in Gaiman's *Neverwhere* and *The Graveyard Book*, and to a lesser extent in *American Gods* (2001). These novels feature a relatively traditional, straightforward narration from beginning to end. The third person narrator is basically univocal and omniscient (extradiegetic), "following the characters' innermost thoughts and feelings ... and [possessing] knowledge of what happens in several places at the same time" (Rimmon-Kenan 95). Following the model of Mendlesohn's portal-quest fantasy, the protagonist is the major focalizer, who gradually becomes familiarized with the fantastic realm, and occasionally gets surprised. The narrative perspective remains one-sided: "we ride alongside the protagonist, hearing only what she hears, seeing only what she sees" (*Rhetorics* xix).[13]

Nevertheless, in spite of the traditional narrative and the more or less conventional and fixed focalization, highly emphasized cognitive differences saturate the novels *on the thematic level.*

Both *Neverwhere* and *The Graveyard Book* describe the supernatural domain as the Underworld. The former places Faerie in the underground system of London, while the latter depicts the ghost world of an ancient cemetery in a small town in England. This similarity explains a significant common element in the two novels: both feature various spatial and time zones. As Alice Jenkins points out, "Places beneath the surface of quotidian life are invested by many fantasy narratives with a peculiar richness of space and time" (32). The Underworld demonstrates Foucault's heterotopias and "heterochronies" by "accumulating time" ("Of Other" 26), encapsulating different historical periods and incorporating relics from various eras. In the fantastic realm of *The Graveyard Book*, fragments of druidical magic have survived. In the Underworld of *Neverwhere*, the "echoes" or "ghosts" of London's "Great Smog" in 1952 have remained tangible. As a character puts it: "'There are little pockets of old time in London, where things and places stay the same, like bubbles in amber,' she explained. 'There's a lot of time in London, and it has to go somewhere — it doesn't all get used up at once'" (228).

The Underworld also juxtaposes numerous spatial zones, including the realm of the dead. In *Neverwhere*, there are "baronies" and "fiefdoms" (29), microworlds that provide privileges and restrictions for their members. In *The Graveyard Book*, the protagonist Nobody Owens or Bod has to learn that "there are the living and the dead, there are day-folk and night-folk, there are ghouls and mist-walkers, there are the high hunters and the Hounds of God. Also, there are solitary types" (63). Thus, the novels portray several realms on the same ontological plane, echoing Foucauldian heterotopias that comprise a whole series of places next to one another (see Figure 4 in the Introduction).

Both novels make it clear that members of a microworld usually cannot see through the boundaries of their own zone: they can hardly imagine, let alone perceive something that lies beyond the limits of their realm. The invisibility of the supernatural domains coincides with "social spaces in our actual world with which the majority of readers are unfamiliar" (Ekman 72). While *Neverwhere* takes it literally that most people intend to neglect homeless citizens, *The Graveyard Book* takes it literally that we tend to forget and ignore our dead ancestors and relatives. The magical invisibility evokes social criticism in these fantasies, evoking such canonized texts as Ralph Ellison's *Invisible Man* (1952).

Thus, Gaiman's subterranean places represent deliberately overlooked social spheres, in a way similar to Terry Pratchett's parodic fantasy fiction, which "is postmodern in the restricted sense that it re-places marginal geographies (such as the sewers) at the heart of its narrative progressions" (Hills, "Mapping" 226). Matt Hills suggests in his essay that when parodic fantasies re-appropriate marginal and vulgar places such as the city sewers, they make use of Henri Lefebvre's "mundus": "Hidden, clandestine, subterranean spaces ... a passageway through which dead souls could return to the bosom of the earth ... [encompassing] the greatest foulness and the greatest purity, life and death, fertility and destruction, horror and fascination" (Lefebvre 242).

In *The Graveyard Book*, quotidian people cannot notice the ghosts of the graveyard. Analogously, in *Neverwhere* perception is extremely restricted for those who approach the fantasy world ("London Below") from reality ("London Above"). Regular Londoners cannot see the fantastic, subterranean — or homeless — characters even if they are right in front of their eyes: "'If you are part of London Below,' said Door to Richard, in a conversational voice, as they walked, side by side, into the next hall, 'they normally don't even notice you exist unless you stop and talk to them. And even then, they forget you pretty quickly'" (186).

The isolation of the protagonist Richard Mayhew from London Above is of cognitive origin: people living in consensus reality simply ignore him, in the same way as they ignore everyone who belongs to the (under)world of homelessness or that of the fantastic. The novel makes "a metaphorical invisibility literal" (Ekman 68) and transforms an existing, widespread message about the homeless into a magic spell: "Out of sight is out of mind. Ignore it and it will go away" (Ekman 64). Thus, Gaiman's fantastic realm is not a fully strange, alien, closed and "self-contained secondary world" (Nikolajeva 36), but an open fantasy realm, a twilight zone at the periphery of our everyday reality. As Ekman puts it, "Gaiman keeps his reader firmly anchored in the actual world" (71).

A rare possibility to eschew social and magical blindness is obtained when the characters participate in ritualistic, carnivalesque events. The "Floating Markets" are such special events in *Neverwhere*, which bring together the various baronies, temporarily suspending the hierarchical distinctions and oppositions between them. Analogously, the Danse Macabre in *The Graveyard Book* unites the poor and the rich, the dead and the living, the primary and secondary world. (It is an interesting feature of Gaiman's Danse Macabre though that one must be either alive or dead to dance it — the liminal character Silas, who is in-between the two states cannot participate.) Another way to break through negligence is via friendship or love: Richard Mayhew, the protagonist of *Neverwhere* recognizes Door at the beginning of the novel, while Bod's real-world friend Scarlett finds the protagonist in her dream and later in the graveyard even when he "Fades."

The character Earl's Court and his world demonstrate the fantastic and social invisibility in *Neverwhere* candidly. Earl's Court lives in his own kingdom, whose boundaries coincide with the boundaries of a subway carriage. His realm belongs to London Below, but it is also situated in the subway system of our consensus reality, London Above. His kingdom is on the borderline, occupies an overlapping realm, and it can maintain its protection and sovereignty *only* because of the limits of human perception. People outside the carriage, especially those outside the fantasy realm, cannot notice his world by seeing through the doors and windows.

> The train slowed down and stopped. The car that had pulled up in front of Richard was quite empty: its lights were turned off, it was bleak and empty and dark. From time to time Richard had noticed cars like this one, locked and shadowy, on Tube trains, and he had wondered what purpose they served. The

> other doors on the train hissed open, and passengers got on and got off. The doors of the darkened car remained closed. The marquis drummed on the door with his fist, an intricate rhythmic rap. Nothing happened. Richard was just wondering if the train would now pull out without them on it, when the door of the dark car was pushed open from the inside. It opened about six inches, and an elderly, bespectacled face peered out at them.
> "Who knocks?" he said.
> Through the opening, Richard could see flames burning, and people, and smoke inside the car. Through the glass in the doors, however, he still saw a dark and empty carriage [148–149].

As the focalizer is the protagonist who more or less belongs to London Above, the question remains open whether characters of London Below (such as the marquis) can see the hidden world through the door glass, or the windows are opaque also for them.

The social and fantastic invisibility can also be explained by the liminal stage that the protagonist has to go through. As Maria Nikolajeva argues, "The passage from the primary to the secondary chronotope in fantasy reflects the archaic pattern of the mythical passage" (75). Ethnographic theories call attention to the fact that participants of the liminal stage have to go through a period of seclusion: "[they are] cut off from the normal social interactions within the village and household" (Turner, "Liminal" 26). This is exactly what happens to many fantasy heroes. Mayhew, for example, has to live in London Below in most parts of the novel without being a proper member of this world. He is a novice who loses his relatives, friends, and properties in the real world, becoming an invisible ghost for his girlfriend, colleagues, and other members of the quotidian society. Turner observes the same phenomenon in archaic communities, where liminality may turn people into "monstrous, fantastic, and unnatural shapes" ("Liminal" 42). He argues:

> The novices are, in fact, temporarily undefined, beyond the normative social structure. This weakens them, since they have no rights over others. But it also liberates them from structural obligations. It places them too in a close connection with non-social or asocial powers of life and death. Hence the frequent comparison of novices with, on the one hand, *ghosts*, gods or ancestors, and, on the other, with animals or birds. They are *dead* to the social world, but *alive* to the asocial world {"Liminal" 27; emphasis added].

During most of the novel, Mayhew remains a novice in London Below, a character who belongs neither to reality nor to the fantasy realm. Instead of being integrated into a new order, he intends to return to his old life, to normality, the dullness of an ordinary life. Because his adventures take place in London Below, however, he becomes more and more integrated into the fantasy realm. After going through the ordeal of the Black Friars, "Richard looked different, somehow ... Hunter scrutinized him, trying to work out what had changed. His center of balance moved lower, become more centered. No ... it was more than that. He looked less boyish. He looked as if he had begun to grow up" (253). After he kills the Beast, he even receives new names: he becomes "the Warrior" (340) and "Sir Richard Maybury" (344).

By the end of the novel the protagonist becomes utterly initiated into the fantastic realm and obtains the possibility to choose between the primary and secondary world.[14] Mayhew's transformation is demonstrated by his highly improved vision and his ability to navigate even in a labyrinth. After killing the Beast and touching its blood to his eyes and tongue, "he ran straight and true through the labyrinth, which no longer held any mysteries for him. He felt that he knew every twist, every path, every alley and lane and tunnel of it" (316–317).

At this point, Mayhew could return to London Above, which would result in — as Maria Nikolajeva observes — a typical ending in a children's fantasy novel.

> The magical journeys in fantasy may be of two principal kinds: *linear* and *circular*. Linear journeys take the protagonist from one world into another ... This type is quite rare in fantasy for children, since it involves a definite farewell to the character's own world.... Circular journeys bring the character back into his own world when the adventure (quest, struggle) is completed. The end of a circular journey often means that the magic is over, either by agreement or by the nature of magic itself [Nikolajeva 42; emphasis in original].

Yet, perhaps because Gaiman's novel is written for (young) adult audience, the protagonist steps out of the circular journey, (re)occupies the linear voyage and chooses fantasyland.

The theme of liminality is also crucial in *The Graveyard Book*, since the text portrays its fantastic realm as a liminal space, a transitory zone between life and death. The protagonist Nobody Owens (Bod) embodies a prophesy, according to which "there would be a child born who would walk the borderland between the living and the dead" (253). His guardian Silas is also "a strange liminal figure ... (described as neither dead nor alive)" (Wolfe, Rev. of *The Graveyard* 19). He belongs to the Honor Guard, a guild that guards the borderlands between the living and the dead, between those who use magic illicitly and unprofessionally for selfish aims ("Jacks of All Trades"), and those who use magic in a proper and honest way.

Cultural criticism is less tangible in *The Graveyard Book* than in *Neverwhere*. In the latter, invisibility, and thus liminality, is interpreted as a social burden by the protagonist. In the former, invisibility is a natural way of existence for the deceased. As Bod's ghost-teacher stresses: "Slipping and Fading, boy, [is] the way of the dead. Slip though shadows. Fade from awareness" (96). Bod is a living character who receives "the Freedom of the Graveyard," hence he can Fade and disappear from the perception of everyday people. The social negligence pertaining to liminality becomes a useful phenomenon here that helps the protagonist throughout the novel. Invisibility is an essential skill that he has to learn via tiresome drills:

> "Try again."
> Bod tried harder.
> "You are as plain as the nose on your face," said Mr. Pennyworth. "And your nose is remarkably obvious. As is the rest of your face, young man. As are you. For the sake of all that is holy, empty your mind. Now. You are an empty alleyway. You are a vacant doorway. You are nothing. Eyes will not see you. Minds will not hold you. Where you are is nothing and nobody."
> Bod tried again. He closed his eyes and imagined himself fading into the stained stonework of the mausoleum wall, becoming a shadow of the night and nothing more. He sneezed.
> "Dreadful," said Mr. Pennyworth, with a sigh [96].

A vital skill that Bod learns and Silas possesses is that they are mostly in control of their own visibility; that is, they can see and be seen by the dead and the living as they wish. Instead of novices, they are guides who are capable of controlling, and mediating between, the two realms.

The divine characters in *American Gods* are in command of their visibility in a similar fashion. During most of the novel, they appear as everyday people. However, when they are riding the "World's Largest Carousel," they can pluralize and blur their appearance, and they can be seen in various bodies and forms simultaneously. Thus, the focal character Shadow goes through the experience of multiplying vision: "The images that reached his mind made no sense: it was like seeing the world through the multifaceted jeweled eyes of a dragonfly, but each facet saw something completely different, and he was unable to combine the things he was seeing, or thought he was seeing, into a whole that made any sense" (131).

Conclusions and Caveats

I have intended to prove in this chapter that Gaiman's "Murder Mysteries" and "A Study in Emerald" form a bridge between detective fiction and fantasy, as they draw on the narrative techniques and thematic conventions of both genres. Gaiman's fiction frequently evokes the rationality of detective fiction, the dread of horror, the escapism of fantasy, the alluring storytelling of fairy tales—but these genre characteristics are constantly undermined by inter- and hypertextual allusions, metafictional games, and ironic perspectives.

Gaiman's fantasy realm is not an escape from reality, but in constant interaction with it. His Snow White is not as docile as Grimms' protagonist, while his stepmother is a more ambiguous character than her original counterpart. Gaiman's horror is usually not as dreadful as that of Poe, Stephen King, or H. P. Lovecraft, since, as Sigmund Freud argues in his well-known essay "The Uncanny," "Even a 'real' ghost ... loses all power of at least arousing gruesome feelings in as soon as the author begins to amuse himself by being ironical about it" (252). Thus Gaiman's fiction, analogously to the fantasies of the New Wave Fabulists, Interstitial Writers, and other "21st Century Stories," can be interpreted as the extension and renewal of conventional canons, especially that of Tolkien's fantasy, providing a new "fuzzy set" for readers of fantastic texts.

Gaiman's short fiction illustrates the all-encompassing influence of postmodernism in popular genres: his stories frequently double or multiply the narrative perspectives, lay bare the process of storytelling, interweave different language registers and textual conventions as well as violate the narrative levels. Thus, they contribute to the general tendency of our time that defines reality "as *constructed* in and through our language, discourses, and semiotic systems" (McHale, *Postmodernist* 164; emphasis in original). His parodic texts demonstrate the contemporary urge to pluralize our critical perspectives, questioning the possibilities of an objective vision, and reacting "against an official language" and "a social and cultural homogeneity" (Hutcheon, *A Theory* 71, 77).

My analysis on "Chivalry" linked Hutcheon's and Booth's theories of irony, arguing that Hutcheon's hermeneutic oscillation and Booth's dual perspectives are foregrounded in Gaiman's oeuvre. Gaiman's texts frequently construct a doubled narrative voice or deploy estranged focalization and so the reading process entails an oscillation between various textual perspectives, forming the reading experience that Mendlesohn associates with her liminal fantasy. An inverted textual perspective is utilized in "Snow, Glass, Apples" and "'I Cthulhu.'" The significance of different perspectives is thematized in his novels *Neverwhere* and *The Graveyard Book*, which deploy traditional narration, but foreground on the thematic level the characters' perceptual differences, the problematics of visibility, and the blurred windows between ontological boundaries. They also describe liminal periods and places in the Turnerian sense, and hypothesize the presence of multiple, juxtaposed, heterogeneous zones in the fantastic realm.

It has to be mentioned here, however, that Gaiman's "postmodern" intertextuality — analogously to perhaps every text that draws on and utilizes an archetypically familiar and popular textual convention — is also institutionally supported, licensed, and developed via communities of publishers and readerships. It could be argued that the "postmodern" liminality and intertextuality of "A Study in Emerald," for example, is a result of target marketing; it targets a niche of science fiction and fantasy fans who are interested in Lovecraft. It becomes economically viable for a publisher to produce an intertextually-specific work, such as the stories in Michael Reaves and John Pelan's *Shadows Over Baker Street* (2003), the anthology in which Gaiman's story first appeared and where a range of authors engage with Holmesian and Lovecraftian themes.

Furthermore, drawing on the well-known convention of the Sherlock Holmes saga simultaneously appeals to genre and high literary criticism, readers of fan culture and mainstream literature. The Holmes stories are, in fact, already canonized to some extent, just as much as certain pastiches with Holmesian topoi, for example, Umberto Eco's *The Name of the Rose* (1980).[15] The same is true of the Cthulhu Mythos: it is enough to refer to the fact that Deleuze and Guattari draw on Lovecraft in *A Thousand Plateaus* several times (240–51), and Jorge Luis Borges wrote his short story "There Are More Things" (1975) in memory of Lovecraft. Thus, in a way similar to Kim Newman, who rewrites classic horror texts such as Bram Stoker's *Dracula* (1897) and Robert Louis Stevenson's "The Strange Case of Dr. Jekyll and Mr. Hyde" (1886), Gaiman's postmodern parodies concomitantly target an "elite" and a subculture audience. (Let us not forget that "A Study in Emerald" also draws on *Dracula* and "Dr. Jekyll and Mr. Hyde," while Newman's "The Red Planet League" appeared in *Gaslight Grimoire: Fantastic Tales of Sherlock Holmes* [2008], an anthology combining the characters of Sherlock Holmes stories with elements of fantasy and supernatural fiction.)

Gaiman's short stories and *The Graveyard Book* (which is a rewriting of Rudyard Kipling's classic *The Jungle Book* [1894]) incorporate both what Matt Hills calls "intertextual cultural capital" and "intertextual subcultural capital" or "popular cultural capital" (*The Pleasures* 173–75), since their allusions are tailored to subculture knowledge as well as to the standards of highbrow literature and theory. In other words, Gaiman's generic, narrative, and thematic liminality is catalyzed or reinforced by *institutional liminality*.

Finally, it is another important caveat that the epistemological and ontological dilemmas, the cognitive and perceptual aspects of Faerie, are crucial in many if not all fantastic texts. Certain gifted or fortunate characters, usually children, can see the supernatural objects, while adults, their parents for instance, cannot. (The reverse occurs, for example, in *The Turn of the Screw*, where only the governess witnesses the fantastic events but the children do not.) Tolkien also highlights that in contrast with our quotidian perception, in fantastic texts "things seen clearly may be freed from the drab blur of triteness or familiarity—from possessiveness" (58). In other words, readers realize certain phenomena when reading fantasy—all sorts of fantasy, not only liminal—that they would otherwise ignore.

Furthermore, Mendlesohn dates back liminal fantasy to Hope Mirrlees's *Lud-in-the-Mist* and Joan Aiken's *All You've Ever Wanted* (1953) — and traces of such a tradition, as my Preface indicates, could be found even earlier. Parody has been eternally present in literature, serving at all times as an unavoidable productive-creative approach to tradition — enough to think about ancient satirical literature. Hutcheon finds a close model to contemporary parodic practice in Renaissance imitation (*A Theory* 10). Bal also stresses that vision was never as unified as the authoritative, prescribed discourse pretended that it was ("His Master's" 383–84).

As Zipes points out, the desire to mock and rewrite fairy tales emerged historically soon after the genre conventions, topoi, characters and motifs had become established in the collective mind of the audience in late seventeenth-century France. The first wave of storytellers (Madame d'Aulnoy, Charles Perrault) was immediately followed by a group of writers in the early eighteenth century, who "enjoyed playing with the motifs and audience expectations" and utilized "clear textual references to a literary genre that had established itself" ("Cross-Cultural" 862, 863). In other words, innovative and mocking fairy tale rewritings are nearly as old as fairy tales themselves: a generation establishing a tradition is almost instantly followed by those who parody the tradition.

Thus, when Gaiman rewrites fairy tales and inverts or doubles traditional narrative perspectives, he is not only a postmodern story writer, but he also follows a long established convention and so he becomes a traditionalist.

CHAPTER 3

Stanislaw Lem: Liminality and the Revenge of the Mirror on Alien Planets

> In some remote corner of the universe that is poured out in countless flickering solar systems, there once was a star on which clever animals invented knowledge. That was the most arrogant and the most untruthful moment of world history—yet only a moment. After nature had drawn a few breaths, the star froze over and the clever animals had to die. (Friedrich Nietzsche)
>
> Far out in the uncharted backwaters of the unfashionable end of the Western Spiral arm of the Galaxy lies a small unregarded yellow sun.
>
> Orbiting this at a distance of roughly ninety-eight million miles is an utterly insignificant little blue-green planet whose ape-descended life forms are so amazingly primitive that they still think digital watches are a pretty neat idea. (Douglas Adams)

As my mottoes from Nietzsche's "On Truth and Lying in an Extra-Moral Sense" and Douglas Adams's *Hitchhiker's Guide to the Galaxy* demonstrate, science fiction texts can recapitulate Nietzsche's sarcastic arguments on human civilization. Adams's novel describes the destruction of our planet not as occurring because humans are brave explorers or enemies of the aliens, but simply due to an intergalactic bureaucratic decision. The fictional guidebook about the Universe finds it adequate to depict Earth with two words: "Mostly Harmless." This cynical approach to the insignificance, contingency and relativity of human culture and sciences, and of humanity as such, is highly tangible in Lem's oeuvre and can be interpreted as a hybridization of (metaphysical) detective fiction and science fiction.

The previous chapters have illustrated that although detective fiction seems to disavow the fantastic, historical and theoretical approaches uncover ample examples of overlapping between the two modes of storytelling: authors from both sides, such as Christie and Gaiman, transgress the limits of their genre norms.

The overlaps between science fiction and detective story, however, are historically somewhat problematic. Until the middle of the 20th century, numerous readers, fans, and critics of science fiction considered detective fiction outdated, emphasizing the "freshness of idea" and the up-to-date technology in their relatively new genre. A certain realism, extrapolative and scientific sensibility as well as sociological depth, was expected from science fiction writers, as readers intended "to gain some mental control of their machine-bound environment," interpreting the genre as a "kind of sociology of the future" (Pierce 9). From a different angle, McHale also emphasizes the differences between the conventions of detective fiction and those of science fiction, associating the shift between the two genres with the cultural shift from modernism to postmodernism (*Postmodernist* 9–11; *Constructing* 247).

Yet it is easy to demonstrate that there are numerous, evident parallelisms between the two genres. The fascination with science, and the occasional residue of a positivist belief in the omnipotence of science, for example, may provide a crucial similarity. As Andy Sawyer argues, "Science fiction, with its sense of wonder and implication that at the same time the universe is knowable, and detective fiction, which suggests that mysteries can be resolved, are both indebted to the scientific method. Both genres, after all, have their roots in the mid-nineteenth century, following Enlightenment rationalism" (174).

I intend to prove in this chapter that Lem's fiction is a blend between detective fiction and science fiction, featuring epistemological and scientific puzzles on an extreme level that bring his stories close to ontology. His fiction, although usually comprises relatively stable and clear narrative structures, displays a dual self-reflection: his novels consciously discuss the limits of science and science fiction.

Thus, I interpret Lem's fiction, especially his *Solaris*, as meta-science and meta-science-fiction. His fiction is also liminal because the characters find themselves in a situation not unlike Lacan's mirror stage, in which Self and the Other, the Subject and Object of representation, become indistinguishable. It becomes obvious for his characters that mirroring is not a neutral and simple phenomenon but it is impregnated by human prejudices, scientific assumptions and paradigms. The mirroring process becomes overtly problematic and turns into a subversive act in so far as the reflection is frequently accomplished with a difference, refraction, oscillation, a rupturing surprise — with the *revenge* of the mirror.

Detection and Science: The Case of Sherlock Holmes

Before analyzing liminal oscillations, scientific reflections, and genre crossing in Lem's fiction, I need to reflect upon the conventionally hybrid nature of detective fiction, namely, the problematic nature of science in these stories. I draw on Conan Doyle's Sherlock Holmes saga to demonstrate that rationalistic detective stories often "expanded the definition of rationality," bringing the genre closer to the "romance of reason" in fin-de-siècle Gothic literature or scientific romance, the works of Bram Stoker, Robert Louis Stevenson, H. G. Wells, and so on (Saler 604–11).

Since the beginning of the genre, "mystery fiction has opened a door to science" (Pierce 11) in so far as it celebrated the power of human intellect and proposed that true knowledge is obtainable, due to "fixed natural laws ... that can lead to the reconstruction of the past even from fragmentary evidence" (Frank 155). Lawrence Frank emphasizes the overt cultural references to rationalism, Darwinian and positivist science in Conan Doyle's Holmes stories, arguing that "the universe of Sherlock Holmes is a Darwinian one" (143). Holmes explicitly refers to the achievements and methods of 19th century scientists such as Charles Darwin, Charles Lyell, and Georges Cuvier. For example, in "The Five Orange Pips" (1891), Holmes points out that "As Cuvier could correctly describe a whole animal by the contemplation of a single bone, so the observer who has thoroughly understood one link in a series of incidents should be able to accurately state all the other ones, both before and after" (112).

By drawing on well-known scientific views of his age, Holmes's investigation intends to improve the method that is restricted to the fragmentary analysis of signs. To eschew the disrupting consequences of infinity, the detective has to posit that each case has a certain unifying structure:

> "From a drop of water," said the writer, "a logician could infer the possibility of an Atlantic or a Niagara without having seen or heard of one or the other. So all life is a great chain, the nature of which is known whenever we are shown a single link of it" [Conan Doyle, *A Study in Scarlet* 17].

The detective asserts that each case has a certain code, a deep structure, and so "the relevant causes are always a finite set.... Holmes cannot go wrong, because he possesses the stable code, at the root of every mysterious message" (Moretti, "Clues" 145). The detective finds a super-code that gives a key for the interpretation of every sign. Yet, this "rationalistic" method implies that Holmes's theory rests on unverified assumptions about a hidden unity and implicit structure. As Frank argues, Holmes's investigation is grounded in "absent evidence ... a hypothetical origin that is never fully available for the detective" (59). Analogously, as Frank observes, Darwin's evidence of the evolution "was compelled to rely on negative evidence ... [as it] demonstrated that species had become extinct; it did not prove that existing species had, in fact, evolved from now-extinct ancestors" (159–60). Thus, Conan Doyle did not only celebrate the optimistic side and positivist views of his contemporary science, but also provided caveats and criticism of the limits of science.

When semioticians analyze the analytical methods of Sherlock Holmes and compare it to the reasoning of Charles S. Peirce, they come to similar conclusions. The critics point out that correct logical reasoning, the rational methods of induction and deduction, are in fact quite rarely used by Conan Doyle's detective. Instead, his investigation rests on unexplainable assumptions, unconscious hypotheses, and "the conjectural method" (Ginzburg 267): "Holmes consistently displays what C. S. Peirce has called abductions" (Truzzi 69). Abduction is formally equivalent to a logical fallacy, which states that if "A" is correct, then "B" is correct; "B" is correct, therefore "A" must be correct.

Abduction consists in one of those *reversals* that de Man foregrounds in his *Allegories of Reading*, the reversal of cause and effect. As Holmes points out in *Study in Scarlet* (1887), the detective's work necessitates "to be able to reason backward" (61), to find the cause behind the effect. The problem is that effects can usually have several causes and so the detective's work rests on the careful deployment and testing of guesses. Holmes enters the labyrinth of *erroneous* causality, which, as Nietzsche points out, can be found in dreams just as much as in wakefulness when "the supposed cause is inferred from the effect and introduced *after* the effect: and all with extraordinary rapidity, so that, as with a conjurer, a confusion of judgment can here arise" (*Human* 18; emphasis in original). Analogous arguments are tangible in Nietzsche's *The Will to Power*: reason, (free) will, consciousness, and the subject are created by similar flawed logic (295–96; see also Shapiro 25–26).

Thus, Holmes's detecting process reveals the inevitably problematic nature of human reasoning. The detective's scientific process is preceded by "an instinct which relies upon unconscious perception" (Sebeok and Umiker-Sebeok 18–19). The perfect logician, such as Holmes or Peirce, must not only be a scientist, but they also have to possess the skills of an artist or pseudo-scientist, demonstrating that "the sciences have grown out of the useful arts ... astronomy has evolved out of astrology, and chemistry out of alchemy" (Sebeok and Umiker-Sebeok 28).

Holmes overtly hovers on the edges of pseudo-science when he draws on craniometry and phrenology. These "disciplines," which are mostly discredited today although they were somewhat accepted in Conan Doyle's age, are manifested frequently in his stories: in "The Blue Carbuncle" (147), *The Hound of the Baskervilles* (452), and *The Lost World* (20, 127). Furthermore,

Holmes once describes a "rather fanciful" theory, a distorted version of evolutionary developmental biology that becomes influenced by feudalistic principles in "The Adventure of the Empty House." He underlines the significance of family trees and argues that "the individual represents in his development the whole procession of his ancestor.... The person becomes, as it were, the epitome of the history of his family" (566).

Additionally, if the detective intends to maintain the public's respect towards his profession, he will also have to hide the contingency behind science: he will have to cheat, use sleights-of-hand, and lie. Holmes utilizes "a little mystification" to find the hiding witness in "The Adventure of the Norwood Builder" ([1903]; 581) and becomes a "master dramatist who receives the homage of his audience" at the end of "The Adventure of the Six Napoleons" ([1904]; 668). He frequently applies disguises "with the thoroughness of a true artist" ("The Adventure of the Dying" 837). Thus, "an element of art and magic is blended into the logic of scientific discovery," and the investigation turns into "a sort of pseudo-science" (Sebeok and Umiker-Sebeok 30). Holmes is not only a chemist, but also a violin player, composer, theatrical artist, pseudo-scientist, and drug addict. (His drug addiction, resulting from psychological neurosis, is foregrounded and exaggerated in Nicholas Meyer's *The Seven Per Cent Solution*.)

The detective becomes somewhat similar to Professor Challenger, the protagonist of Conan Doyle's science fiction stories (Moskowitz 157, 168). Professor Challenger creates, heralds, and in the end proves fantastic extrapolations of his contemporary scientific theories: for example, that prehistoric animals still exist on Earth, ether can alter and so become poisonous, our planet is an all-encompassing living organism, and so on. Although eventually he manages to prove the correctness of his shocking hypotheses, due to his eccentric behavior he is often characterized as a fake scientist, a clown figure who desperately needs the attention of the public. As his colleague in the "The Poison Belt" says, he is "a born charlatan, with a kind of dramatic trick of jumping into the limelight" (180).

As critics often point put, the most vulnerable aspect of Conan Doyle's scientific views was spiritualism (Saler 607). Although spiritualism does not feature in the Sherlock Holmes stories, it attains great significance in his Professor Challenger stories. In *The Land of Mist* (1926), spiritualism competes with accepted scientific standpoints and eventually seems to establish a new scientific paradigm (244). Professor Challenger becomes convinced of the verity of supernatural phenomena and ghostly visitations, realizing that "he, the champion of scientific method ... had, in fact, for many years been unscientific in his methods" (411).

The combination of the character Sherlock Holmes with science fiction themes, therefore, is implicit in Conan Doyle's oeuvre. Pastiches, parodies and adaptations almost immediately turned this implicit connection into explicit (Saler 600). A story in August Derleth's Solar Pons series, for example, brings together the detective with the Cthulhu mythos. More recent adaptations openly play with mixing the "rationalistic" tradition of the Holmes saga with the fantastic: enough to mention here Alan Moore's comic book series *The League of Extraordinary Gentlemen* (1999–), which juxtaposes Sherlock Holmes's arch-nemesis Moriarty with H. G. Wells's characters, Count Dracula, Mr. Hyde, the James Bond saga, and so on (Hemmingson 375). Holmes accepts the verity of supernatural phenomena in several stories of J. R. Campbell and Charles Prepolec's *Gaslight Grimoire*. In Peter Calamai's "The Steamship Friesland," for example, Holmes solves the case with the help of a ghost and by heeding Conan Doyle's advice on spiritualism. The similarity between Holmes and Professor Challenger and the possibility of blending their fictional worlds have also been recognized by popular culture. Manly and Wade Wellman's *Sherlock Holmes's War of the Worlds* (1975), for example, is a sequel to the Holmes and Challenger stories, a science fiction novel in which the two protagonists have to fight against H. G. Wells's Martians.

The point is, Conan Doyle's detective stories do not only celebrate science but also reveal their limitations, foreshadowing complex science fiction texts, for example those of Stanislaw Lem. As Frank argues, Conan Doyle "provided a critique of the historical [and scientific] imagination quite as sobering as that emerging from the stories of Edgar Allan Poe ... or, ironically, from the writings of Lyell and Darwin" (155–56). Physicians such as Dr. Bell, paleontologists like Cuvier, biologists like Darwin, and geologists like Lyell have realized that their field often becomes "a narrative science" (Frank 172). The scientist deploys and analyzes tiny and hidden items, encoded signs or fragmentary clues in order to create an account of chronological series that looks complete but rests on gaps and guesses. Thus, the scientific investigation results in "lies-to-children" (Pratchett, Stewart and Cohen 41), or "a fictional construct, a history" (Frank 163), demonstrating that narrative is a basic human tool to (mis)understand the universe: "a metacode, a human universal on the basis of which transcultural messages about the nature of a shared reality can be transmitted" (White 6).

In other words, Conan Doyle's science fiction and detective stories reflect and somewhat react against the idea that positivist science constructs edifices of accumulated knowledge, that the universe is a mystery to be solved and the scientist is a puzzle-solver (see Kuhn 35–42).

Lem's Generic Liminality between Detective Fiction and Science Fiction

Isaac Asimov's robot stories (for example *I, Robot* [1950], *The Caves of Steel* [1954], and *The Naked Sun* [1957]) embody an additional well-known overlap between detective fiction and science fiction when they depict a murder or psychological puzzle in a highly technologized environment. Asimov's texts are telling examples of such genre crossing, influencing many writers: as Christian W. Thomsen argues, "The conflicts that Asimov pointed out were taken up by successors and exploited in much more intricate ways" (31). Although Lem expressed harsh criticism over Asimov's robot stories in his essay "Robots in Science Fiction," he might have used them as a starting point in his own fiction, for example, in *More Tales of Pirx the Pilot* (1968).

Analogously to Asimov, who draws on recurring detective-psychologist characters (Elijah Baley, R. Daneel Olivaw, Susan Calvin) who investigate the possible errors of programming the robots, Lem's Pirx and Ijon Tichy investigate when dangers arise "not from men and machines so much as from their collision, because the reasoning of men and computers [or robots] was so awfully different" (Lem, "Ananke" 208; see also Kandel 379).

To investigate the case of a hiding alien or android who is masqueraded as a human forms a widely used motif in popular culture — enough to think about Robert Heinlein's *The Puppet Masters* (1951), the television series *V* (1983–84; 2009–), Ridley Scott's *Blade Runner* (1982), Philip K. Dick's *Do Androids Dream of Electric Sheep?* and "Second Variety" (1953). Analogously, Lem's "The Inquest" portrays the protagonist Pirx's dilemma to find the android within his crew, thus evoking a detective fiction situation. Pirx undertakes the task to test a new generation of androids on a space mission without knowing which of the crew members are human. All five astronauts — the suspects — look equally innocent or guilty, but one or two of them are androids: "the culprits." Pirx's task is even more complexified by the crew members, who, similarly to the famous prisoner's dilemma in game theory, can choose between indicting the others or remain silent, and between admitting or rejecting the charges. Eventually, the android is exposed, since he constructs "a kind of murder machine" to kill the crew. Pirx thwarts his plans and defeats the android, but he becomes the antihero of metaphysical detective stories because his "lack of resoluteness," his "bumbling human decency" and unintentional mistake (158–61) solves the case instead of his genius.

In other cases, Pirx hunts for a robot gone berserk ("The Hunt") or for an excessively adventurous, almost human automaton ("The Accident"). In *Peace on Earth* (1987), Ijon Tichy and various secret services investigate the mechanical and computerized systems, the artificial intelligence units of the

Moon, where possibly a superweapon against the Earth has been developed. They try to reconstruct the forgotten moments of Tichy's reconnaissance mission, since a mysteriously performed corpus callosotomy erased his memories. An obese, depressive secret agent who is "pushing sixty" becomes the "Sherlock Holmes" of the case, but he can provide only a fraction of the final explanation and the case remains partly unsolved (221–34). Furthermore, he and Tichy cannot prevent the final, apocalyptic events of the novel, again evoking the role of the antihero and the "defeated sleuth" in metaphysical detective stories (Merivale and Sweeney 8).

In "Ananke," Pirx plays not only the role of the detective, but also that of the murderer when he ascertains that the fatal accident of a space ship is due to his former colleague, the mentally unstable Cornelius, who suffers from anankastic or obsessive-compulsive disorder. Because he cannot verify his investigation with proofs, he drives Cornelius into suicide with a telegram that contains the title and the most famous sentence of a detective story by Edgar Poe, "Thou Art the Man" (1844). In *Fiasco* (1986), Pirx becomes the clue and (perhaps) the victim: after an accident on Titan, the crew of the space ship *Eurydice* brings back a vitrified body into life, either that of Pirx or that of another pilot, Parvis. The identity of the body is unsuccessfully investigated by "criminologists, forensic experts," physicists who examine the personal belongings of the victim and who are "also sleuths, in a way" (72).

Lem's "The Mask" (1976) also features a protagonist-narrator who resembles both a detective and a murderer. A highly intelligent robot hides in a woman's body, almost deceiving even itself, since besides its (supposedly) genuine memories of its own construction it has artificial memory implants of various individual personalities. Suspicious signs (lumps in her arm, contradictory memories, overly deep footprints) urge her to examine the human body "as a masterful detective might examine the scene of a crime" (204). She is manifested as a typical representative of the mastermind detective, devoid of passion, possessing "elegantly parsed vocabulary ... logical phrases, syllogisms ... [and] this feeling of terrible tedium in matters of sex, the cold contempt, the distance" (203). When she incises her body to reveal her true identity, her programming turns her into a hunting machine, whose job is to assassinate Arrhodes, an enemy of the King: the detective overtly obtains the role of the murderer.

Furthermore, certain clues indicate in this masterly written story that the protagonist might not be the only cyborg disguised as human. The guests of the royal ball act "as if everyone there were party of the same conspiracy ... a host of mechanically dancing mannequins" (193), and the monk who helps finding Arrhodes tells her: "'You are my sister'" (226). His statement remains an enigma even after the end of the story, as it is not revealed whether the monk has referred to the human(e) personality traits of the machine or to his own artificiality.[1] Analogously, the ambiguous ending does not reveal whether the automaton could resist its murderous programming: she waits passively but with compassion for the death of her (loved) prey, who is killed by a human abductor instead of the machine.

Lem's *The Investigation* and *The Chain of Chance* draw on and subvert detective fiction traditions, combining them with science fiction, ghost stories, essay-esque philosophy and theories of science. There are, however, significant differences between the two novels: while the former is a rewriting of British-European crime fiction evoking the genre traditions of Agatha Christie, Conan Doyle, and Georges Simenon, the latter imitates the American hard-boiled tradition and spy stories (Steiner 453; Swirski, *From Lowbrow* 153–56). The former is a Kafkaesque "anti-mystery" (Jarzebski, "The World" 81), which pretends to provide a final answer but, in fact, eschews narrative closure; the latter, however, confirms the possibility of a final explanation in detective fiction. As Swirski argues, "Where the latter novel [*The Chain of Chance*] climaxes in a resolution, the investigation from 1959 [*The Investigation*] is crowned with fiasco and a flurry of muddled hypotheses" (*From Lowbrow* 81).

The Investigation describes Lt. Gregory's investigation over dead bodies that return to life for a short period in the English countryside. The text is a modernist anti-detective novel, which is saturated by symbolically dense descriptions of sinister, mysterious, alienating buildings and places, such as the flat of Chief Inspector Sheppard, that of Gregory, the oddly desolate eerie London, the foggy countryside, and so on. As T. R. Steiner argues, "The book becomes exotic, its London not the familiar metropolis of Conan Doyle or Creasey but a *mitteleuropäische* Kafkaesque shadow city" (453; emphasis in original). The novel refuses to give a final, prevailing explanation for the mystery and maintains the possibility of various alternate explanations: the strange crimes may have been committed by the mastermind scientist, statistician Sciss, or they form a supernatural event, or they embody an accident resulting from the coincidence of random events; they might be the consequences of a lorry driver's crazy amok, the manifestations of the driver's visions, the Chief Inspector's own deeds, and so on.

The Chain of Chance is another distorted detective story that bears certain science fiction traits. The setting is an alternate Europe, a slightly futurized and somewhat dystopian Italy and Paris, roughly in the same year when the book was published (1976). At the age of eighteen, the protagonist volunteered to fight in the Second World War, but now he is an ex-astronaut in his early fifties. More precisely, he is a former back-up astronaut, who probably took part in the Mars mission but did not become a member of the landing crew due to his hay fever. He investigates the mysterious deaths of balding, middle-aged American and Western-European tourists in Naples, repeating the final deeds and journeys of one of the victims.

Somewhat regrettably, the ending of *The Chain of Chance* transforms it into "the rational variant" of *The Investigation* (Swirski, *From Lowbrow* 158). The conclusion provides a final, prevailing solution, explaining the strange deaths with the accidental combination of cosmetic and pharmaceutical chemicals with cyanide in roasted almonds. Thus, the genre formula is significantly less sabotaged than in the previous case: although the criminal is missing and the detective's successful investigation is due to random events, the final solution of the private eye becomes overarchingly dominant, indicating that the hidden cause behind the mysterious events can be apprehended. The ending does not even provide a twist: certain characters indicate early on that the deaths could be the consequences of a "biochemical trap," a chance "combination of different substances," and that an "adversary who relies on a strategy of chance can only be defeated by the same strategy" (Lem, *The Chain* 123, 124, 126).

Lem draws on the conventions of the detective-puzzle in his well-known science fiction novels, as well. But these allusions are often quite obscure, because his puzzles are manifested with a critical edge to indicate "the erroneousness of pretending to a final solution or total knowledge of any complex situation" (Suvin, "The Open-Ended" 219).

His celebrated novel *Solaris* is centered on a scientific puzzle, portraying in detail the enigmatic nature of an intelligent ocean in a distant planet, which sends "visitors," the embodiments of repressed memories and desires, to the space station of the scientists. The novel explains in detail how scientific and psychological explanations of the alien life form "replaced one enigma by another, perhaps even more baffling" (19). Furthermore, when the protagonist-narrator Dr. Kris Kelvin arrives at the space station, he finds his colleague dead and so he has to face "the mystery surrounding Gibarian's death" (25). Thus, Kelvin occasionally takes the position of the psychologist and the detective, resembling in his efforts (as well as in his name) Susan Calvin in Asimov's robot stories, but his efforts remain unconvincing. Instead of solving puzzles and unraveling mysteries, Kelvin keeps on citing unverified theories.

Analogously to *Solaris*, an alien world, in this case a future society on Earth, is manifested as a complex enigma in *Return from the Stars*.

Lem's enigmas, in a way similar to, but more overtly than Conan Doyle's puzzles, reveal the inadequateness of science, the historical and contemporary inadequacy of conceptualizing the world with anthropomorphic and patriarchal theories (Swirski, *Between Literature* 71). Thus, the seemingly traditional prose in Lem's fiction conceals a dual self-reflection: one that can be identified with Lem's awareness of literary or science fiction traditions, a "metageneric" self-consciousness (Philmus 66, 76), and the other that derives from reflecting scientific models, cultural and philosophical theories (Swirski, *Between Literature* 74).[2]

In the rest of this chapter, based on the analyses of Neil Easterbrook and Istvan Csicsery-Ronay, I interpret Lem's fiction, especially his *Solaris*, as meta-science and meta-science-fiction, in order to analyze postmodern liminality, the poststructuralist interpretation of transgression in his oeuvre. I intend to outline the epistemological problematics in his fiction, which question the distinguishable nature of genuine and virtual experiences, scientific and pseudo-scientific research, original and representational, corporeal and mirrored images, human and mechanical consciousness.

Meta-science: Naming, Decoding, Madness

Csicsery-Ronay describes Lem's fiction as "metacommentary," indicating the overt criticism of cultural constructions such as science, myth, literature, and religion in his novels ("How not to" 387). These constructions, which intend to explain the universe, diffuse into various contradictory theories and create a flux of ideas without final resolution or reconciliation. In Foucauldian terms, the texts indicate the multiplicity of discourses, "discontinuous practices, which cross each other, are sometimes juxtaposed with one another, but can just as well exclude or be unaware of each other" ("The Order" 67).

The validity and "truth" of scientific explanations depend on the discipline or paradigm that created them. Foucault's disciplines open the discourse but also confine it with a prescribed "set of methods, a corpus of propositions considered to be true, a play of rules and definitions of techniques and instruments" ("The Order" 59). Thomas S. Kuhn's paradigms follow and contradict each other, providing theories with certain freedom but also constraining the scientific perspective (Kuhn 37). Strict conditions given by paradigms prove to the postmodern reader that "scientific revolutions," the substitution and succession of paradigms do not necessarily mean progress, but draw attention to problems in the history of science. As Kuhn argues, "The member of a mature scientific community is, like the typical character of Orwell's *1984*, the victim of a history rewritten by the powers that be" (166).

Creating names and special terms that draw on and modify the conventions of language is an essential process of the scientific method. The character Snow in *Solaris* points out that "We have named all the stars and all the planets, even though they might already have had names of their own" (184). Scientific language, like language as such, originates from the human intellect and so inevitably humanizes the world. As the narrator of *Solaris* argues, appellation gives way "to the temptations of a latent anthropomorphism or zoomorphism" (116), or at least, in case of cautious Solarists, of "geocentrism" (111). Nietzsche also underlines the anthropomorphic nature of naming, categories and concepts: "If I define the mammal and then after examining a camel declare, 'See, a mammal,' a truth is brought to light, but it is of limited value. I mean, it is anthropomorphic true and true and contains not a single point that would be 'true in itself,' real, and universally valid, apart from man" ("On Truth" 251).[3]

Lem's satirical *The Futurological Congress* (1971) also suggests that appellation, "morphological forecasting" and "projective etymology," provide a key to (mis)understand the future and the unknowable. In a way similar to Freudian psychoanalysis, according to which slips indicate the operations of the unconscious, Lem's character suggests that strange misnaming, slips of the tongue indicate the unknown. Future inventions, objects, and events can be predicted by examining potential, upcoming expressions of language. The crackpot scientist Trottelreiner argues that

> man can control only what he comprehends, and comprehend only what he is able to put into words. The inexpressible is therefore unknowable. By examining future stages in the evolution of language we come to learn what discoveries, changes and social revolutions the language will be capable, some day, of reflecting [106].

Besides naming and taxonomy, the ambivalences of encoding, decoding, and translation also reveal the metaphorical, anthropomorphic, and arbitrary nature of language. A translated word does not refer to the same image of reality as the original; thus, as Nietzsche argues, "The various languages, juxtaposed, show that words are never concerned with truth" ("On Truth" 248). The problematics of translation and decoding form a recurring theme in Lem's fiction; one of his novels — *His Master's Voice* (1968) — is solely about the incapability of earthly scientists to translate and interpret an alien "message."

In *Memoirs Found in a Bathtub* (1971), a character says that "everything is code" (67): every natural phenomenon (a rose, starlight, etc.) and every literary work is encoded. The problem is that deciphering these codes leads either to unanswerable questions, unsolvable dilemmas and confusion, or to complete babble. The protagonist's mission is deciphered by a computer as "there will be no answer," while the same machine translates Shakespeare's poetry as "tra la la," and it "will reduce our monuments of literature, creations of genius, immortal works, all to complete gibberish!" (69).

The problematics of such pseudo-code lead to despair and tragedy in the novel, while they are described humorously in one of Lem's robot stories, "Tale of the Three Storytelling Machines of King Genius" (1967). Trurl builds a robot-adviser for a king, who accepts the machine, but rejects to pay the constructor's fee and dismisses the engineer. Trurl intends to take revenge, but the mastermind robot, the Perfect Adviser, undermines his efforts, protecting the interests of the king. Consequently, Trurl writes an innocent letter to the Adviser that is interpreted, due to the paranoia of the king and his secret service, as an extremely complicated code that hides semi-meaningful, complex coded messages, such as "Roll the locomotive's aunt in cutlets" (190). The Adviser realizes Trurl's plan and warns the king that Trurl has only created "the illusion of a code" (191). Yet, the King disbelieves and destroys the Adviser, allowing Trurl to finally take his vengeance. Trurl's "crude, primitive" strategy is based on pseudo-code and the assumption that "the presence of a code would have been a simple matter; its absence, however, led to complications" (194).

In *His Master's Voice*, insanity and undecipherable language are interrelated, as the novel indicates that often a seemingly insane theory comes up with a revolutionary solution. In the novel, only a "crackpot" idea assumes that there is a *message* in the neutrino emission coming from space, since a "stream of information — human speech, for example — does not always tell us that it is information and not a chaos of sounds. Often we receive a foreign language as complete babble" (40).

When Foucault underlines the significance of metaphors in the language of disciplines ("The Order" 60), he draws on medical science as an example, which has been analyzing madness for centuries. The language of madness can be interpreted as an alternate language to that of reason, and is therefore often forced to remain mute and unheard: "This whole immense discourse of the madman was taken for mere noise" ("The Order" 53). In *Solaris*, the messages of the planet are also unheard, "described as a symphony in geometry, but we lack the ears to hear it" (121).

Historically, the language of the madman has also been attributed with strange powers, with "the power of uttering a hidden truth, of telling the future, of seeing in all naivety what the others cannot perceive" (Foucault, "The Order" 53). The speech of the Other implies mythical and religious discourses: "There was a widely held notion (zealously fostered by the daily press) to the effect that the 'thinking ocean' of Solaris was a gigantic brain, prodigiously well-developed and several million years in advance of our own civilization, a sort of 'cosmic yogi,' a sage, a symbol of all action and for this reason had retreated into an unbreakable silence" (24). Silencing the other and enhancing it with a mythical omniscience and omnipotence are interrelated phenomena.

A theoretician in the novel also points out that "Solaristics is the space era's equivalent of religion: faith disguised as science. Contact, the stated aim of Solaristics, is no less vague and obscure than the communion of the saints, or the second coming of Messiah. Exploration is a liturgy using the language of methodology" (172). The problematic nature of science may lead to an emptied-out religious discourse; as Peter Nicholls argues, "The novel can plausibly be read as having nothing to do with God, but merely having to do with the semantic necessity ... of using religious vocabulary when confronted by phenomena not explicable in terms of human intellect" (63).

A further similarity between the language of the madman and that of Solaris is evoked by the central character of the novel. The psychologist Kelvin is interested in astronomy, and becomes a member of the Solaris-project due to Gibarian, the "proper" scientist, who cannot deal with the "visitors" and so commits suicide at the beginning of the novel. Kelvin (whose name may be an allusion to the British physicist William Thomson, Lord Kelvin) is only slightly more successful than Gibarian, perhaps because he "makes no effort to use his psychological knowledge" (Yossef 57). The language of the alien is understood or translated neither by scientists nor by the slightly incompetent psychologist in the novel, although Kelvin eventually gives a case study of Solaris, characterizing it as "a god limited in his omniscience and power, fallible, incapable of foreseeing the consequences of his acts, and creating things that lead to horror. He is a ... sick god, whose ambitions exceed his powers and who does not realize it at first" (197).[4]

Nietzsche argues that the procedures we use to understand the universe gain their power via long term establishment, as "after long use [they] seem solid, canonical, and binding to a nation" ("On Truth" 250). Foucault dates these procedures back to 16th century England ("The Order" 55). Since Solaristics is a relatively new discipline whose object resists any theories, it has not managed to establish prescribed and stable rules, language and methods: it has no governing paradigm. As Darko Suvin points out in his essay on Lem and *Solaris*, the "Reliance on familiar imaginative frameworks is erroneous in radically new situations" (221). Consequently, no scientific theory can provide a stable discourse; as Daniel Walker argues, "no paradigm can be established so that the work of normal science can begin. Thus, normal science comes off as absurd" (162).

The novel demonstrates a special and overt example of Foucault's argument that "we must not imagine that the world turns towards us a legible face which we would only have to decipher; the world is not the accomplice of our knowledge" ("The Order" 67). Lem depicts a universe that evokes H. P. Lovecraft's stories, whose horror stories rest on the depiction of human helplessness and contingency, foregrounding the characters' "motelike unimportance in a blind and chaotic universe which neither loves them nor even finds them worthy of notice" (Burleson 12).

Solaris resists human attempts to render the planet familiar, legible and calculable for humans; thus science, in a way similar to Conan Doyle stories, becomes extremely similar to pseudo-science, astrology to astronomy. The first appearance of the "visitors" of Solaris, for example, is described in a book full of "pseudo-science, inspiring eccentrics to explore freakish by-ways ... an invaluable period document as much for the historian as for the psychologist of science" (77). This book, which is linked more to astrology than to astronomy, becomes crucial in understanding the alien planet's behavior.

His Master's Voice confirms that the problematic points of scientific paradigms often arise on the borders of science and pseudo-science or swindle. The alien messages are discovered by a character who "made his living as a supplier, and banker, and even spiritual comforter for the kind of maniacs who in earlier times confined themselves to building perpetual-motion machines and squaring the circle" (36), and by a bogus scientist who belongs to the "multitude of con men and crackpots [who] inhabit the domain that lies halfway between contemporary science and the insane asylum" (38). In *Solaris*, the ago-old wishful dream of astrology comes true, when the alien planet encapsulates, radiates upon and dominates human emotions and lives.

Meta-Science-Fiction: Irony and Gender in *Solaris*, *Return from the Stars*, and *The Chain of Chance*

A prime example of Lem's conscious utilization and parody of science fiction conventions is in "Pirx's Tale" (1968). The story describes the unsuccessful adventure of Pirx when, due to his unskilled and physically incapable crew, he cannot record his encounter with the ship of an ancient alien civilization. His story, therefore, can be interpreted as a parable of a failed contact between humanity and the aliens. The first person narrative, however, is undermined by the introductory paragraphs. In these passages, Pirx makes a distinction between "trashy" sci-fi and proper science fiction, "good books" that truthfully describe the cosmos — and renders his own story as the former! The narrator-protagonist emphasizes:

> I'll take sci-fi, the corny, easy-to-read stuff, where everything, the cosmos included, is so tame. But it is an adult tameness, full of calamities, murders, and other juicy horrors, yet all quite harmless, because it's bull, from A to Z: scariness to make you smile.
>
> The story I'm about to tell is just such a spook tale. Only this one actually happened [4].

Analogously, an adventure-packed and spooky science fiction book becomes a mise-en-abyme in *Fiasco*. Mark Tempe (the resurrected Pirx or

Parvis) reads a story of explorers who disturb the inner structure of a termite society, which is in war with red ants. The human explorers interfere with the war, capture a mysterious object from the kernel of the termite city and so become the targets of attack by various insects all over the world. Later on, the astronauts of *Eurydice* go through similar adventures, entering a similar war on Quinta: an extraterrestrial technological instrument or organism is described as a "moth" (149) and a spiderweb (319), Tempe as a "fly" (262), reconnaissance devices as "bee's eyes," and earthly civilization is characterized as a "human anthill ... lost in the boundless reaches of the Universe" (248).

Gary K. Wolfe's science fiction "icons" are mediating devices between order and chaos, self and the Other, natural and artificial, human and alien; they are mythical images "of the barrier between known and unknown" (Wolfe, *The Known* xiv). Lem's novels often evoke these icons and dichotomies, and make them problematic: as Mark Rose argues, *Solaris* is "a highly self-conscious fiction that is as much a work of generic criticism as it is a new text in the genre" (82). The rocket, space ship, space station, astronaut, and the labyrinthine city are such science fiction icons in Lem's *Solaris*, *Return from the Stars* and *The Chain of Chance*, drawn on in a way similar to "Pirx's Tale" and *Fiasco*: the reader cannot be sure when the trashy sci-fi elements turn into "proper" literature. It remains unnoticed when/if the anthropomorphized space turns into the alien, unascertainable Universe, where "humans will never feel at home" ("Pirx's Tale" 3).

It is virtually a truism of science fiction criticism that the rocket is a phallic symbol (Wolfe, *The Known* 20). Elyce Helford analyzes the opening scene of *Solaris*, Kelvin's journey from "mothership" Prometheus to the space station in a similar fashion. Helford from a Lacanian and feminist perspective argues that "[t]he planet, in this discursive context, is constructed as passive receptacle, the inactive and unresisting object of male desire" (169). She interprets the ocean of the alien planet as a feminine symbol, and the library of the space station as a haven from the unknown and frightening female otherness: "This windowless space is centered in the station and the ocean is completely shut out" (170).

The destination of Kelvin's shuttle, however, is the space station, not the planet. Helford reads the ocean "as a great womb, a womb which cradles and protects the fetal Kelvin within the amniotic membrane of the space station" (170). Her description implies that the space station — with the exception of the library — has become part of the alien planet, evoking the unity of the amniotic membrane and the womb of the mother. In this case, would the space station, which is an astronautic edifice and a symbol of human construction, become an image of contact? Would it provide synthesis or liminal space between human and alien?

In my interpretation, the traditional understanding of liminality is questioned in Lem's oeuvre, but I will try to illustrate that its postmodern interpretation, the liminal play of oscillation, becomes highly detectable.

Helford argues that "Lacanian theory provides a suggestive framework for explaining Kelvin's psychic development on Solaris" (173). She is not the only critic who believes in the protagonist's development: as Csicsery-Ronay points out, "Most critics agree that in his concluding words Kelvin has attained a new state of alertness and awareness. His formerly aggressive drive for Contact has given way to a more serene receptivity" ("The Book is" 9). My reading, however, in a way similar to that of Csicsery-Ronay, questions the protagonist's "psychic development," as the novel's ambivalence and irony undermines the attempts to read it as an allegory of psychological progress.

Helford does not emphasize (although she certainly mentions) the irony of the novel, that is, the critical attitude often present in Kelvin's narration. Although Kelvin spends much time in the library, he reads the scientific books with an ironic overtone *even at the beginning of the novel*. The protagonist realizes early on the inadequateness of scientific theories: his comments, therefore, frequently demonstrate a parodying distance from the scientific theories.

> The second volume of Hughes and Eugel, which I was still leafing though mechanically, began with a systematization that was as ingenious as it was amusing. The table of classification comprised three definitions: Type: Polythera; Class: Syncytialia; Category: Metamorph.
>
> It might have been thought that we knew of an infinite number of examples of the species, whereas in reality there was only the one — weighing, it is true, some seven billion tons [20].
>
> Veubeke, director of the institute when I was studying there, had asked jokingly one day: "How do you expect to communicate with the ocean, when you can't even understand one another?" The jest contained more than a grain of truth [22].

What is more, irony is significant and overt in some of the books themselves, such as in Grastrom's pamphlet. It is a "fifteen page booklet (his magnum opus!), [in which] Grastrom set out to demonstrate that the most abstract achievements of science, the most advanced theories and victories of mathematics represented nothing more than a stumbling, one or two-step progression from our rude, prehistoric understanding of the universe around us. He pointed out correspondences with the human body ... in the equations of the theory of relativity, the theorem of magnetic fields and the various unified field theories" (170).

Furthermore, the implications of an ironic reading are tangible in Lem's *Return from the Stars*, a novel somewhat similar to *Solaris*. The dense prose of the text, perhaps influenced by Ernest Hemingway (Freedman, *Critical Theory*

97), evokes chivalry and masculinity, but it is in contrast with the protagonist's vain attempts to make contact with an alien, albeit human civilization. The novel becomes a feminist parody of patriarchal and scientific views — occasionally indicating the possibility that it is in fact a patriarchal parody of feminist views.

Hal Bregg, the protagonist-narrator in *Return from the Stars*, is an astronaut who returns from a space mission of "a hundred and twenty-seven years Earth time and ten years ship time" (28). He intends to understand — and conquer — the alien culture, which is "ahead" of his due to more than a hundred years of "development," via relationships with women. The male team of the space ship, the homoerotic relationship between Bregg and Olaf is in conflict with the female representatives of a slightly feminine earthly society void of peril and violence. The space ship as a masculine symbol underlines the female characteristics of the planets that the astronauts intend to conquer, including the Earth.

Bregg's physical superiority (he is taller and stronger than most men of the future) evokes chivalry, the "Knights of the Holy Contact" in *Solaris*, especially when he "saves" the life of an actress in the simulated perilous adventure of an amusement park called "Merlin's Palace" (89). He is a pilot and an amateur scientist who loves mathematics and who is proud of his ability to always decide objectively. Nevertheless, when he returns to Earth he becomes "savage" and embodies the aggressive drives of the unconscious. He usually reacts to his conflicts with passive, non-responding women aggressively:

> She stood submissively. Her head fell back, I saw her teeth glistening; I did not want her, I wanted only to say, "But you're afraid," and for her to say that she was not.... Had she been afraid only as a woman is of a man, a strange, even threatening, unknown man, then I wouldn't have given a damn; but this was something else. I looked at her and felt anger growing in me. To grab those naked white arms and shake her... [40].

Bregg is a character highly similar to John, the astronaut-detective in *The Chain of Chance*, the masculine hero of hard-boiled detective fiction, who also saves a girl, and who is openly cynical about the "feminist underground" movement of his age (7). John, although he spent much less time in space than Bregg, also feels alienated from the society that he returns to: he is "the observer 'literally' from 'out of this world,' unwittingly alienated from it ... by the experience of space" (Steiner 458). His passion for alien planets is overtly associated with sexual drives when he misinterprets the erotic movie poster of a round-the-clock cinema: "The first evening I almost ducked inside, after mistaking the rosy-pink spheres on the posters for planets. Not until I was standing in front of the box office did I notice my mistake: displayed on the poster was an enormous fanny" (4).

Such episodes illustrate that although Lem promotes criticisms that emphasize that in his books "problems of knowledge play the part that love and erotic adventures do for other writers" (Swirski, *Between Literature* 73), scientific and erotic adventures, epistemological and emotional conundrums are inseparable in several of his stories. On Ijon Tichy's fourteenth voyage in *The Star Diaries*, for example, Tichy encounters a society where one can buy "scrupts," but only if he has a woman around. As Tichy is single, he cannot obtain a "scrupt," no matter how much he would like one, and thus the reader will never find out what kind of an alien (pornographic?) product the "scrupt" is (111–12).[5]

In *Return from the Stars*, the future society uses a vaccine to wipe out most of the unconscious and aggressive drives, initiating the process of "betrization," and so "They have killed the man in man" (Lem, *Return* 153). They have obliterated the scientist, the sportsman, and the chivalrous knight in man: the job of surgeons is done by robots, combat sports are extinct, love and extreme emotions can hardly be found, and so on. The "Knights of the Holy Contact," therefore, become absurd and ridiculous, since their intension to conquer the Universe is futile from the point-of-view of the future society. The idea of a space mission is exposed as an absurd folly both as a scientific problem and as a dangerous challenge:

> It is difficult to put into words the feeling that came over me — because if they had truly succeeded in making acceleration independent of inertia, then all the hibernations, tests, selections, hardships, and frustrations of our voyage turned out to be completely needless; so that, at that moment, I was like the conqueror of some Himalayan peak who, after the indescribable difficultly of the climb, discovers that there is a hotel full of tourists at the top, because during his lonely labor a cable car and amusement arcades had been installed on the opposite side [112].

John, the protagonist in *The Chain of Chance*, characterizes space travel in a similar fashion. He describes antigravity and motion sickness in the space ship as a pitiful comedy of human errands, distorted versions of housecleaning and bathroom activity:

> Who can describe the still-life spectacle that takes place in orbit? Just when you think you've got everything tied, secured, magnetized, and taped down with adhesive, the real show begins — that whirling swarm of felt-tip pencils, eyeglasses, and the loose ends of cables writhing about in space like lizards. Worst of all were the crumbs, hunting for crumbs with a vacuum cleaner...
> Or dandruff. The hidden background of mankind's cosmic steps was usually passed over in silence. Only children would dare to ask how you pee on the moon....
> The whole thing was ridiculous. We kept at it till the cerebral congestion and the hardening of the intestines went away... [9–10].

Bregg and John are portrayed simultaneously as heroic and pitiful astronauts, masculine and emasculated characters. The latter character is described in the first two chapters of *The Chain of Chance* as a hard-boiled detective and spy with a dangerous, complex secret mission. But, as Steiner observes, the reader's expectations soon meet with anticlimax: "Lem creates more suspense than the conventional thriller — and nothing happens. The contract ... that suspense will explode into violence is violated" (458).

Furthermore, John, who suffers from hay fever and turns out to be fifty years old and slightly balding, participated in dangerous and heroic missions twice without actually contributing to the success of these missions. First, he enlisted in the commandos at the age of eighteen, but got wounded before he could enter combat in the Normandy invasion. Second, he became a member of the Mars project, but never actually landed on the planet because of his hay fever. Thus, he was specially trained twice to become a member of an elite, heroic male community, only later to be unselected in both cases. As the character says:

> Somewhere in my files, they must have written the word "allergic" — in other words, defective. Because of that diagnosis I became a backup astronaut — a pencil sharpened with the best possible instruments so that in the end it couldn't be used to make a single dot. A backup Christopher Columbus, as it were [20].

It is ironical that when he intends to do something heroic and masculine (note the phallic metaphor of the sharpened pencil!), he fails — but when meeting the challenge off-guard, he succeeds to some extent. He is accidentally present during a terrorist attack at the airport of Rome, saving Annabella, a young French girl. When he gives up his attempts to reveal the mystery in Naples, he randomly bumps into the solution.

Return from the Stars ends when Bregg refuses the invitation to the next space mission, breaks up with his male friends and returns to his "gold and white" home, staying with his wife. Similarly to *Solaris*, the novel ends with the protagonist's somber monologue, indicating that he has learnt form his adventures; he has become wise and understanding towards the alien, personified as earthly women.

> [F]or the first time I — alone but not a stranger to the Earth — now subject to her and her laws — for the first time I could, without protest, without regret, think of those setting out for the golden fleece of the stars....
>
> The snow of the summit caught fire in gold and white, it stood above the purple shadows of the valley, stood powerful and eternal, and I, not closing my tear-filled eyes, got up slowly and began to walk across the stones, to the south, to my home" [*Return* 247].

The complex nature of Lem's novels, however, undermines the solemn meditations with irony; Bregg's misogynist behavior questions his final, enlightened attitude. Thus, I disagree with Ann Weinstone, who argues that Kelvin in *Solaris* eventually "has stopped seeing, writing or even thinking. He has, at least momentarily, ceased *representing*" (186; emphasis in original). My reading of Lem questions the possibility to evade representation, mirroring and repetition. Quite the opposite: Lem's oeuvre problematizes and keeps in focus thinking and representation, which the characters can never elude.

Solaris as Fort-Da

As Easterbrook argues, the feminist-psychoanalytic interpretation of *Solaris* (and, I would add, *Return from the Stars*) becomes problematic if one just applies these theories to explain the protagonist's behavior or psychic "development." Lem's novels often provide a reading experience that "seems to invite an extremely conventional psychoanalytic interpretation but which contains a series of radically unconventional devices that deflect or defer any possibility of employing a traditional, especially psychoanalytic ... strategy" (Easterbrook, "The Sublime" 177). In fact, Lem indicates that Freudian theory is just one geocentric discourse among many, another anthropomorphic, explanatory story or "lie-to-children." As the narrator in *His Master's Voice* points out, Freud "has become the Ptolemy of psychology, for now, with him, anyone can explain human phenomena, raising epicycles upon epicycles: that construction speaks to us, because it is aesthetic. He converted the pastoral model into one that was grotesque, unaware that he remained a prisoner of aesthetics" (10).

Nevertheless, the poststructuralist implications of Freudian and Lacanian psychoanalysis are crucial in my interpretation of *Solaris*. I do not intend, however, to use these theories merely to analyze the psyche or mental "development" of the protagonist, but to connect them to a postmodern interpretation of liminality. As Easterbrook argues, the novel "shifts from the psychoanalysis of one man's duplicitous guilt to the question of the possible distinction between origins and ends, originals and copies, presentations and re-presentations" ("The Sublime" 188). Thus, although the possibility of personal psychological development becomes highly dubious, the poststructuralist understanding of liminality and mirroring remains meaningful and relevant in these novels.

Poststructuralist theories posit that, instead of going through a "rite of passage" or psychic development, a constant oscillation characterizes the subject. Foucault, based on Lacan, underlines the hidden, problematic and elusive nature of the Other. The position of the Father, the Authority which "links space, rules and language within a single and major experience," must be absent when one encounters it (Foucault, "The Father's" 81). The Other, the image of God or Father is tangible only when it disappears: "The gods are *here* only by being *there*" (78; emphasis in original). Lacan's "Phallus," the signifier that defines desire and provides values for the subject, is accessible "only through a threat — a threat of ... privation," and hence "it can play its role only when veiled ... [and] by its disappearance" (Lacan, "The Signification" 281, 288).

The Other requires an "inaccessible presence" and a "tangible absence," a game of appearance and disappearance: "a form which is nothing in itself but which designates the *Limit* in all its aspects" (Foucault, "The Father's" 76, 79; emphasis in original). The situation can be characterized with the "fort-da" phenomenon, a Freudian-Lacanian term to describe the infant's game of appearance-disappearance with a wooden reel and a piece of string.

This game, in Freud's theory, is translated as seeing and not seeing the mother ("Beyond" 15). The game is crucial for Lacan as well, but he associates the importance of the "fort-da" with the subject's initiation into language, with the birth of desire (see Silverman 169–176). The subject, designated by a primary rupture, comes to existence due to this game of frontiers:

> For the game of the cotton reel is the subject's answer to what the mother's absence has created on the frontier of his domain — the edge of his cradle — namely, a *ditch*, around which one can play at jumping.
> This reel is not the mother reduced to a little ball by some magical game ... [but] it is a small part of the subject which detaches itself from him while still remaining his, still retained [*The Four Fundamental* 62; emphasis in original].

Lacan's analyses of the fort-da game relate to Derrida's theories, which stress the play of sameness and difference, absence and presence, interiority and exteriority. Derrida points out that "Play is always play of absence and presence, but if it is to be thought radically, play must be conceived of before the alternative of presence and absence. Being must be conceived as presence or absence on the basis of the possibility of play and not the other way around" ("Structure, Sign and Play" 369; see also *Dissemination* 93, 157).[6]

Kelvin's relationship with the planet Solaris can be described with such a play, the constant alteration of appearance and disappearance, delimitation and transgression. The compulsion to repeat the game of presence and absence, totality and rupture, is highly tangible in *Solaris* (see Easterbrook, "The Sublime" 183). There is a constant back and forth, "fort-da" movement in the novel, in a way similar to Franz Kafka's *The Castle*. Csicsery-Ronay claims that "the planet is Kelvin's Castle. Whether it will yield its secret or not, Kelvin insists that it has a secret to yield, and that he has been 'called' to plot its dimensions" ("The Book is" 15).

Analogously, in *Memoirs Found in a Bathtub* the protagonist intends to find and decode his mission, which would give an all-encompassing meaning to the presence of "the Building." Although he occasionally seems to achieve a breakthrough and find an interpretation that would explain his role in the Building, eventually he is deprived of any success. Lem's world, recapitulating Kafka's *The Castle*, indicates that there should be a unity, an all-encompassing discourse to understand the Other, but his novels remain a medley of incongruous units.

To understand and decode the self-alien encounter, the characters would need a totalizing language. Their success rests on the Derridean center which is outside the system, "a base, a sort of Archimedean point, which in itself is not rational" (Jarzebski, "Stanislaw Lem's" 367). This central, and at the same time outer, point of reference constantly appears and disappears for the characters. As Csicsery-Ronay argues, the "alien intelligence provides humankind with a glimpse of its longsought Archimedean point in the universe only to show how inaccessible it is" (Csicsery-Ronay, "The Book is" 15).

The final and frequently quoted scene in which Kelvin encounters the ocean can persuasively illustrate the "fort-da" play in *Solaris*. The character steps on the surface of Solaris for the first time and puts his gloved hand into the ocean. The jelly of the planet, temporarily mesmerized by the hand, envelopes while resisting to touch it. Kelvin utilizes the phenomenon, raising his hand, and thus a wave of ocean is "attached" to his body. As the narrator explains, "A flower had grown out of the ocean, and its calyx was molded to my fingers. I stepped back. The stem trembled, stirred uncertainly, and fell back into the wave, which gathered it and receded" (203). He *reverses* the events that have happened to him: this time he provides the Other for the ocean, who follows the alien body but is incapable of taking a grip on it; therefore, he hides his hand and gives it back again, repeating the game several times.

In the first chapter of *Fiasco*, nature behaves in a similar way. When the pilot Parvis walks on the frozen volcanic surface of Titan, the various volcanic formations remind him of earthly landscapes, but at the next moment they reject that reminiscence. Recognition and its deprivation follow each other rapidly: "Whatever he saw was both totally alien and extremely familiar, reminding him continually of something that in the next minute would always allude him ... because here things seemed ... [as if] they could never complete themselves, never achieve full realization, never decide on a conclusion, on a destiny" (31–32).

In *Solaris*, the constant emergence and discrediting of scientific paradigms manifest the constant appearance and disappearance of the alien. Although Kelvin seems to believe that eventually he can reach a limitless discourse, the communion with the Other, the character, in fact, merely drives the limits further away (see Foucault, "The Father's" 83).

Liminal Spaces: Labyrinths

In Jean Baudrillard's typology, the first subgenre of science fiction is the ideal, "romantic," utopian subgenre, in which the "model"—the alien planet, simulacrum or mirror image—is overtly different from the "original" and more developed than the Earth (*Simulacra* 121–22). But, as many critics observe, utopian settlements, which are frequently placed on islands or in strictly delineated cities, evoke notions that writers consciously intend to avoid: the utopian city is centralized, stable, xenophobic, confined, and so on (Wolfe, *The Known* 88–90).

Many cities and buildings in science fiction and postmodernist literature, therefore, in order to eschew utopias, frequently evoke the image of the labyrinth. Such texts try to embody Nietzsche's wishful exclamations: "If we desired and dared an architecture corresponding to the nature of our soul (we are too cowardly for it!)—our model would have to be the labyrinth!" (*Daybreak* 104).

The labyrinth is a major image in Lem's fiction (see Jarzebski, "The World" 81). In *Fiasco*, both the termite city and the extraterrestrial civilization form a city of labyrinthine mounds, where the contact with extraterrestrial societies becomes "a maze without an exit" (191). In *Solaris*, it is the "cyclopean surface structures" that are characterized as labyrinthine (Nudelman 180). The "symmetriads" are enormous geysers, pillars, chaotic formations resembling fluid, labyrinthine cities, which suddenly become organized, solid and symmetrical. Their symmetrical phase coincides with their passivity and death: after becoming symmetrical, the "symmetriads" soon subside into the ocean, stop being active and resemble ruined cities that archeologists can investigate. The active, living formation turns into a passive object: "The structure stabilizes itself, and the partly submerged symmetriad ceases its activity. It is now possible to explore it in complete safety by making an entry near the summit, through one of the many syphons which emerge from the dome" (Lem, *Solaris* 119).

The labyrinth, which "always [features] some kind of enigma," and which "is always connected to the cognition of something new and unknown" (Nudelman 178, 181), can be read as a science fiction icon, a detective fiction motif, a psychoanalytical image, a mythical and Jungian symbol (von Franz 175–78), and a barrier between the known and the unknown. It can be related to the rite of passage, the fantastic portal and the initiation rituals, embodying liminal space in the traditional sense when it forms an obstacle that a novice/protagonist has to go through so that he or she could gain a new identity. This is what happens, for example, in Guillermo del Toro's fantasy film *Pan's Labyrinth* (2006).

However, in the works of Lem, Borges, Dick, and postmodern writers such as Eco and Italo Calvino, the liminal nature of the labyrinth eschews narrative closure, teleological process and individual development. In these texts, the question frequently arises and remains unanswered: is there in fact a center, a hidden knowledge that lies at the heart of the labyrinth? Is the labyrinth a conquerable obstacle between the known and the unknown? Or, as Wolfe argues, does the text "focus on the barrier itself" (*The Known* 34), on the labyrinth in its own right? In other words, will the labyrinth become similar to the science of Solaristics, described once by Kelvin as "an increasingly tangled maze where every apparent exit led to a dead-end" (169)?

Lem's novels usually do not transcend "Solaristics," as they lack the exit from the labyrinth. The final explanation to the mysteries is missing, or becomes ambiguous and ironic. The text itself becomes a labyrinth, not just its description, in a way similar to metaphysical detective stories, which are "designed in the form of a textual labyrinth" (Merivale and Sweeney 9). The fictional universe becomes "a labyrinth made of labyrinths. Each leads to another" (Lem, *Fiasco* 116).

A prime example of such hesitation and textual labyrinth is in Lem's "Tale of the Three Storytelling Machines of King Genius." The story has an extremely complex narrative structure with at least three levels of embedded tales, which become supplemented by feedback loops, metalepses between the narrative levels. The complex, multiply embedded plot is centered around a virtually constructed dream entitled "Mona Lisa, or The Labyrinth of Sweet Infinity." The frame of the dream-story depicts a king who becomes the target of his adviser's murderous plans. The adviser intends to assassinate him by luring him into the infinite maze of imaginary worlds created by a dream machine. His plans fail several times, as the king's cowardice and greed help him to escape from the hallucinatory, erotic temptations. Finally, however, he enters "Mona Lisa," a dream that simply repeats his reality, opening itself to the infinity of mirrors and embedded worlds. Lem's tale becomes a Borgesian parable, for the king finds himself "trapped and wrapped in dreams as if in a hundred tight cocoons, so that even when he managed, straining with all his might, to free himself from one, that didn't help, for he immediately fell into another ... lost in a labyrinth of dreams" (231; see also Hayles, *Chaos Bound* 128).

Furthermore, the labyrinth is an image of controversies. As Karsten Harries argues, Nietzsche's treacherous labyrinth "appears as a shifting figure — now a prison from which he seeks to escape, now a seductive other" (35). The complex nature of the labyrinth leads to controversial psychic states, such as the opposing but inextricably interwoven emotions of claustrophobia and agoraphobia, the fear of closed and infinitely open spaces.

A telling example for the ambiguity of the Nietzschean labyrinth is the labyrinthine structure in *Memoirs Found in a Bathtub*. The novel portrays an underground fortress, the headquarters of an intelligence agency, the so-called "Building." It soon turns out that the "Building" and its "missions" can be investigated endlessly by the protagonist, but they still construct a prison, an inescapable labyrinth, a closed space for him. Open and closed spaces, infinity and confinement, chaos and order, emptiness and fullness enfold into each other constantly in Lem's fiction, evoking Borges's "The Two Kings and the Two Labyrinths" (1949), in which the desert becomes a labyrinth. Such mazes evoke the poststructuralist understating of liminality and labyrinth, which is dominated by "the uncanny experience of reaching a frontier where there is no visible barrier.... One may move everywhere freely within this enclosure without ever encountering a wall, and yet is it limited. It is a prison, a milieu without origin or edge" (Miller 154).

In *His Master's Voice*, the information that has been beamed from space acquires a labyrinthine inner structure. There is a constant double-edged suspicion around the message. On the one hand, the fear is tangible that there is no code, that the message has no meaning and content: the neutrino transmission becomes "so densely coded with information that it is virtually indistinguishable from noise" (Hayles, *Chaos Bound* 122). In that case, the labyrinthine message would conceal only a void. On the other hand, the complicated nature of the message evokes the possibility of an open-ended discourse, the infinity of meaningful interpretations.

Lem's infinitely ambiguous message evokes Derrida's interpretation in *Spurs* of Nietzsche's styles, images, aphorisms and fragments, which "remain indefinitely open, cryptic and parodying. In other words, the text remains closed, at once open and closed" (137). Simulation and truth, veiling and bluntness, meaning and meaninglessness, fragmentariness and totality become irrevocably intertwined: the text "should remain forever secret. But not because it withholds some secret. Its secret is rather the possibility that indeed it might have no secret, that it might only be pretending to be simulating some hidden truth within its folds" (133).

Lem's female characters and labyrinths are just as much contradictory and subversive as Nietzsche's women figures and labyrinths: it is never quite clear whether the woman should be submissive or a feminist, truthful or deceptive; whether the labyrinth is a never-ending rhizome or a much simpler structure with a center — in other words, whether the labyrinth belongs to Type 1, 2 or 3 in Umberto Eco's typology (*Semiotics* 80–84).

Bregg, the protagonist and narrator in *Return from the Stars*, also encounters a labyrinth when he first arrives on Earth. The city, his birth place is in a sense a utopia where violence has been entirely obliterated, but it also becomes a complete maze for him, as incomprehensible as "the labyrinths of the station" (49) where his plane arrives. Traditional, symmetrical edifices have been substituted by asymmetry, "mountain-building." Because the consequences of inertia have been wiped out, navigation in the buildings is extremely difficult for the protagonist, who lacks the ability to decide if an elevator descends or ascends. The character has difficulty in detecting his own presence in the building, illustrating the contemporary architectural trend that "cultivate[s] the labyrinthine qualities of urban environments by interweaving interiors and exteriors ... through the creation of an interior sense of inescapable complexity, an interior maze" (Harvey 83). Thus, the labyrinthine building becomes a liminal space between inside and outside, in a way similar to Benjamin's arcades (*Charles Baudelaire* 54), Charles Jencks's postmodern, labyrinthine architecture (87–96), and McHale's "liminal, in-between space ... of postmodernism" (*Constructing* 158).

In *Return from the Stars*, both the streets and the terminal are comprised of several levels, which are connected by escalators and elevators. The whole city manifests "soft," labyrinthine, postmodern space (Harvey 5–6) and fluid architecture always in flux and motion, where "Solid masonry and concrete, the ultimate image of dead matter, seem to come alive with movement" (Jencks 211; see also Jameson, *Postmodernism* 45). As Lem's narrator-protagonist puts it: "It was hard to rest the eye on anything that was not in motion, because the architecture on all sides appeared to consist in motion alone, in change, and even what I had initially taken to be a vaulted ceiling were only overhanging tiers, tiers that now gave way to other, higher tiers and levels" (Lem, *Return* 9).

The image of the labyrinth also appears in Lem's detective fiction. In *The Investigation*, the city of London is described as labyrinthine; in *The Chain of Chance*, Rome's flight terminal is "known unofficially as the Labyrinth" (32). The building encapsulates entrapment and protection, anti-terrorism and terrorism: it is promoted as one of the safest terminals on Earth, but perhaps consequently, it soon becomes the target of a terrorist attack. When the protagonist saves a young girl from the blast by jumping off of a bridge in the terminal, he falls into a foamy liquid which was designed to save people and soften the impact of a detonation, yet in fact nearly suffocates many of the victims.

Lem's labyrinthine cities, buildings, and messages demonstrate the overarching urge in contemporary literature to portray ambivalent and infinite structures. Labyrinths are frequently utilized in mainstream postmodernist fiction, science fiction, and metaphysical detective fiction, because mazes can illustrate unsolved mysteries, the absence of narrative closure, and the lack of successful detection: in such texts "the mystery is a maze without an exit" (Merivale and Sweeney 9).

Furthermore, the theme of the labyrinth can be linked to another crucial theme in contemporary fiction: mirroring, the troubling experience in the house of mirrors. Luce Irigaray points out that when male scientist-detectives investigate the (female) Other, by surveying the unconscious and transforming woman into an object, they often use or create mirrors. The quest for the Other is governed by the Law of the same; the object of man's desire and investigation is a "faithful, polished mirror, empty of altering reflections. Immaculate of all auto-copies ... candid in their self-ignorance" (136). Nevertheless, although a feminist approach or literature may aspire to reinterpret woman's role as a *faithful* mirror, it does not automatically have to eschew *specular image as such*: as Irigaray says, "if it is indeed a question of breaking (with) a certain mode of specula(riza)tion, this does not imply renouncing all mirrors" (143). Concave mirrors and other disrupting glass surfaces can easily confuse the patriarchal scientist: they "deconstruct the logical grid of the reader-writer, drive him out of his mind, trouble his vision to the point of incurable diplopia [double vision]" (142). Consequently, not (only) the woman as an object, but (also) the male subject will feel entrapped or confined in the labyrinths of mirrors, thus experiencing crucial epistemological and ontological uncertainties: "Everywhere he runs into the walls of his palace of mirrors, the floor of which is in any case beginning to crack and break up" (137).

Mirroring with a Rupture: Monsters, Doubles, and Dolls

Baudrillard's second subgenre or second era of science fiction, which encompasses texts manifesting "an expanding universe" (*Simulacra* 123), recalls space operas. Such texts (in a way similar to his first subgenre) evoke the image of mirroring, as extraterrestrial settlements often reflect the social system, values, and body images of the Earth. Space travels, exploration and encounters with "strange new worlds" are frequently covert repetitions of human life, resembling historical colonization.

Solaris reflects this phenomenon, criticizing other texts of the genre. A frequently quoted passage of *Solaris* stresses that "We take off into cosmos, ready for everything: for solitude, for hardship, for exhaustion, death. Modesty forbids us to say so, but there are times when we think pretty well of ourselves.... We think of ourselves as the Knights of the Holy Contact. This is another lie. We are only seeking Man. We have no need of other worlds. We need mirrors" (72).

Mirroring, however, can easily turn into a subversive act. Poststructuralist and feminist theories, as well as Lem's texts, emphasize that reflection is typically accomplished with a difference, a refraction, a rupturing surprise — with the *revenge* of the mirror. (See, for example, Bacchilega 10; Irigaray 142; Baudrillard, *Simulacra* 1–14.) Mimicking resemblance causes "gender trouble" (J. Butler vii–ix) and the "menace" of the subaltern (Bhabha 86). This rupture can be forged with many different techniques: it can be achieved, for example, by means of the *unexpected* appearance of the mirror.

This is exactly what takes place in several of Lem's novels, usually at the beginning of the stories. In *Return from the Stars*, Bregg accidentally glimpses the mirror image of his overly muscular masculine body when he is wandering lost in the labyrinths of the terminal. Kelvin goes through a similar experience in *Solaris*, envisioning a ghost. Mark Tempe, when he realizes that he will become a member of the crew landing on Quinta, becomes distressed, opens a wrong door by mistake and faces his own mirror image in *Fiasco*. In *The Investigation*, Gregory walks into a glass-roofed dead end alley and so he mistakes his own mirror image for another person, a "stranger," who has something "askew" around his crotch.

> I looked in. A large, broad-shouldered man looked in from the opposite side. Myself in a mirror.... I felt a little like laughing, but mainly I was nonplused [*Return* 13].
>
> A narrow looking glass, built into the locker room, reflected part of the room, and out of the corner of my eye I caught sight of something moving. I jumped, but it was only my own reflection. Underneath the spacesuit, my overalls were drenched with sweat [*Solaris* 13–14].
>
> Mark ... did not remember if he said good-bye or even if he said anything. Or how he got back to his cabin. He did not know what to do with himself. Going to the closet, he opened the wrong door by mistake, saw his face in the mirror, and murmured:
> "You'll see the Quintans" [*Fiasco* 110].
>
> "What does he want?" Gregory wondered. The two men scowled at each other. In the shadows the man's broad face was hidden ... and his belt was all askew, with its end twisted loosely around the buckle. There was certainly something wrong with the buckle, Gregory thought, but he had enough problems without worrying about that too. He moved as if to walk past the stranger but found his path blocked....
> The stranger ... was himself. He was standing in front of a huge mirrored wall marking the end of the arcade. He had mistakenly walked into a glass-roofed dead end.
> Unable to escape the feeling that he was really looking at someone else, Gregory stared at his own reflection for a moment. The face that looked back at himself was swarthy, not very intelligent, perhaps, but with a strong, square jaw that showed firmness ... although more than once he had decided it was only pigheadedness [*The Investigation* 33–34].

The unexpected, and hence uncanny, appearance of the mirror image manifests the latent fear of Lem's characters in these novels (see Freud, "The Uncanny" 248). It also anticipates their further anxieties, epistemological crises, individual and gender dilemmas, which come to the surface in the later chapters. These episodes evoke Lacan's description of the mirror experience, which states that the imago "symbolizes the mental permanence of the I, at the same time as it prefigures its alienating destination" (Lacan, "The Mirror" 2). The mirror experience leads not only to self-formation but also results in self-alienation: the self simultaneously resists and revels in, ignores and embraces the mirror image. Under this estranged mirroring and representational process, "Recognition is thus overlaid with misrecognition," as Laura Mulvey observes (201).

Another possible form of the revenge of the mirror may be its exaggerated submission, lack of resistance, and blatant death. As Baudrillard says, "To reflect the other's desire, to reflect its demand like a mirror, even to anticipate it: it is hard to imagine what powers of deception, of absorption, of deviation — in a word, of subtle revenge — there is in this type of response" ("The Masses" 213). Analogously, Lem's *Return from the Stars* candidly reveals the masculine protagonist's struggle to dominate over submissive women when Bregg falls in love with a woman called Eri without actually seeing and understanding her: he admits that for a while he has no idea what color her hair is. The female character reacts to Bregg's aggression with overt and exaggerated submission and passivity. She dies, disappears, or fades away in the mirroring process — even her name indicates something illusive, intangible and airy:

> She was cold, slippery, like a fish, a strange, alien creature, and suddenly in this touch, so cool, lifeless — for she did not move at all — I found a place of heat, her mouth, I kissed her, I kissed and I kissed.... It was utter madness. She did not defend herself. Did not resist at all, was as if dead. I held her arms, lifted up her face, I wanted to see her, to look into her eyes, but it was already so dark, I had to imagine them [173].

Such episodes reveal the futility and blindness of the protagonist's urge to make contact with the Other, which behaves in the same way as Baudrillard's object of simulation, reacting "by a *parodic* behavior of disappearance" ("The Masses" 213; emphasis in the original). The aim of exploration, the Woman, becomes analogous to Baudrillard's "Tasadays," the dead objects of ethnology (*Simulacra* 8). The death of the scientific object can be interpreted as a protest, self-defense strategy, or revenge: "By dying, the object takes its revenge for being 'discovered' and with its death defies the science that wants to grasp it" (*Simulacra* 7).

The third possible origin of the rupture in mirroring may be that the boundaries between object and the reflected image, activity and passive reflection, the original and the imitation, become blurred. When the distinction between the original and the mirror image falls under doubt, the situation demonstrates poststructuralist liminality: instead of clear-cut distinctions, there is a constant *reversal*, an oscillation between the two poles of representation. As Derrida stresses regarding speech and its representation, phonetic writing: "What is intolerable and fascinating is indeed the intimacy intertwining image and thing ... to the point where by a mirroring, inverting and perverting effect, speech seems in its turn the speculum of writing, which 'manages to usurp the main role'" (*Of Grammatology* 36).

Science fiction texts often make it problematic to distinguish between the original and the mirror image by questioning priority. Did the humans create robots to duplicate themselves, or was it the other way around? Hayles analyzes the interwoven relationship of mirror image and the "original," emphasizing the constant feedback loops in Lem's short story collection *Cyberiad* (1967). She argues that in Lem's stories "neither human nor robot can logically claim to be 'original.' Conversely, neither one is merely a copy to be used for another's pleasure" (*Chaos Bound* 129). Or, as Lem's characters put it, "robots and palefaced are joined by a reciprocal bond" ("Tale of the Three" 244), since "Sometimes men build robots, sometimes robots build men. What does it matter, really, whether one thinks with metal or with protoplasm?" ("Altruizine" 263).

As Derrida observes, ruptured, distorted, and inverted mirroring may also lead to monstrosity: "The perversion of artifice engenders monsters" (*Of Grammatology* 38). Monsterized characters become the manifestations of our repressed fears of and hatred towards the Other. The monster is a key element of the horror genre, an "interstitial" being, a "culturally impure" character who "breach[es] the norms of ontological propriety ... an extraordinary character in our ordinary world" (N. Carroll 16, 31–35). But the monster is also a science fiction icon (Wolfe, *The Known* 151), a frequent image of human contact with the alien: "today, our monsters are robots, cyborgs, genetically altered creatures, and aliens who ... confuse, destroy and recombine oppositional dualisms such as human/nonhuman, biological/mechanical, male/female, and the like" (Weinstone 173–74).

Either way, the monster often becomes a widely utilized symbol of (terrifying) hybridity, invincibility, and transgression. In *Solaris*, the "visitors" can be read as monsters, since they blend human and alien characteristics, their bodies are almost indestructible and their appearance seems, for a while, unstoppable. A prime example of liminal monstrosity occurs also in Lem's "The Mask," in which the narrator-protagonist cyborg constantly searches, tests, and transgresses for its inner "invisible barrier[s]" (184), thus "discovering its own limits" (181). "She" continually questions her identity, hovering on the threshold between dreaming and awakening, human and artificial consciousness, organic and programmed memories, autonomous and subdued existence.[7] After freeing herself of her human flesh, she becomes a terrifyingly alien figure whose appearance and hunting for a human frighten the country folks, in a way similar to Mary Shelley's monster in *Frankenstein*. Her liminal personality, however, remains to some extent tangible: she hesitates until the very end of the story between following its own will and fulfilling the programmed task, between becoming a rescuer and a murderess, "bride and butcher" (238).

Besides monstrosity, the mirror image is often associated with the appearance of the Double. As Nudelman observes, the visitors in *Solaris* can be read as Doubles, since the astronauts "are fated to meet with 'themselves/not themselves,' with their Doubles, with an enigmatic, epistemic double consciousness" (185). The main source of horror in the novel is the Freudian uncanny (unheimlich), the encounter with the Double, one's unconscious memories personified in the "visitors," as the characters have to relive their pasts and face formerly familiar but repressed, deliberately forgotten emotions and situations.

As Freud argues, the uncanny effect of the Double originates from a reflection that becomes *too accurate*: "An uncanny effect is often and easily produced when the distinction between image and reality is effaced, as when something that we have hitherto regarded as imaginary appears before us in reality, or when a symbol takes over the full functions of the thing it symbolizes" (Freud, "The Uncanny" 244). A hypothesis in contemporary robotics, the "Uncanny Valley," confirms that overly realistic robots create repulsion in the users. The protagonist in *Return from the Stars* faces such problems when he is shocked by humanoid robots who serve customers at airplanes and female dresses that are decorated with animate, blinking eyes.

Such an excess is another possible method to create specular rupture, mirroring revenge: the object of investigation becomes a mirror that *overfulfils* its task. The planet does not only create an imago, but overly realistic, omnipresent clones as well. The Double, the "visitor" reflects not only the exterior, the peaceful surface of the present and the conscious, but also the inside, the buried traumas of the past and the unconscious. What is more, the mirror does not only reflect, but also embodies the image. As Darko Suvin argues, "Man always projects his mental models upon the foreign universe: on Solaris, the universe obligingly materializes one projection" ("The Open-Ended" 219).

Thus, Lem's *Return from the Stars* and *Solaris* portray two typical, but somewhat contradictory, vengeful strategies of the object of the mirror. In the former, the disobedience of the alien world (on planet Earth) is achieved by parodic *passivity*, disappearance, and blatant death. In the latter, the defiance of the alien planet utilizes *exaggerated* reflection, hyperconformist simulation, *overly active* acceptance: too much mirroring, excessively dynamic and accurate reflections.[8]

Another manifestation of the uncanny Double manifests itself in the figure of the doll. In *Solaris*, a doll is described in the log and interrogation of Andre Berton.[9] Berton is a pilot on a mission to find a lost Solarist, but he himself gets lost in the fog. Perhaps the most uncanny part of the story occurs when he glimpses the giant face of a two or three year old child in the ocean, a face "like a doll in a museum, only a living doll" (82). Freud, in "The Uncanny," analyzes E.T.A. Hoffmann's "The Sandman" (1816), in which a source of fear is a doll, an automaton that evokes the "[u]ncertainty whether an object is living or inanimate" (230), and whether one can control its own body or not. Analogously, the doll in *Solaris* seems to be controlled by a non-human force when it systematically goes through every possible human gesture and movement, as if the alien planet "had wanted to make a study of what this child was capable of doing with its hands, its torso, its mouth" (82).

The ability to lose control over one's body, the human body as dominated by an alien force or a machine, is a constant nightmare of science fiction. Thus, the doll becomes another science fiction icon, a not-too-distant relative or precursor of the image of the robot. It manifests or at least foreshadows the problematic nature of drawing distinctions between human and artificial, mechanical operation and organic brain, authentic and synthetic life forms.

In *Solaris*, the gigantic size of the doll also contributes to its uncanny effect: "this child was extraordinary large. Enormous, in fact. Stretched out horizontally, its body rose twelve feet above the ocean" (81). Although the proportions of the child's body feature a big head, and not the exaggerated body parts that Bakhtin finds in medieval literature (enlarged genital organs, belly, nose, mouth and buttocks), Lem's image still resonates with Bakhtin's grotesque, enlarged body. The grotesque body rests on topsy-turvy hierarchies, "the bodily hierarchy turned upside down" (*Rabelais* 309), and on transgression, as "the limits between the body and the world are weakened" (313). The grotesque body "swallows the world and is itself swallowed by the world" (317). Analogously, in *Solaris* the inside world of the subject becomes open and vulnerable to outside forces. Berton's living doll is created, controlled, and subsequently destroyed by the ocean, which invades the dreams and thoughts of the astronauts.

There is transgression *within* the body as well, displaying the combination of opposites: "The grotesque image of the body is to show two bodies in one: the one giving birth and dying, the other conceived, generated and born" (Bakhtin, *Rabelais* 26). Berton describes the face of the child analogously, comparing it to a mask that features contradictory emotions simultaneously: "one half gay, the other sad, one half scowling, and the other amiable, one half frightened and the other triumphant" (83).

Another doll-like figure with grotesque body gains a significant role in *Fiasco*. In the first chapter of the novel, Parvis embarks on a mission to find Pirx with the help of a "strider" — a mecha-like machine which has been envisioned in several Hollywood movies, for example, in James Cameron's *Aliens* (1986) and the Wachowskis' *Matrix Revolutions* (2003). Lem's mecha forms a doll or a bizarre body because it has no head, no sexual organs (originally the entrance to the machine was placed on its groins, but the users detested the connotation), and because its movements are the repetitions or extensions of human movements. Operating such machines evokes symbiosis between man and machine, evoking a feeling of omnipotence in the user:

> He had achieved, again, the familiar state that veterans called "fusion of man and strider." The boundary between himself and the machine had disappeared; its movements were now his movements" [26].

Soon after the idyllic union of man and machine, however, Parvis falls into the traps of Titan, misled by his own reflection. He finds himself in an enchanted realm, in Shakespearean "Birnam Wood," a "snowy" forest of web-like obstructs that block his movements. Man and the machine find themselves stuck in white syrup, confined in an artificial womb and forming "an enormous white doll, an eccentric snowman" (45). Like several other Lem stories, omnipotence rapidly turns into impotence when Parvis loses control over the mecha and becomes the doll of a higher power, moving "like a puppet on strings" (40).

Conclusions and Caveats

My starting point in this chapter was that traditional detective fiction is a genre that evokes Enlightenment, philosophical and scientific rationalism. I intended to demonstrate, however, that, as Conan Doyle's stories indicate, the pure reason of 19th century "normal science" was already conscious of its limits. Thus, even conventional detectives and thinkers such as Holmes and Professor Challenger deviate from the rigidities and constrains of a stable norm, anticipating certain problematics of Lem's fiction.

Furthermore, self-conscious detective fiction and science fiction conventions characterize Lem's texts, creating generic liminality in his oeuvre. As for thematic liminality, the represented or mirror image questions the priority of the "original" via various strategies — unexpected appearance, passivity, reversal, and overacceptance — and so gains semi-independence: this is what I call "mirroring with a rupture" or "the revenge of the mirror" in such texts. The inability to judge whether one encounters the real or a simulated image, original or a replica, Self and the Other, is a crucial experience in Lem's novels, contributing to a long-established genre convention, manifested as early as in E.T.A. Hoffmann's fiction. Thus, his novels illustrate that Freudian and Lacanian psychoanalysis, especially theories of the mirror, can be useful to explain and subvert science fiction icons such as the Monster, the Double, the labyrinth, the "alien" planet, the astronaut hero, and so on.

Lem's texts can be interpreted as metaphysical detective stories in so far as they evoke the norms of detective fiction, but they describe the universe without the presence of meanings, without an all-encompassing code that would clarify the mysteries. By means of their ironical or open endings, his novels often eschew narrative closure. (*The Chain of Chance*, in my opinion, is an exception in this sense.) Thus, Lem's fiction becomes similar to other metaphysical detective stories, which "composed in equal parts of parody, paradox, epistemological allegory (Nothing can be known with any certainty), and insoluble mystery ... self-consciously question the very nature of reality" (Merivale and Sweeney 4).

Lem's analysis of Dick's novels may equally well characterize his own works: "Instead of unraveling puzzles, he leaves the reader at the end on the battlefield, enveloped in the aura of a mystery as grotesque as it is strange" (Lem, "Philip K. Dick" 135). Lem's characters also remain lost and confused on the battlefield after trying to find an Archimedean point, a viewpoint outside their discourse. They end up hovering on the boundaries, in a labyrinth or pseudo-labyrinth, playing with the limits of the inside and outside — or, to approach it from another angle, they become the victims of such a play.

Finally, two caveats must be discussed. First, although Lem intends to avoid totalizing descriptions and discourses, by using language "not even Lem can entirely avoid metaphor. In selecting the sea as a sign [in *Solaris*], Lem employs a familiar image of the nonhuman, one already invested by ancient usage from Homer and Shakespeare to Melville and Verne with the idea of the infinite" (Rose 84; see also Malmgren, *Worlds Apart* 42–43). Lem also follows a long generic tradition when he describes the alien with figures of insects in *Fiasco* and *The Invincible* (1964), and when he portrays a sentient planet in Solaris. Professor Challenger in Conan Doyle's "When the World Screamed" already suggests that a planet (the Earth in this case) is "a living organism" that ignores humanity completely (443–44), and that "a common ambition of mankind [is] to set the whole world talking" (461).

Language inevitably comprises long-established metaphors and anthropomorphisms when a story depicts the alien; perhaps the single alternate that the genre can undertake is to avoid using language. For example, the narrator in Borges's "There Are More Things" describes the alien monster only indirectly, by observing its belongings, and he stops the narration when he should describe the monster. Lem's *Fiasco* ends analogously: when the earthly ambassador lands on the foreign planet and finally meets the aliens, the rest of the crew destroys the planet and so neither the crew nor the reader will find out what sort of creatures the Quintans are. (Nevertheless, as the novel can easily be interpreted as a didactic parable about the psychologically dramatic consequences of war, Lem's anthropocentrism becomes somewhat tangible here.)

Second, although Lem's novels demonstrate a poststructuralist understanding of epistemological and ontological questions, feminist and psychoanalytic problems, many of his shorter works trivialize and parody these dilemmas. As Thomsen argues, these stories keep Lem "from becoming a didactic bore.... Lem, the satiric clown, relativizes his own standpoints as a passionate ... cultural critic" (38). The significance of random events and the contingency of human intellect play a crucial and tragic role in *The Investigation* and *The Chain of Chance*. On the other hand, as Jarzebski argues, in his other works Lem fabricates "many jokes about humanity being an ugly by-product" of random universal events, Brownian motion ("Stanislaw Lem's" 366). Ijon Tichy's eight voyage, for example, explains the origins of life on earth as the prank of two drunken space vagabonds, "Gorrd" and "Lod" (*The Star Diaries* 35–36).

The problematics of individual and programmed consciousness, original and created world become overt in many of Lem's short stories and it is difficult to decide when the serious discussion of these issues turns into parody. Numerous examples of these borderline cases can be found in *The Star Diaries* and *The Cyberiad*. In "The Seventh Sally," Trurl, a robot-engineer (who is a robot himself) programs a pocket universe, an enormously realistic virtual reality for a megalomaniac king. The story raises serious (?) questions about the distinctions between artificial and genuine personality, and about the fundamental rights of a created being. The sarcastic ending, however, reveals that the virtual universe has turned against its monarch, removed the king from the planet, only keeping his boots, utilizing them as artificial satellites.

Lem's another recurring character, Ijon Tichy, witnesses similarly ambiguous adventures. He meets Professor Corcoran, a crackpot scientist who firmly believes in the famous brain-in-the-vat skepticism. Consequently, he creates his own vats, engineering artificial but humanistic delusions for machines, a reversed version of the Wachowskis' *The Matrix* (1999); this time a human mastermind forges virtual reality for artificial brains. The professor does all this not because he revels in deception, but because he enjoys the role of a God who keeps out of his created world (Lem, "Further Reminiscences"

35–51). Although the science fiction motif of virtual and human realms seems to be portrayed somewhat seriously here, it obviously becomes the object of sarcasm a few pages further when Tichy describes legal wrangles aroused by the appearance of extremely intelligent washing machines, and by a human who turns himself into a throng of robots, forming a new planet (89–110).

These stories can be interpreted both as satirical science fiction parodies, and, since Lem himself draws on these issues seriously in many cases, as self-parodies. A prime example of such self-deprecating irony is an embedded story in "Tale of the Three Storytelling Machines of King Genius," in which Klapaucius meets a crazy, unappreciated philosopher, Chlorian Theoreticus the Proph, who reiterates many principles of Lem's serious fiction. Evoking *Solaris* and *His Master's Voice*, Chlorian Theoreticus argues that

> each civilization ... eats its way into the Universe, turning cinders and flinders of stars into toilet seats, pegs, gears, cigarette holders and pillowcases, and it does this because, unable to fathom the Universe, it seeks to change that Fathomlessness into Something Fathomable, and will not stop until the nebulae and planets have been processed to cradles, chamber pots and bombs, all in the name of Sublime Order, for only a Universe with pavement, plumbing, labels and catalogues is, in its sight, acceptable and wholly respectable [241].

His treatise, however, meets only with the complete silence of the audience: nobody is in interested in his deep arguments. What is more, he evokes ridicule when another of his philosophical pieces becomes the victim of the printer's carelessness as a typo distorts the subtitle from *A Peek into the Future* into *A Pee into the Future*. Interestingly enough, several of Lem's own works, when translated into English, suffer similar — although less conspicuous and ludicrous — distortions due to typos and mistranslations (see Swirski, *From Lowbrow* 172–73).

Chapter 4

Philip K. Dick: Urbanity, Liminality, Multiplicity

> The cyberpunks, being hybrids themselves, are fascinated by interzones ... Cyberpunk has little patience with borders (Bruce Sterling)
>
> The first thing to realize about parallel universes, the *Guide* says, is that they are not parallel. (Douglas Adams)

Homi Bhabha emphasizes the possibility of liminality in contemporary urban societies, especially in the suburbs of the immigrants when he argues that "the liminality of the Western nation is ... the colonial space played out in the imaginative geography of the metropolitan space; the repetition or return of the postcolonial migrant to alienate the holism of history" (168). Critics reflecting on Bhabha's postcolonial theory further emphasize the social and spatial nature of his hybridity, observing that liminality is "a space in its own right rather than a mere dividing line" (Fludernik, "Carceral" 68), and that "we get to inhabit *the* limen" (Lugones 77; emphasis in original).

Yet questions arise: in what way is social, postcolonial, and narrative liminality related to architectural liminality as it is formed in the cities? How can liminal space be created, or at least catalyzed by architecture and urban design? As Grosz ruminates, "How to *think* architecture differently? ... How to see dwelling as something other than the containment and protection of subjects? In short, how to think architecture beyond complementarity and polarization, beyond subjectivity and signification?" (127; emphasis in original). Referring to the influential writings of Deleuze and Guattari, she also poses the question: "Can architecture incorporate/appropriate or cannibalize nomadology or rhizomatics" (127)?

Cyberspace and Bukatman's broader term "paraspace" are spatial formations that might provide a basis for this new, alternative architecture and spatial thinking. As I explain later in this chapter, I apply the term "cyberspace" with a double meaning. On the one hand, cyberspace indicates the spatiality of existing and fictional digital universes, "the virtual space of computer memory and networks" (Whittle 6) such as the internet, online societies, the matrix, and so on. On the other hand, the term may refer to the virtualization of our social and cultural life, the mediatization of our everyday reality. Paraspace is a somewhat different and broader term, denoting, mainly in fiction and literary criticism, a partly invisible and largely mental, "rhetorically heightened 'other realm,'" which includes cyberspace, but it can also refer to the worlds of telepathy, drug-induced hallucinations, derangement, simulacra, time travel, quantum physics, "urban zones," and "cyber zones" (Bukatman, *Terminal* 157).

Oppositions such as the "inside" and "outside," "here" and "there," "near" and "far," that have been recording for centuries "the degree of taming domestication and familiarity ... of the surrounding world" (Bauman 13) are utterly reinterpreted in cyberspace and paraspace. This new, virtual reality can be just as much objective and "outside" the human as it is subjective and "inside;" equally near and far, public and private, invigorating and fatal (see, for example, Virilio 58–59, 88). The idea of rigid limitations and distinctions is eroded (Haraway 35). Meanwhile, our everyday "reality" becomes mediated or simulated, transformed into a fluctuating, unstable space by architecture, social life, dreams, hallucinations, media images, and computer programs. As Jencks observes, contemporary architecture revels in this "ultimate liminal experience" when "space-time looses visual coordinates": "All boundaries are thus broken, borders transgressed, and experience thereby ... [is] turned inside-out" (95–96).

This is how the contemporary city becomes an estranged and fantastic place; the liminal space of reversed hierarchies forms the "image of the carnivalized city, the city as permanent carnival" (McHale, *Constructing* 251). Concomitantly, the digital realm, "the landscape of cyberspace ... reveals the architecture of its liminality" (Swanstrom 19), becoming the new, electronic Frontier. As David Tomas argues, cybernetic technologies mediate between human and mechanical life forms, constituting "a postindustrial 'rite of passage' between organically human and cyberphysically digital life-forms" (33).

In what ways do the multiplied virtual realities demonstrate and subvert the traditional understanding of liminality? Do virtual realities derive from modern or postmodern ideas, images, and architecture? How do Dick's virtual realities prefigure the cyberpunk visions of cyberspace? Can human characters such as the designer, programmer, and traveler control the flux of the cyberspace? Does Dickian cyberspace and paraspace liberate the individual, or does it just lead to new forms of anxiety and confinement, becoming a new instrument of control in the interest of the State? How is virtual space related to the virtualization of time and history? I tackle such questions in this chapter to characterize Dick's oeuvre, especially his proto-cyberpunk stories, alternate histories, and narrative deviations, in the context of liminality.

Virtual Cities: Modernism, Postmodernism, Nostalgia

When delineating the history of cyberspace, critics often characterize two distinct models of urban culture and architecture in the 20th century.

Modernity has established a space that is based on increasingly rapid transportation, planning and mapping. As Bauman argues, "Engineered, modern space was to be tough, solid, permanent and non-negotiable. Concrete and steel were to be its flesh, the web of railway tracks and highways its blood vessels" (17). In modernity, urban planning and mapping "colonizes space" (de Certeau 121). Modernist architecture is "like logic and beauty, a born enemy of confusion, spontaneity, chaos, messiness ... [and] its strategic principles are standardization and prefabrication" (Bauman 42). The German Bauhaus, for example, promoted the utilization of industrially fabricated elements, and the American Art Deco favored clear view inside and outside the building, utilizing straight lines, white walls, symmetry, and high towers with stepped spires (see Figure 8 on page 127).

In modernity, even the possibility of perfectly designed cities, that of Utopian settlements, was postulated. Corbusier envisioned a city where an omnipotent plan ("le Plan dictateur") judged upon every building. The designer then supposedly gains ultimate control over the city and its citizens, their present and future: it was believed that the architect "must not only comprehend the spirit of his age but also initiate the process of changing it" (Harvey 19).

To strengthen the dominance, the "monopoly" of the designer, the establishment of new cities became a prerequisite. As Bauman observes, modernist projects had to start from the zero point (41–42). Thus, it was no longer the map that imitated the actual territory, but the territory followed the map, ruling out obscurity and ineffective mazes. The modernist city is the map resurrected in a transparent form, intending to create lucid, practical, unambiguous, well-lit environments.

The idea of the perfectly planned city is questioned by postmodern architecture, the labyrinthine "soft city" (Harvey 5–7). In this new, more obscure, somewhat simulated space, concrete corporeality and conscious plans are questioned, and maps lose their meanings; as Baudrillard argues, such territory and its representation "disappears in the simulation" (*Simulacra* 2). Jencks (53–55) and David Harvey observe that, unlike modernism, postmodernism intends to utilize its historical background, albeit in fragmented forms, revealing palimpsest-like architecture and signifying "a break with the modernist idea that planning and development should focus on large scale, metropolitan-wide, technologically rational and efficient urban *plans*" (Harvey 66; emphasis in original). Postmodernism is grounded in multiple, dispersed, decentralized spaces, heterogeneous urban environments, as postmodern urbanization accepts the necessity of catering to every taste, recognizing the needs of divergent social groups and creating "cities within a city" (Harvey 67–76).

Postmodern urbanity frequently evokes references to cyberspace, the unimpeded information flow, and the rapid and cheap forms of communication. The human environment becomes McLuhan's "global village," in which, instead of the production, circulation and fetishization of commodities, contemporary capitalism "gives way to the 'proteinic' era of networks, to the narcissistic and protean era of connections, contact, contiguity, feedback and generalized interface that goes with the universe of communication" (Baudrillard, "The Ecstasy" 127). Thus, as Jameson argues, postmodern architecture and technology no longer favor "[the modernist] representation: not the turbine, not even Sheeler's grain elevators or smoke stacks, not the baroque elaboration of pipes and conveyor belts, nor even the streamlined profile of the railroad train ... but rather the computer" (*Postmodernism* 36–37). Paul Smethurst differentiates the modern and postmodern chronotope in a similar fashion: "If the time-spaces of modernism were constituted in cities and suburbia, and traversed by motor vehicles, aeroplanes, electromagnetic devices and the cinema, postmodernism is constituted in cyberspace and transmitted through electronic media" (3).

The giant flashing screen in *Blade Runner* is the symbol of the postmodern city, representing "our only architecture today: great screens on which are reflected atoms, particles, molecules in motion ... gigantic spaces of circulation" (Baudrillard, "The Ecstasy" 130). Analogously, Manuel Castells depicts our everyday reality as "real virtuality" and "the world of make believe" (373). The result of his "real virtuality" is the "global city phenomenon": in Castells's "global cities" or "megacities," the traditional model of space, "the space of places" is transformed, succeeded by "the space of flows." The space of flows is characterized by the postmodern flux, the network, in which "no place exists by itself, since the positions are defined by flows ... [and] places do not disappear, but their logic and their meaning become absorbed in the network" (412).

Thus, contemporary social theories stress that our cities become postmodern, fluid environments, "which can only be represented *in motion*" (Jameson, *Postmodernism* 45; emphasis in original). Additionally, the matrix, the immaterial virtual space, is depicted with metaphors that refer to urbanity, such as buildings, gates, boulevards, street lights, and so on (Mitchell 108–26).

Science fiction, especially Dick's fiction and cyberpunk literature, depict virtual and corporeal cities in a highly similar fashion. Their fictional cities are postmodern, fluid environments, always in motion. In Dick's "The Commuter" (1953) and "Adjustment Team" (1954), the protagonist's environment is secretly reshaped by hidden forces, foreshadowing Alex Proyas's cult-film *Dark City* (1998). In Gibson's *Idoru*, Japanese skyscrapers are constantly moving due to nanotech technology: "The entire facade of one of the new buildings seemed to ripple, to crawl slightly" (83).

In cyberpunk, the American metropolis is often characterized in comparison to a computer program (Gibson, *Neuromancer* 43; see also Luckhurst 206), while the matrix is depicted with images that refer to material cities. In Gibson's *Mona Lisa Overdrive*, for example, the matrix is described as "all the data in the world stacked up like one big neon city" (16). Thus, both virtual and material cities can be characterized by the chaotic architecture of postmodernism. As Dani Cavallero points out in *Cyberpunk and Cyberculture*,

> Gibson radically questions the association of cyberspace with a clean and rationalized geography.... Neither Gibson's cyberspace nor the material buildings and streets presented in his fiction abide by the rules of modernity, where the machine is often idolized as a means of fabricating mathematically pure, inorganic environments [144].

Nevertheless, cyberspace can easily become a utopian environment as well, evoking certain modernist dreams. As the corporeal world does not provide freedom in the dim future of cyberpunk, the matrix needs to provide privileges, pleasant "dwelling" space, even luxury. This is how, as Michael Benedikt argues, cyberspace brings back the archetypical and utopian image of the Heavenly City, celebrating "weightlessness, radiance ... peace and harmony through rule by the good and wise, utter cleanliness" (15).

Harvey emphasizes in his survey on modern and postmodern architecture that "there is much more continuity than difference between the broad history of modernism and the movement called postmodernism" (116). The postmodern break with modernism does not exclude the possibility of modernist echoes: utopian and Art Deco architecture remains influential, appearing for example, in Charles Moore's highly postmodern Piazza d'Italia in New Orleans (Harvey 95). Jencks also states that postmodernism "is historically specific, rooted in conventions ... evolutionary, not revolutionary, and thus it contains Modern qualities" (87). Somewhat refining Jameson's arguments, Harvey underlines that "Stressful though the current condition undoubtedly is, it is qualitatively similar to that which led to ... various modernist reconceptualizations of space and time" (305). Modernity, especially avant-garde, often displayed an affinity towards "totalizing chaos," heterogeinty, and fragmented history (Harvey 11).[1]

The impact of avant-garde on science fiction and cyberpunk visions is tangible and hardly surprising. The daring visions of Italian Futurism emphasized the speed of cars, streamlined trains and airplanes instead of computerized cyberspace — "with Gibson it is the ice-breaking console that substitutes for the race car" (Csicsery-Ronay, "The Sentimental" 230). Nevertheless, there is contiguity between the celebration of vehicles and computers: the "auto eroticism" or "mechanic eroticism" of avant-garde (Francis Picabia, Marcel Duchamp) foreshadows J. G. Ballard's "proto-cyberpunk" novel *Crash* ([1973]; see Dery 188–90). Furthermore, Gibson's fiction, especially his early short story "The Gernsback Continuum" (1981) provides ample examples that interweave computers and "the locomotives, automobiles, and airplanes of the Machine Age" (Bukatman, "Gibson's" 86). Numerous characteristics relate the cyberpunk movement to modernist, especially avant-garde movements, and so cyberpunk is often characterized as an avant-garde, neo-futuristic movement and phenomenon (McCaffery 9; Grant 43; Csicsery-Ronay, "The Sentimental" 229).[2]

In Dick's fiction, the interrelatedness of visual, interactive media and avant-garde art is recognized, which is a central argument in Benjamin's concept of modernity. As Benjamin stresses, avant-garde artists frequently created a spectacle similar to the "variety" of the new media: "Dadaism attempted to create by pictorial — and literary — means the effects which the public today seeks in the film" ("The Work" 237). The interrelatedness of the new media and avant-garde art is articulated in Dick's *Radio Free Albemuth* when mystical and drug-induced visions are compared to abstract paintings by Paul Klee as well as the extremely quick editing of films and music videos:

> It resembled a modern abstract painting; I could almost name the artist, but not quite. Rapidly, at the terrific rate of permutation which in the TV field they call flash-cutting, the frame of balanced, proportioned colors gave frame to another frame, equally attractive. Within a few given seconds I had seen no less than twenty of them; as each frame, each abstract, appeared, it once gave way to another. The overall effect was dazzling. Paul Klee, I said to myself excitedly [99].

The contemporary economic and cultural era is, after all, often interpreted as "the Third Machine Age" (Jameson's *Postmodernism* 36). Recent science fiction and cyberpunk writers frequently locate their origins in the previous Machine Ages: steampunk, for example, is usually set in an alternate 19th century of computerized steam motors. Science fiction and cyberpunk texts describe not only up-to-date, digital technology, but also decaying, old, analogue machines: computers are supplemented by references to hardly functioning televisions, cars, old-fashioned calculators, typewriters and photography (Luckhurst 211). In Dick's proto-cyberpunk *Do Androids Dream of*

Figure 8: The Chrysler Building (1928–1930) and modernist urbanism in New York (Wikimedia Commons).

Electric Sheep?, the future wasteland of San Francisco is saturated by "broken and semi-broken appliances" and "dead machines" (18), while the semi-organic androids are described as traditional machines, material commodities: "the variety of subtypes passed all understanding, in the manner of American automobiles of the 1960s" (14).

Filmic images, the visualized cities of cyberpunk also blend architectural paradigms: *The 13th Floor* features a simulated Los Angeles in the 1930s, while the retrofitted film noir images of *Blade Runner*— a film based on Dick's *Do Androids Dream of Electric Sheep?*— embody modernist visions of the city, in a way similar to Fritz Lang's *Metropolis* (1927).[3] The headquarters of the Tyrell Corporation, "the Tyrell pyramid," as Peter Wollen argues, invokes "a style which shaped Los Angeles during the 1920s through the designs of ... Frank Lloyd Wright" (239). The tower also evokes modernist urbanism in New York, especially "the Chrysler Building, a superb Art Deco icon" (Bukatman, *Blade Runner* 62). A slightly similar, white pyramid shaped "skyscraper" appears in the cyberworld images of *Johnny Mnemonic* (1995) at the very beginning of the film, whose script was written by Gibson.

Dick's fiction candidly illustrates the way postmodernists intend to utilize and, at the same time, to challenge, contradict, and parody the influence of modernist visions. His texts, in a way similar to cyberpunk fiction and films, demonstrate not only that postmodern thinkers and artists emphasize and exaggerate their divergence from modernism, but also that the culture and architecture of modernism "remains as a force influencing present-day reality in its old artifacts and as a still-present alternate universe which continues to coexist next to reality" (Westfahl 90). As Svetlana Boym observes, the idea of progress almost always coincides with nostalgic cultural trends, evoking (self-)reflective nostalgia, which "can be ironic and humorous. It reveals that longing and critical thinking are not opposed to one another" (50). Such reflective nostalgia appears, for example, in hidden but influential elements of the city, forgotten places and haunted buildings, ruins: the "unintentional monuments of urban environments" (Boym 78).

Virtual Cities: Mapping and Traveling

Roland Barthes's essay "Paris Not Flooded" provides a lucid example which demonstrates that modernist and postmodernist principles of urbanization can overlap. Barthes describes the Parisian flood as a media-phenomenon that creates a spectacle for the masses. The flooded city evokes Jameson's "fluid" architecture and Harvey's postmodern "architecture of the spectacle" with "its sense of surface glitter and transitory participatory pleasure, of display and ephemerality, of *jouissance*" (Harvey 91; emphasis in original). Nevertheless, it also evokes the utopian, modernist dreams of city creation, "the euphoria of reconstructing the village or neighborhood, giving it new roadways" (Barthes, "Paris" 33). The spectacle in Paris, as Barthes argues in his essay, foregrounds "childhood myth[s]," the experience of play and modeling, as

Figure 9: The historicizing Bradbury Building (1893) in Los Angeles, featured in *Blade Runner* (photograph by Carol M. Highsmith, Library of Congress).

well as a sense of security and human dominance: "The spectacle was singular but reasonable" (31). The catastrophic event gains a reassuring nature in the newspapers, since it manages to verify for the public "that the world is manageable" (34).

Dick's texts often describe virtual realities in a similar fashion: virtual reality creates the space of a public spectacle, but still remains somewhat "manageable." It is especially manageable for certain privileged characters: dreamers, planners, designers and hackers, who lack authority in quotidian reality but become omnipotent in the virtual world. Dick's "Small Town" (1954), for example, depicts the creation of a virtual city in such a fashion. The protagonist, Verne Haskel, is a lower-middle class character similar to Arthur Miller's Willy Loman, who becomes the sole creator of a model that imitates trains and his own city to the utmost precision. He constructs a neat, lucid model, a "minute town, each facet in perfect order" (342). After a while, however, the perfect imitation does not provide ample satisfaction, and the character gradually transforms the model according to his personal needs, dreams, and principles. His improved, utopian urban environment reflects modernist principles, in a way similar to the short-lived co-op buildings of Dick's *Martian Time-Slip*, which "reflect the utopian aspirations of urban planning boards and modernist architects" (Bukatman, *Terminal* 50). Such housing structures reveal the ultimate power of the urban planner, and the "forced democratization and egalitarianism of taste" (Harvey 80).

> He had cleared the slum area, the old rundown stores and houses and streets. The streets were wider and well-lit.... The wealthy district had been altered. There were now only a few of the mansions left — belonging to persons he looked favorably on. The rest has been cut down, turned into uniform two-bedroom dwellings, one story, with a single garage each.
> The city hall was no longer an elaborate, rococo structure. Now it was low and simple ... [Dick, "Small Town" 350].

The creation of this virtual reality evokes Borges's "The Circular Ruins": Haskel, in a way similar to the magician of Borges's story, gradually builds up his own artificial reality which he can, to some extent, solidify and make real. Haskel "didn't merely dream about an escape world. He actually constructed it — every bit and piece" (352–53). The twist ending — again evoking "The Circular Ruins" — indicates that Haskel does not only become a creator, but also a character in his artificial city: he escapes into his modeled universe, bringing his wife and other acquaintances with him. The characters have to understand that they have become puppets in Haskel's model; analogously, the dreamer in Borges's story realizes with terror in the end that "he too was a mere appearance, dreamt by another" (78).

Another architect who uses the model and the map for city construction is Ted Barton in Dick's *The Cosmic Puppets* (1957). Barton returns to his home town after many years, but he only finds a simulacrum-world instead of his own reality. He realizes, however, that the process of *remembrance* can reconstruct his former town. The problem is that many people are incapable of remembering correctly. Dick's characters create, therefore, a perfectly authentic map in order to help people remember. The (re)construction of the city strictly follows the map, evoking Bauman's description of modernist architecture:

"These maps," Hilda said, "are to be considered adequate symbols of the territory below ... *the symbolic representation is identical with the object represented*. If the symbol is accurate, it can be considered the object itself. Any difference between them is purely hypothetical" [Dick, *The Cosmic* 115; emphasis in original].

[In modernist projects] the map precedes the mapped territory: if the city is, from its creation and for the duration of its entire history, simply a projection of the map upon space ... [then] the map turns into a frame in which urban realities yet to arise are to be plotted, deriving their meaning and function solely from the site allocated to them within the grid [Bauman 41].

Besides the planner and the architect, another figure who can traverse, control, or at least take a grip on virtual realities, is the traveler. Such characters represent and renew the modernist phenomenon of "motion sickness," Benjamin's flaneur; they become "traveller-voyeurs," who are "the logical forerunner[s] of the 'Net junkies'" (Virilio 38).

Social theorists from Karl Marx onwards emphasize that modernization culminates in "the reduction of spatial barriers" (Harvey 109). Bauman, referring to modernist and postmodernist changes in urban environments, stresses that "Space stopped being an obstacle" (77), as our contemporary space, in a certain sense, is limitless: "There are no natural borders any more, neither are there obvious places to occupy" (77). Nevertheless, social barriers between the rich and the poor still exist and the idea of traveling, movement, and flux is highly significant: it is "the society of travelers" that we live in (96). As the whole society is obsessed with speed and traveling, "we are all on the move" (77), and social distinctions are reflected by the various forms of traveling.

Evoking Deleuze and Guattari's nomads and other itinerants, Bauman divides the contemporary city populations into "tourists" and "vagabonds." They embody the nomads, the flaneurs who travel within and between contemporary cities: rivals and alter egos of each other. The tourists, whether business travelers or actual sightseers, are the voluntary participants of geographical movement. In a way similar to Benjamin's flaneur, the tourist does not merely see the sights and examine the merchandise of the city, but also becomes a commodity: "he goes to the marketplace as a *flaneur*, supposedly to take a look at it, but in reality to find a buyer" (Benjamin, *Charles Baudelaire* 34;

emphasis in original). Bauman's vagabonds, however, are formed by the byproducts, the waste of the industrial society (92), and they are *forced* to move around. They lack the money and freedom that tourists possess: "the vagabond is a flawed consumer" (96). Unlike the tourist, who collaborates with the State and the tourist industry as well as the industry as such, the vagabond is the disobedient victim of the State.

But which category does the commuter, the suburb-dweller, and the protagonist of Dick's short story "The Commuter" belong to? Commuting, to some extent, lacks voluntariness, thus resembling the movement of the vagabond. But the commuter is not a flawed consumer, especially if he lives in an exquisite neighborhood, in upper-middle class suburbia. The commuter usually has a social position analogous to that of the tourist. Perhaps the commuter is a liminal character, fluctuating between the role of the tourist and that of the vagabond. Nevertheless, he is different from both groups in a crucial respect: although commuting is a form of traveling, the commuter is not a "traveller-voyeur," not a flaneur with drifting, digressive strolls, but simply someone who passes to and fro repeatedly in a confined periphery, mainly ignoring the landscapes and his fellow travelers (see Benjamin, *Charles Baudelaire* 44).

Either way, the commuter is definitely an itinerant who lives a mobile life; no wonder, therefore, that he becomes a traveler between alternate universes in Dick's "The Commuter." The story features a character similar to Verne Haskell, another feeble, middle-class worker, named Ernest Critchet this time:

> The little fellow was tired. He pushed his way slowly through the throng of people, across the lobby of the station, to the ticket window. He waited his turn impatiently, fatigue showing in his drooping shoulders, his sagging brown coat [129].

Critchet intends to buy a commute book to Macon Heights, a suburb which somehow has disappeared from the map of the train company. It is a town that has not been built, because the local council voted against the project seven years ago by a single vote. The middle class dreams and desires of the public, however, change reality in the "twilight zone" of the story — literally, since the transformation takes place soon after sunset (133). A new version of reality comes into existence, in which the council votes in favor of the suburb. Thus, a middle class utopia is formed, in which women know their places, carrying "grocery bags and little wire carts," and things are in perfect order: "Automobiles drove slowly back and forth. A sleepy little suburban town. Modern, upper-middle class. A quality town. No slums here. Small, attractive houses" (137).

Dick's stories recapitulate modernist and postmodernist theories, demonstrating that contemporary space, our present-day world, is based on speed, traveling and flow. Whether it is the modernist, corporeal urban space or the postmodern, digital space of flows, the flux remains crucial and undisputable. The real question is who controls these flows: as Harvey puts it, which "individuals or powerful groups dominate the organization and production of space through legal or extra-legal means" (222)?

Deleuze and Guattari argue that the power of the State is grounded in the "capture of flows of all kinds, populations, commodities of commerce, money or capital ... [creating] fixed paths in well-defined directions, which restrict speed, regulate circulation" (*A Thousand* 386). Virilio also states that cyberspace is a potent instrument for the State to strengthen its cultural and symbolic power. Cyberspace has become the new American frontier, a cultural and media construction that contributes to Americanization and globalization (19–27).

John Perry Barlow argues contrarily in his online essay "Crime and Puzzlement" (1990). Analogously to Virilio, he compares early cyber-societies to the Frontier, but Barlow's Frontier and cyberspace is the space of counterculture, anti-establishment and sociopathy[4]:

> Cyberspace, in its present condition, has a lot in common with the 19th Century West. It is vast, unmapped, culturally and legally ambiguous, verbally terse (unless you happen to be a court stenographer), hard to get around in, and up for grabs. Large institutions already claim to own the place, but most of the actual natives are solitary and independent, sometimes to the point of sociopathy. It is, of course, a perfect breeding ground for both outlaws and new ideas about liberty.

It is an interesting question, therefore, whether the adventurer in cyberspace is an outlaw or an agent of the authority. Is it a criminal or a detective; a hacker who goes through virtual spaces freely and illegally, or a guard of the State who maintains surveillance, perfecting the system of Foucault's panopticon? Science fiction provides ample examples for both: petty criminals, drug users become the explorers of paraspace (for example, in Dick's *A Scanner Darkly* or Jeff Noon's *Vurt* [1993]) as often as detectives do (in Pat Cadigan's *Tea from an Empty Cup* [1998], Alfred Bester's *The Demolished Man* [1953], Dick's *Do Androids Dream of Electric Sheep?* and "The Minority Report" [1956]).

Cyberworlds and Simulacra

As Bukatman's observes in his *Terminal Identity* (49), Dickian cyberworlds recapitulate Guy Debord's writings on the society of the spectacle, and Baudrillard's simulacra. Dick's texts reveal that our contemporary culture has become the culture of schizophrenics, simulacra, and ephemeral media images "predominantly concerned with the production of signs, images, and sign systems rather than with commodities themselves" (Harvey 287).

Interestingly enough, postmodernism occasionally highlights the *positive aspects* of simulacra, schizophrenia, and delirium. In Deleuze and Guattari, schizophrenics are "cut off from reality" and so "they resemble philosophers." Schizophrenics also have a special relation to language, when they "mistake words for things" (Deleuze-Guattari, *Anti* 23). The schizo constantly creates, renews, reinterprets, and reassembles languages and codes:

> As for the schizo, continually wandering about, migrating here, there, and everywhere as best as he can, he plunges further and further into the realm of deterritorialization, reaching the furthest limits ... It may well be that these peregrinations are the schizo's own particular way of rediscovering the earth. The schizophrenic deliberately seeks out the very limit of capitalism ... He scrambles all the codes [*Anti* 35].

The schizoid delirium means to renounce one's ego and identity: the schizoid "is somewhere else, beyond or behind or below these problems" (*Anti* 23). Schizophrenic delirium leads to traveling to other worlds, exploring other space-time continuums, and nomadism. The celebration of schizophrenia is also related to reveling in the surface and affirming simulacra (Harvey 53–54). Simulacra are non-original entities, "optical or linguistic effects," "surface effects" (Deleuze 7) that elude the authority of the original, of Plato's Idea. As Deleuze points out, Plato's simulacrum differs from the "copy," as the latter is based on depth and the similarity of the Same, while the former is on difference and the surface. Thus, contemporary philosophies frequently stress the affirmation of simulacra; Deleuze, for example, argues in *The Logic of Sense* that "The simulacrum is not a degraded copy. It harbors a positive power which denies *the original and the copy, the model and the reproduction*.... Simulation is ... a Dionysian machine" (263; emphasis in original).

The main character is a schizo who faces such simulacra in Dick's *Time Out of Joint*. Ragle Gumm is a traveler who "picked up a nomadic outlook" (33) in a strictly sedentary, conventional, immobile society. He is a "bum" without meaningful activities, who makes his living by successfully participating in a newspaper puzzle. He lives with his sister, and has no permanent, gainful, nine-to-five job. Still, he participates somewhat joyfully in suburban life, watching television, meeting the neighbors, having an illicit relationship with a housewife, trying out new "fads" such as the café espresso, and so on. He lives in a nostalgic simulacrum world, which is grounded in his own memories of and desires for a utopian, mitigated 1950s. He has chosen and created his own dreamworld, which serves as a means of survival in the dystopian future. In a way similar to Verne Haskel, Gumm prefers his modeled world to the barren reality, living "in a protracted childhood ... hobby [world], like gluing together model Spads" (39). Furthermore, even though eventually he seems to renounce the simulated dreamworld, the novel keeps it dubious whether future experiences "will prevent him from withdrawing [into his hallucinated realm] the next time the going gets tough" (Wolk 119; see Fitting 227).

Problems arise, of course, when a simulation goes awry; for example, when Ragle Gumm's simulated world starts to fall apart. In *Time Out of Joint*, the protagonist finds objects turning into labels, slips of paper:

> The soft drink stand fell into bits. Molecules.... In its place was a slip of paper. He reached out his hand and took hold of the slip of paper. On it was printing, block letters:
> SOFT-DRINK STAND
> Turning away, he unsteadily walked back, past children playing, past the benches and the old people. As he walked he put his hand into his coat pocket and found the metal box he kept there.
> He halted, opened the box, looked down at the slips of paper already in it. Then he added the new one.
> Six in all. Six times [40].

The event indicates that, in a way similar to Deleuze and Guattari's schizo, Gumm mistakes words for things (see Rossi, "Just a Bunch" 203–07). As Dick's character ruminates: "Word doesn't represent reality. Word *is* reality. For us, anyhow" (44; emphasis in original).

The relatively beneficial nature of simulated time-space is a crucial motif in Dick's *Ubik*, as well. In this novel, a universal, omnipresent and ever-changing product, the "commodity of commodities, Ubik [itself]" becomes the ultimate simulacrum "which permits the maintenance of appearance" (Bukatman, *Terminal* 96). Although the novel describes the terrifying and deteriorating effects of simulation, the over-advertised Ubik is the only tool that can stop the deteriorating process engendered by the demonic character Jory. The characters have to face that their reality goes through an accelerated aging process: money loses its value, food, coffee, and cigarettes get stale and dry within a few hours. Ubik, the ultimate commodity is a necessary, life-preserving tool, as virtual life inevitably approaches entropic death even without Jory — and "there are Jorys in every moratorium" (Dick, *Ubik* 204). Simulation in this case becomes a useful force, a means to prolong life, albeit a simulated one, in a way similar to "Adjustment Team," in which a relatively peaceful world and a utopian society are founded by simulation: "A society [of intellectuals] will be founded. More and more educated men will transfer an increasing amount of time to this international society. Purely national research will suffer a slight but extremely critical eclipse. The war tension will somewhat wane" (283).

Dick himself refers to his frequent use of simulacra and his fascination with schizophrenic traveling to alternate realities when he writes in his "Notes" that "once you have mentally opened the door to the reception of the notion of *fake*, you are ready to think yourself into another kind of reality entirely. It's a trip from which you never return. And, I think, a healthy trip ... unless you take it too seriously" (376; emphasis in original).

Of course, the simulacra and simulated worlds are often experienced in fiction and analyzed in theory with much less positive enthusiasm. Baudrillard, for example, argues that simulacra obliterate the very possibility of any meaningful social activity: "People no longer look at each other, but there are institutes for that. They no longer touch each other, but there is contactotherapy. They no longer walk, but they go jogging, etc." (*Simulacra* 13).

Dick's works often evoke Baudrillard's devastated world and destructive simulacra. Dick's interpretation of his own works in "How to Build a Universe" is most revealing when, foreshadowing Baudrillard, Dick describes a situation where the fake elements of Disneyland blur the distinctions between reality and simulacra. The hypothetical event contributes to our overarching confinement in inescapable delusions:

> In my writing I got so interested in fakes that I finally came up with the concept of fake fakes. For example, in Disneyland there are fake birds worked by electric motors which emit caws and shrieks as you pass by them. Suppose some night all of us sneaked into the park with real birds and substituted them for the artificial ones. Imagine the horror the Disneyland officials would feel when they discovered the cruel hoax. Real birds! And perhaps someday even real hippos and lions. Consternation. The park being cunningly transmuted from the unreal to the real, by sinister forces [Dick, "How to" 13–14].

> Disneyland exists in order to hide that it is the "real" country, all of "real" America that is Disneyland (a bit like prisons are there to hide that it is the social in its entirety, in its banal omnipresence, that is carceral). Disneyland is presented as imaginary in order to make us believe that the rest is real, whereas all of Los Angeles and the America that surrounds it are no longer real, but belong to the hyperreal order and to the order of simulacrum [Baudrillard, *Simulacra* 12].

Thus, simulations are quite rarely celebrated by Dickian characters: humans are rather repelled by simulacra, even if they somewhat accept their necessity. In Dick's *Martian Time-Slip*, a simulated environment is created by the Martian Public School to maintain the illusion of Earth and humanized automata teach the children. Although the son of the protagonist Jack Bohlen accepts and feels comfortable in the school environments, Bohlen is repelled by the teaching machines, as he believes that they "are going to rear another generation of schizophrenics ... teaching them to expect an environment which doesn't exist for them" (85).

The novel demonstrates that the characters experience Deleuzian schizophrenia in an ambiguous manner. On the one hand, schizophrenia leads to precognition, to a heightened state of mind, enabling the characters to unveil the simulations: "Instead of psychosis, he had thought again and again, it was more on the order of vision, a glimpse of absolute reality, with the façade stripped away" (Dick, *Martian* 81). On the other hand, schizophrenia also leads to isolation from the public world, and to alienation from the society; as Bukatman argues, Dick's fiction "explores the alienation that results from seeing *through* the spectacle" (*Terminal* 48; emphasis in original).

In Dick's novels, virtual realities are described many times with disastrous, tragic overtones, as they result in dangerous, devastating delusions. His simulacra evoke Baudrillard's arguments on contemporary media and simulation, which often lead to confinement, death, and fake phenomena that become "*artificially resurrected under the auspices of the real*" (Baudrillard, *Simulacra* 8; emphasis in original). In *Ubik*, the cyberspace of computers is inhabited by the semi-resurrected dead, creating the space of "half-life" and the institutions of "moratoriums." In half-life, the subjects are forcefully "purged of their death" (Baudrillard, *Simulacra* 11), confined in a liminal space somewhere between life and death. As Joe Chip, the protagonist of *Ubik* observes: "'I don't like moratoriums,' he said.... This is an unnatural place, he thought. Halfway between the world and death" (77, 85).[5]

What renders simulacra even less appealing is that the schizo traveler who moves across paraspaces can fall into traps and peril for various reasons. First, the traveler is persecuted by the State, which intends to control the movements of its citizens. As Grosz argues, the State organizes and regulates the movements of the city-dwellers, "function[s] as a solidity, a mode of stasis," and lets "no body outside of its regulations: its demands for identification and documentation relentlessly records and categorizes" (107). The State wants its citizens to have a stable identity, precisely what schizophrenics lack. As Deleuze and Guattari observe, "The schizo is constantly subjected to interrogation, constantly cross examined ... the questions put to him are formulated in terms of the existing social code: your name, your father, your mother?" (*Anti* 13–14).

The authorities try to control and forbid the escape to cyberspace on the pretext that the entry to cyberspace — or Bukatman's paraspace — is often enhanced by means of drugs. Schizophrenia and psychedelic states of mind in Dick's works are therefore often coupled with paranoia, a constant, inexplicable fear of an omnipotent enemy. A prime example is his *A Scanner Darkly*, where the schizophrenic drug user envisions himself being cross-examined by the authorities:

Maybe I'm weaving or something, he thought. Fucking goddamn fuzzmobile saw me fucking up. I wonder what.
  COP: "All right, what's your name?"
  "My name?" (CAN'T THINK OF NAME)
  "You don't know your own name?" Cop signals to other cop in prowl car. "This guy is really spaced."
  "Don't shoot me here.... At least take me to the station house and shoot me there, out of sight."
  To survive in this fascist police state, he thought, you gotta always be able to come up with a name, your name. At all times. That's the first sign they look for that you're wired, not being able to figure out who the hell you are [9].

The episode evokes Derrida's "errant" movement in his *Dissemination*, the passage of "an outlaw, a pervert, a bad seed, a vagrant, an adventurer, a bum ... [who is w]andering in the streets, he doesn't know who he is, what his identity — if he has one — might be, what his name is, what his father's name is" (143). Like the drug user who is incapable of producing meaningful, ever-new statements, Derrida's errant "repeats the same thing every time he is questioned on the street corner, but he can no longer repeat his origin" (143–44).

Second, the traveler may get injured or might lose sanity in cyberspace, and such accidents frequently influence reality and repeat themselves in real life. In numerous science fiction texts and films, if a character is injured in virtual reality, his or her corporeal body will suffer similar injuries. As Virilio argues, since the first "computer-aided suicide, we know that mere tapping on a keyboard can become a risk-behaviour" (41). In Dick's fiction, a good example is the empathy box of Wilbur Mercer in "The Little Black Box" (1964) and *Do Androids Dream of Electric Sheep?* In both stories, Mercer's physical pain is experienced in cyberspace and so the escape to virtual reality leads to physical injuries and mental distress.[6]

The cyberworld in *A Maze of Death* (1970) and "I Hope I Shall Arrive Soon" is a world to escape to from the maddening effects of "sensory deprivation" on a long space-journey. In both cases, the escape is not successful and so virtual experiences lead to depression, constantly recurring (virtual) death, and paranoia. Instead of utopia, Dick's cyberspaces and dreamworlds lead to dystopia, destruction, murders and nightmares.

In "I Hope I Shall Arrive Soon," the protagonist Victor Kemmings is a victim of a computer error on a space ship, rendering him unable to fall into "cryonic suspension" during the ten year-long journey. He can, however, fall into a semiconscious state, lingering between sleep and consciousness: "Virtually unconscious, but unfortunately still able to think" (359). He is in an unpleasant liminal state, which is quite similar to the situation that the eight central characters of Dick's *Eye in the Sky* (1957) find themselves in: "None of them was fully conscious.... Eight persons were tossing and shifting, alternating between wakefulness and sleep" (124, 125). This situation renders the mind extremely vulnerable: "[Kemmings] had to depend totally on the goodwill of the ship. Suppose it elected to feed him monsters?" (Dick, "I Hope" 360).

The ship, however, does not abuse its power and tries to become Kemmings's psychologist: the computer intends to "feed" him his positive but partly forgotten, buried memories. This is where the problem arises: instead of the pleasant experiences, his unpleasant memories, the traces of his guilty conscience start to dominate, "contaminating" his dreams: "He has integrated his early fears and guilt into one interwoven grid, the ship said to himself" (366).

Kemmings relives his early childhood experiences, such as the realization of death, and the experience that the world comprises of entities that have their own will that is different from that of the self as it is formulated in Freud's reality principle. In Dick's story, the young Kemmings destroys plants in the sandbox and helps the family cat kill a bird. Analogously, Freud argues that the little child transforms into play traumatic experiences, but in play he takes the role of the master: "By repeating it ... as a game, he took on an *active* part" ("Beyond" 16; emphasis in original).

Such events are one of the first manifestations of the reality principle, which remains tangible throughout life. As Freud formulates, we are "obliged to *repeat* the repressed material as a contemporary experience instead of ... *remembering* it as something belonging to the past" ("Beyond" 18, 23; emphasis in original). Thus, unpleasant memories, such as those relating to his childhood experiences and unsuccessful marriage infiltrate Kemmings's hallucinations: nightmares, dreadful memories saturate and devastate his paraspace, and he loses sanity both in cyberspace and in reality. His mental breakdown is represented by physical decay in objects, when his "whole house is collapsing" (362). His environment starts to decompose, disappear and fade, in a way similar to the aging objects of *Ubik*. Such events can be explained as the results of Freud's death instinct, primeval drives which "arise from the coming to life from inanimate matter and seek to restore the inanimate state" ("Beyond" 44).

Analogously, in *A Maze of Death*, the cyclic, meaningless loops of paranoia dominate the virtual lives of the characters, rather than the free nomadic movements of the schizophrenic (Enns 72–75). In Dick's novel, traveling in space is manifested as a flawed movement when, due to technical errors, the space adventure becomes an aimless, insipid, tragic roaming. The astronauts repeat this experience in their cyberworld in a slightly distorted form: instead of new and exhilarating virtual dreams, a God-like entity, the "Form Destroyer" devastates their cyberspace. The characters are murdered (virtually) one after the other in mysterious circumstances in an isolated place that they cannot leave, reiterating Agatha Christie's *And Then There Were None* ([1939]; also known as *Ten Little Indians*).

Dick's "I Hope I Shall Arrive Soon" and *A Maze of Death* unmask and subvert science fiction and cyberpunk clichés. Such clichés reveal a similarity between the naïve, utopian belief in space exploration and the celebratory belief in the freedom of cyberspace when the adventurer-hero of space journeys transforms into the explorer of cyberspace (McHale, *Constructing* 248–50). As Virilio argues, naïve techno-junkies, "Internauts take themselves for cosmonauts ... like overgrown fairy-tale children, cross the space between the real and the figurative, reaching as far as the interface with a virtual paradise" (42). In Dick's stories, both space exploration and cyberspace are deprived of freedom, leading to meaningless repetition, endless loops, technical errors, and entropic death.

Another—the third—possible danger for the traveler is that he may get lost in the plurality of universes. As I have argued before, certain science fiction characters can control and find directions in the newly formed, fluid, limitless city space. (Case in Gibson's *Neuromancer* to a certain degree, for example, and Verne Haskel quite extensively remains in charge.) Yet many characters lose control and wander aimlessly in the "soft" cities, such as the protagonist Leo Bulero in *The Three Stigmata of Palmer Eldritch* and the characters in *Eye in the Sky*. In the former, it remains dubious throughout the novel whether there is an exit from the mazes of paraspace. In the latter, Jack Hamilton becomes lost and captured in his own labyrinthine house, when the basement turns into a semi-organic maze in which all ways lead downstairs to a lethal trap in the cellar (196–99). Such fictional events buttress Jameson's argument about the unmappable and alienating nature of hyperspace:

> [W]e ourselves, the human subjects who happen into this new space, have not kept pace with that evolution ... [since w]e do not yet possess the perceptual equipment to match this new hyperspace.... This latest mutation in space—postmodern hyperspace—has finally succeeded in transcending the capacities of the individual human body to locate itself, to organize its immediate surroundings perceptually, and cognitively to map its position in a mappable external world [*Postmodernism* 38, 44].

Being lost in alternate universes and simulacra may derive from the lack of clear-cut boundaries. A paraspace is often infiltrated by another alternate reality: experiences in a "new" world are permeated by memories coming from previous worlds. Symptoms of an earlier life disturb and confuse the characters when Freudian slips, misspelled and erroneous surnames indicate memories of a previous life. In *Time Out of Joint*, the names Keitelbein and Kesselman are mistaken, especially when the protagonist gets stranded at the edges of the simulation, "Caught in a between place" (104). In *The Three Stigmata of Palmer Eldritch*, the suitcase psychiatrist mispronounces the name of his clients, both that of Mayerson and that of Bulero. In the latter novel, there is such a Freudian slip in the very beginning when Mayerson talks to his psychiatrist, which questions the presence of any "reality" throughout the novel.[7]

Furthermore, mistakes in fixed and permanent motor activities also indicate that a simulated realm has been infiltrated by memories from a previous life. Such events happen to characters in *Time Out of Joint* who experience errors in their habitual, quotidian acts. Taking the same stairs every day, a character has to realize that a step is missing from the stairs that lead to her house. Another person, acting purely on instinct, reaches for a light cord instead of a light switch. Such bizarre episodes indicate that a character's environment has been artificially changed and penetrated by another world.[8]

Being lost in the mazes of simulacra, it may become impossible for characters to return to reality. The characters of *Ubik* remain in the deteriorating "half-life," never finding their way back to a stable reality. The paraspace created by telepaths, precogs, and moratoriums provides a labyrinth, an unsolvable mystery for Joe Chip and Glen Runciter. Kemmings has to live through the simulated version of his arrival on the planet recurrently in "I Hope I Shall Arrive Soon"; thus, even when he eventually returns to reality and actually arrives at his destination, he is unable to accept the genuine, static nature of his environment. In "The Commuter," the vice-president of the train company, Bob Paine needs to realize that the middle class desires of perfect order spread beyond the boundaries of the suburban paraspace: they reach and saturate the city center, transforming reality and Paine's life categorically. His eccentric lover turns into a perfect housewife, while he is indiscernibly lured into the peaceful home of a happy family by the presence of his adorable (but previously nonexistent) baby.

Dick's works strengthen Virilio's arguments that our reality disappears, or at least becomes blurred and vague, since virtual reality "destroys cultures which are precisely situated in the space of the physics of the globe" (Virilio 9). Real cities and other traditional geographical constructions disappear or turn into the periphery, "throwing into question not so much the nation-state, but the city, the geopolitics of nations" (Virilio 10; see also Boym 80).

The simulated model destroys the original world in Dick's "The Electric Ant" (1969), as well. The story features a semi-organic android that has to face the partly artificial nature of his existence. He decides to conduct experiments with his cognitive and perceptive system by manipulating his punched tape brain. After going through various hallucinatory visions, after too much experimentation with the technological aspects of his perception, the mechanical body of the experimenter breaks down. The typically Dickian twist ending reveals that due to the machine's breakdown, the "real" world as such disappears for all the characters. Dick's story demonstrates Virilio's caveats that our techno-culture and the "contemporary sciences are engaging ... in the eclipsing of the real, in the aesthetics of scientific disappearance" (3).

The story also brings up another crucial aspect of virtual realities: that of the hybrid body, the body as a portal between virtual spaces and reality.

Mind Invasion

The cyborg-body provides a crucial motif for science fiction and cyberpunk. Contemporary social theories also stress that as the boundaries between corporeal and virtual space become blurred, the individuals form hybrids of human and the machine; we are all cyborgs now (Mitchell 13–15; Haraway 35).

A fundamental condition for establishing virtual reality is the loss of boundaries between man and the machine, that is, interactive connection and unimpeded information flow between the user and the computer: a relationship that vaguely resembles sexual intercourse. Baudrillard describes this phenomenon as "a new form of schizophrenia," when the subject faces the terror of "the unclean promiscuity of everything which touches, invests and penetrates without resistance, with no halo of private protection, not even his own body, to protect him any more" ("The Ecstasy" 132). Bruce Sterling names this experience "body invasion" and "mind invasion" (346). The former refers to prosthesis, artificial organs of the human body. The latter means that technological instruments and media equipment stimulate and manipulate dreams, memories, and emotions of the human brain.

Dick's texts often portray "body invasion"—enough to mention here Palmer Eldritch's "stigmata," the prostheses of eyes, teeth, and hand, or Hoppy Harrington's artificial limbs in *Dr. Bloodmoney* (1965). Nevertheless, I find it more worthwhile to explore the wide range of mechanical and media devices, the various forms of mind invasion in order to describe the "posthuman" liminal existence in his works.

The robot-protagonist in "The Electric Ant" and the "simulacra" (androids) in *We Can Build You* are controlled by punched tape memory constructions. In *Valis* (1981) and *Radio Free Albemuth* (1985), the protagonist's mind joins an "intergalactic communications network," a "long-abandoned telephone" service (113). The schizoid and autistic characters and their supposedly successful treatment evoke filmic metaphors in *Martian Time-Slip*. *A Scanner Darkly* is saturated by various technological instruments that imitate the human mind: the protagonist, a police informant is described as "the effective screening device [that] carried the information" (105). The mentally disturbed mind imitates a "closed loop of tape" (66), a recording that repeats the same message over and over again. Further, the mind becomes similar to a faulty computer that is unable to process new data, "Repeating his last instruction" (265). The burned-out mind is compared to a broken device: "wires cut, shorts, wires twisted, parts overloaded and no good, line surges, smoke, and a bad smell" (66). The consciousness of a drug addict is described with images of a clock radio:

> All of a sudden they sit up, like a machine cranked from position A to position B ... the mind of a junkie being like the music you hear on a clock radio ... it sometimes sounds pretty, but it is only there to make you do something. The music from the clock radio is to wake you up; the music from the junkie is to get you to become a means for him to obtain more junk, in whatever way you can serve. He, a machine, will turn you into *his* machine [159; emphasis in original].

Dick's description of reciprocal and faulty machines here evokes Deleuze and Guattari's "desire machines," which are "binary machines ... one machine is always coupled with another.... This is because there is always a flow-producing machine, and another machine connected to it that interrupts or draws off part of this flow.... Desiring machines work only when they break down, and by continually breaking down" (*Anti* 5, 8).

The origin of the technical transformation of the human brain goes back to at least as early as the 19th century. In the age of the typewriter and the phonograph, the mechanical influence on the human brain and body was often described with an emphasis on the inferior role of the human. The machines standardize, vivisect the body, in so far as they divide and classify sensual experiences. A typical example of media historians is that early typewriters did not render visible that which was being typed: one could write, but not read at the same time (see, for example, Bukatman, "Gibson's" 76).

The data inscribe themselves on the human mind and body, while the subject becomes a passive device, a blindly chosen victim as it happens to the convict in Franz Kafka's "In the Penal Settlement" (1914). Friedrich Kittler, drawing on Nietzsche's philosophy and Kafka's story, says: "If something is to stay in the memory it must be burned in: only that which never ceases to *hurt* stays in the memory" (Kittler 196; Nietzsche, *On the Genealogy* 61; emphasis in original). The protagonist in Dick's *Lies, Inc.* (1964, 1983, 1984) has a similar experience due to a psychedelic trip when he thinks that an alien force rewrites and reprograms his mind: "he could not fashion in any manner whatsoever a change in the flow of sense-data flowing in on him; the authority of the data, their absoluteness and degree, again reduced him to a passive device which merely registered the stimuli without responding" (108). The drug-induced experiences have an analogous effect in *A Scanner Darkly*, as the addicts are *obliged* to watch films: "Another fantasy film rolled suddenly into his head, without his consent" (18). In "What the Dead Men Say" (1964), a psychotic mind invades and controls all the communication channels and media such as the radio, television, telephone, telegraph, and the newspapers, in the form of "a monologue": obscure, droning but domineering messages that eliminate "authentic communication" (269). Analogously, psychokinetically empowered radio messages sent from the Earth almost kill the astronaut Walt Dangerfield, whose satellite transmitter becomes a devastating device in *Dr. Bloodmoney*: "He had been stricken by careful instruments issuing up from the very world which he struggled to contact. If he could have cut himself off from us, she thought, he would be alive now. At the very moment he listened to us, received us, he was being killed" (274–75).

Such overbearing machines and media equipment do not just fragment the body and evade the mind, but they make people identical, standardizing their experience. Critics from Marx onwards emphasize that early machines, especially machines in the factory, drill, subdue, and empty out the laborer: "To work at a machine, the workman should be taught from childhood, in order that he may learn to adapt his own movements to the uniform and unceasing motion of an automaton" (Marx 460). The resulting "absurd kind of uniformity" of city dwellers, of the urban pedestrians who "adapted themselves to the machines and could express themselves only automatically" (Benjamin, *Charles Baudelaire* 133), is reflected in films of the early twentieth century, for example *Metropolis* and Charlie Chaplin's *Modern Times* (1936) as well as contemporary movies such as *The Matrix* and *Animatrix* (2003).

The human mind, as a passive device completely subdued and controlled by data, can be linked with mysticism, as well. Kittler argues that the victims of the data-flow "are 'virtually compelled to invent gods'" (196). Kittler analyzes Daniel Paul Schreber's paranoid visions, according to which his "hallucinations are facts effectuated by the discourse of the Other" (297). In other words, "God occupies Schreber's nervous system" via "rays" in "nerve-language information channels," that is, deploying a telepathic method (298). This is a theory or delusion very similar to the central idea in Dick's *Valis* and *Radio Free Albemuth*. In the latter novel, "the wisdom of God" reaches the character via hallucinations, information beams of "an intergalactic communications network" (113). The communication, no matter how benign, is forced upon the subject: "The AI operator of Albemuth's station, an artificial intelligence unit, had raised me at some prior time and was holding the contact open. Therefore information reached me from the communications network whether I liked it or not" (111).[9]

These passive devices are often substituted by an *active* interface between human and machine due to the influence of cinema, television, and the computer. As early as the beginning of the 20th century, photography and film changed both the production and the reception of art. As Walter Benjamin points out, the reception of new art forms involves interaction, active "consumption," unlike traditional art, which required "aura" and passive contemplation. Rapidly moving and constantly changing images constitute "the shock effect of the film, which, like all shocks, should be cushioned by heightened presence of mind" ("The Work" 238).

Marshall McLuhan stresses that unlike "mechanical" instruments of the 19th century, the contemporary media, especially television, provide decentralized and interactive stimuli: they are "integral and decentralist in depth, just as the machine was fragmentary, centralist, and superficial in its patterning of human relationships" (7–8). Such a decentralized, communal, interactive, and entertaining experience is described in Dick's *Eye in the Sky*—rather ironically though. Jack Hamilton dreams about a machine that would produce high fidelity music, combining the experience of three people who listen to three different compositions: "The brains of the three men are removed and wired together by the core of the Hamilton Trinaural Sound System, the Hamilton Musiphonic Ortho-Circuit. The sensations of the three brains are mingled in a strict mathematical relationship, based on Planck's constant" (29).

This theory of the interactive human subject, the coexistence of active and passive roles in the psyche is significantly less common in Dick's texts than the paranoid visions of blindly chosen subjects, humans as passive devices, and mystical forces invading the brain. In his fiction, the influence of machines on the brain often correlates with mental illness as it is demonstrated by N. Katherine Hayles's interpretation of the Dickian "schizoid android." The schizoid android is a frequently used, mostly female character in Dick's fiction, appearing, for example, in "What the Dead Men Say." The mentally unstable Kathy Egmont manipulates people with the help of machines and media equipment, treating humans as if they were machines themselves.

The "schizoid android" is a femme fatale who lacks empathy due to her mental illness, either schizophrenia or autism, and behaves like a robot, representing "the coming together of a person who acts like a machine with a literal interpretation of that person as a machine" (Hayles, *How We* 161). In Dick's *We Can Build You*, Pris Freuenzimmer is described by the male first person narrator as such a character when she falls in love with another schizoid android, Sam K. Barrows. Barrows appears "as if ... the shaved dome of his skull, had been lopped off and then skillfully replaced with some servo-system or some feedback circuit of selenoids and relays, all of which was operated from a distance off" (34). The mentally ill Pris behaves like a machine and handles other people as if they were machines: "She must see only the most meager outer part of people.... She had an ironclad rigid schematic view, a blueprint, of mankind. An abstraction. And she lived in it" (34, 189).

Analogously, in Dick's *Clans of the Alphane Moon* (1964), the most aggressive clan of mentally ill people, those who completely lack empathy, are responsible for designing and maintaining machinery. His *Do Androids Dream of Electric Sheep?* also confirms that "schizoid and schizophrenic human patients" cannot be distinguished from androids: "A small class of human beings could not pass the Voigt-Kampff scale. If you tested them in line with police work you'd assess them as humanoid robots" (33). These examples candidly demonstrate that the images of cyborgs and those of mental disorder are strictly intertwined in Dick's fiction.

Christian Metz argues that the spectator accepts the role of film-watching with great enjoyment, since primal fantasies are re-experienced in the cinema. The spectator plays both an active and a passive role, as we are both the camera and the screen — we both release and accept data: "The film is what I receive, and it is also what I release, since it does not pre-exist my entering the auditorium and I only need close my eyes to suppress it. Releasing it, I am the projector, receiving it, I am the screen" (51).

Analogously, in certain stories by Dick, film machinery not only results in devastating mental illness but also provides remedy for the brain. In *Martian Time-Slip*, the human brain is manifested as a film producing and film recording machine. According to the fictional psychiatrist Dr. Glaub, the mental problem with autistic children is due to errors in the cognition of time, as the environment around the child "is so accelerated that he cannot cope with it, in fact, he is unable to perceive it properly, precisely as if he faced a speeded-up television program, so that objects whizzed by so fast as to be invisible" (44). The cure for the autistic child, therefore, also involves television: "this new theory would place the autistic child in a closed chamber, where he faced a screen on which filmed sequences were projected slowed down.... Both sound and video slowed" (44).

Dick was somewhat familiar with the experiments of neurosurgeons such as Wilder Penfield (Enn 71; Wolk 109–10), who argued as early as 1959 that "the stream of consciousness in the human brain can be electronically reactivated" (1719). During his experiment, the patients started to hallucinate or recall memories when their mind was stimulated with electrodes, "as though a wire recorder, or a strip of cinematographic film with sound track, had been set in motion within the brain" (1719). Dick also heard about James Olds, who found the pleasure center of the brain. Dick's *We Can Build You* includes a direct reference to Penfield and Olds (10); in *Do Androids Dream of Electric*

Sheep? a mood organ belongs to the brand "Penfield," while *The Simulacra* (1964) features a character named Wilder Pembroke (see Wolk 111).

The similarities between mechanical behavior and mental disorder as it is described by Dick may also derive from Rollo May's anthology of psychological essays *Existence: A New Dimension in Psychiatry and Psychology* (1958). Dick was fairly familiar with the book (Enn 75; Wolk 102), whose contributors, psychologists influenced by existentialism and phenomenology, recognize the machine-like nature of the schizophrenic and his world. Eugene Minkowski, for example, describes the disrupted temporality of his schizoid patient, who handles his fellow human beings as if they were machines or robots. As Minkowski puts it, for the schizoid "Men were no longer perceived as individuals with their personal and individual values but became pale, distorted shadows moving against a backdrop of hostility. There were not living men ... [but] only schematic mannequins" (135).

Alternate Timelines

Dick's fictional worlds exemplify the contemporary urge "to challenge the idea of a single and objective sense of time or space" (Harvey 203). In postmodernism, both space and time ceases to have "materialized and tangible dimensions" (Harvey 293), presenting the multiplicity of virtual, fictional, and simulated plateaus. Dick's simulated and multiplied realities demonstrate Jameson's weakening historicity, Harvey's postmodern condition, and Smethurst's postmodern time-space "where society loses that sense of belonging customarily found in traditional constructions of place. In postmodernity, this is not only a geographical problem, but also an historical one, with society losing sense of its place in history as well" (Smethurst 222).[10]

Time Out of Joint provides only a covert, implicit example of multiple universes, and yet it has received great attention by critics. In his *Postmodernism*, Jameson reads the novel as a text that subverts historical sense. Science fiction as such, he claims, often eludes or undermines the historical thinking of modernity. Citing the Hungarian critic Georg Lukács, Jameson argues that the historical novel in the 19th century represented the philosophy of middle class, when the bourgeoisie intended to create a new world view, a historical sense with progress in order to establish their recently gained authority. Science fiction, however, reflects our postmodern age, in which "we no longer tell ourselves our history in that fashion ... because we no longer experience it that way, and indeed, perhaps no longer experience it at all" (283–84). Science fiction and historical novel have an inverse relationship, because "if the historical novel 'corresponded' to the emergence of historicity, of a sense of history in its strong modern post-eighteenth-century sense, science fiction equally corresponds to the waning or the blockage of that historicity" (284). *Time Out of Joint* articulates a contemporary issue, the postmodern lack of belief in a tangible history when historical sense vanishes or at least gets irrevocably absorbed in mediating corpuses such as popular culture, since "we are condemned to seek History by way of our own pop images and simulacra of that history, which itself remains forever out of reach" (25).

Dick's novel is set in the fifties' America, as Jameson puts it in *Postmodernism*, "a small town Utopia very much in the North American frontier tradition" (283). The suburban utopia turns out to be a hallucination, a more or less successfully reconstructed space-time created by the dreams and fantasies of the central character Ragle Gumm and by other characters who intend to maintain the simulacra with various (but hardly detailed) masquerading devices. Gumm lives in the late 1990s when a nuclear war, a "civil war" between the inhabitants of the Earth and those of the Moon devastates the world. He gets exhausted by the war so much that he dreams another "reality," a reality constructed by his childhood memories of small-town happiness.

Many critics highlight *realism* in the novel; Jameson, for example, argues that "indeed, of the great writers of the period, only Dick himself comes into mind as the virtual poet laureate of this material: of squabbling couples and marital dramas, of petit bourgeois shopkeepers, neighborhoods, and afternoons in front of television, and all the rest" (*Postmodernism* 280). Umberto Rossi stresses Dick's *social criticism*, claiming that the world of the mainstream adult family, the Nielsons, is undermined by a non-adult family into which Gumm belongs. The childish characters represent a counterculture resistance against the mainstream consumerist culture, and the fake nature of the suburban utopia reveals the unreality of utopist propaganda in the 1950s (Rossi, "Just a Bunch" 197).[11]

My reading underlines that Dick creates a nostalgic and *pseudo-realistic* novel. It soon becomes clear that it is not *exactly* the fifties that comes into view: Marilyn Monroe is unknown, since her life and fame did not fit into the simulacra, people do not listen to the radio any more, they do not know the whiskey brand Jack Daniels, and so on. Nevertheless, this world has characteristics similar to the "real" fifties, such as the constant fear of a nuclear war or catastrophe (which actually occurs in Dick's *Eye in the Sky*), and the beginnings of "the society of the spectacle," the overarching influence of television. Thus, the novel manifests Svetlana Boym's reflective nostalgia, which maintains a distance from the past instead of faithfully recreating it: "This type of nostalgic narrative is ironic, inconclusive and fragmentary" (50). Such a text suggests multiple narratives, "explores ways of inhabiting many places at once and imagining different time zones" (xviii). The object of longing, the past, is not a utopian place but a blatantly artificial world or simulacrum: "It is in ruins, or, on the contrary, has just been renovated and gentrified beyond recognition" (50).

The lure of consumerism is also tangible in the novel: unlike in other Dickian stories where computers and drugs connect to alternate realities, here it is the quotidian happiness with the diverse merchandise of a supermarket that brings Ragle Gumm to the simulation. The protagonist as a child was fascinated by the town's mall or supermarket. When he dreams about and relives his childhood, he returns to and gets completely lost in the supermarket, which becomes the border zone between reality and the dream-world.

> *He entered the store and reached out for his free sampling, trembling....*
> *"Do you enjoy this?" the woman asked. "Roaming around here in the different stores while your parents are shopping? ... Is it because you feel that everything you might need is available here? A big store, a supermarket, is a complete world in itself?"*
> *"I guess so," he admitted....*
> *He looked around him and saw that he was in the pharmacy department. Among the tubes of toothpaste and magazines and sunglasses and jars of hand lotion. But I was in the food part, he thought with surprise. Where the samples of food are, the free food. Are there free samples of gum and candy here? That would be okay* [181; emphasis in original].

Dick's *Man in the High Castle* is another pseudo-realistic novel, which again makes it clear that American science fiction especially in the fifties and sixties often demonstrated the overarching fear from enemies of the U.S. (Jameson, *Postmodernism* 283). While *Time Out of Joint* depicts the similarities between alien attacks and communist invasion, *Man in the High Castle* investigates the possible outcome of the defeat of the Allies in the Second World War. Dick's fictional world becomes the inverse of the actual historical situation: instead of Germany, it is the U.S. that is divided into zones, providing an apt environment for the collusion of opposing intelligence agencies, especially those of Japan and Germany. The reversed hierarchies and relations make the novel similar to Dick's "Faith of Our Fathers" (1967), in which the U.S. is defeated and invaded by Communist powers.

Both texts manifest ample examples of a reversed political situation, in which the U.S. gains the inferior role. Oriental characters, in the midst of the growing "easternization" of the world, hunt for the relics of the culture of the defeated West: Mr. Tagomi collects "authentic" relics from the almost extinct Western culture in *The Man in the High Castle*, while party cadres engage in rodeos in their spare time, practicing "the esoteric imported art from the defeated West of steer-roping" (198) in "Faith of Our Fathers." The short story is set in Hanoi, a city that gains central power in the fictional world order, where American characters have to move to and learn the Cantonese language if they want a political career.

In both stories, there are two possible ways of escape from the dystopian world: one is provided by simulacra and alternate realities, and the other with the pleasure and power of literature and irony. The novel contains a mysean-abyme, a fictional alternate history within the novel, *The Grasshopper Lies Heavy* by Hawthorne Abendsen. In the novel-within-the novel, the political situation is similar to our own reality in the sense that the Allies won the Second World War. Nevertheless, the two dimensions are not identical: in Abendsen's novel, China does not become a communist power, Hitler is put on trial instead of committing suicide, and the British Empire remains intact. Thus, the fictional novel and Mr. Tagomi's brief experience of an alternate reality (220–26) indicate the presence of several parallel worlds, which can provide some kind of hope in the semi-apocalyptic, dystopian situation. As a character ruminates:

> Suppose eventually they, the Nazis, destroy it all? Leave it a sterile ash? They could; they have the hydrogen bomb....
> Will that put an end to all life, of every kind, everywhere? When our planet becomes a dead planet, by our own hands?
> He could not believe that. Even if all life on our planet is destroyed, there must be other life somewhere which we know nothing of. It is impossible that ours is the only world; there must be world after world unseen by us, in some region or dimension that we simply do not perceive [234].

In "Faith of Our Fathers," the alternate realities derive from drug-induced experiences. In the reversed fictional world of the story, however, everybody takes drugs each day; the special psychedelic experience, therefore, comes from using anti-hallucinogenic snuff. Furthermore, a singular reality cannot be restored even with the help of the anti-hallucinogenic substance: the characters experience twelve different versions of reality, twelve manifestations of the God-like entity that rules their world.

Dick's short story also demonstrates the power of literature and the significance of irony in a totalitarian state. The protagonist, the young party cadre Chien needs to find out if a poem is "the work of a dedicated progressive, a loyal party member," or that of a "petit-bourgeois imperialist" (200). His puzzle compels him to decide whether the poem is a praise of the political leader, or it is "satirizing the Absolute Benefactor's promulgations" (201). The enigma turns out to be insolvable—without outside help, without knowing the historical background of the poet, he would be unable to decide. His dilemma demonstrates de Man's views on irony, which state that "an ironic temper can dissolve everything, in an infinite chain of solvents. It is not irony but [only] the desire to understand irony that brings such a chain to a stop"

("The Concept" 166). Dick's story and de Man's essay stress that the ironical use of language is merely stopped by our *will* to end irony.

The Second World War, or perhaps an alternate second world war is manifested in Dick's *Ubik*, as well. The novel's paraspace manifests a reversed time flow, a process of aging backwards, in a way similar to his other novel *Counter-clock World*. The characters of *Ubik* go back in time and eventually return to the era of the Second World War, or that of *a possible* Second World War. Joe Chip reads newspaper headlines of the European fronts, but the events that he reads about never happened in our reality.

> A fresh-looking newspaper lying at the far end of the overstuffed sofa attracted his attention. He picked it up and read the date: Tuesday, September 12, 1939. He scanned the headlines:
> FRENCH CLAIM SIEGRFIED LINE DENTED
> REPORT GAINS IN AREA NEAR SAARBUCHEN
> Major battle said to be shaping up
> along the Western front
> Interesting, he said to himself. World War Two has just begun. And the French thought they were winning it. He read another headline.
> POLISH REPORT CLEAMS GERMAN FORCES HALTED
> SAY INVADERS THROW NEW FORCES INTO
> BATTLE WITHOUT NEW GAINS [131].

It is still possible of course that the character confronts *our* Second World War, since the official news and headlines often mitigate the events of a conflict, exaggerating the victories and concealing the losses. It remains uncertain for the reader: does the episode reveal the presence of alternate histories, or does it simply demonstrate the unreliability and manipulative nature of the media?

Analogously, there is a unique and extremely untrustworthy historical account in Dick's *Lies, Inc.* The novel features a history book that is unreliable for various reasons. Just to name a few: first, the fictional history book has been published in multiple editions, which cannot be all correct, since they include mutually exclusive explanations (A. Butler, "LSD" 274). Second, the history book reflects a time structure similar to the reversed time of Carroll's *Through the Looking Glass*: it contains events that have not happened yet. Third, as it aspires to be a "complete history," it depicts various timelines, including subjective, hallucinatory paraspaces: "Each of the paraworlds is explained" (Dick, *Lies* 150). Fourth, the book itself may be a tool in the hands of intelligence agencies that deliberately confuse the public about the true nature of events, a device of Lies Inc.

Dick's novels exemplify that teleological history, history as a linear set of events, and the idea of a true account of events are questioned in 20th century philosophy and science fiction. They evoke Hutcheon's postmodern historiographic metafiction, which is a literary category considerably similar to the popular subgenre alternate history. Andy Duncan, for example, defines alternate history as "not a history at all, but a work of fiction in which history as we know it is changed for dramatic and often ironic effect" (209). Hutcheon's historiographic metafiction "plays upon the truth and lies of the historical record ... [when] certain historical details are deliberately falsified in order to foreground the possible mnemonic failures of recorded history and the constant potential for both deliberate and inadvertent error" (*A Poetics* 114).

Robert H. Canary reads the science fiction of the sixties as texts of innovative ideas about escaping linearity. He draws on Dick's *The Three Stigmata of Palmer Eldritch*, in which reality is altered and fractured due to time travels, and the future, present, and past are merged, creating labyrinthine timelines. Even the phrase "parallel worlds" should not be used any longer, as reality is a "seamless web" (Jameson, "Progress" 156), a network without center, a bunch of chaotic timelines that occasionally correlate.[12]

I cannot, therefore, agree with Canary when he claims that Bulero, representing mankind, fights against and eventually defeats Palmer Eldritch, a divine character who strives for the infinity of timelines. Canary argues that "in *The Three Stigmata of Palmer Eldritch*, there is an objective historical reality, and men are able to shape it.... Palmer Eldritch's new drug induces mystical union with Palmer Eldritch, and no one wants it; the wholly other is seen as the absolute evil" (90). Canary states that the novels of Dick "still employ a basically realistic strategy," as the author is "directly concerned with the rules which govern our experience of historical reality; to conceive of such work as a sharp break with that of the 1950s world would, I believe, exaggerate the significance of the changes" (91).

My argument against this interpretation is twofold. First, although Leo Bulero represents mankind and confronts Eldritch, he intends to maintain multiple paraspaces selling his own drug "Can-D," which brings its users to a nonexistent world, similarly to Eldritch's "Chew-Z." Bulero also intends to shape reality with the help of his employees who have paranormal skills and look into the future: thus, he is aware of and exploits multiple universes throughout the novel.

Second, even if Bulero pursues a solid timeline, it remains dubious whether his victory is achieved. Bulero remains considerably uncertain throughout *The Three Stigmata of Palmer Eldritch* whether he has returned to reality or he remains under the influence of drugs forever: "Say, I bet this still isn't real, Leo said to himself.... I'm still under the influence of that one dose; I never came back out—that's what's the matter" (Dick, *The Three* 202).

There are signs even at the very end of the book that reality has not been reconstructed. Eldritch's stigmata, the prostheses of eyes, teeth, and hand, the signs of divinity and of a realm ruled by Eldritch appear on characters even at the very end of the book (203). Language problems remain tangible when, for example, Leo Bulero forgets his own name (204), a phenomenon that manifests the breach of a simulated realm in Dick's fiction, as I have pointed out before.

I rather agree with Ian Watson, therefore, who claims that "one rule of Dick's false realities is the paradox that once in, there's no way out" (71). Peter Fitting's reading on *Ubik* and *The Three Stigmata of Palmer Eldritch* also emphasizes the open-ended nature of the texts, indicating that no paraspace gains a final ontological priority. Both novels end with an unconvincing explanation "in a completely ambiguous fashion, thus precluding any final and definitive interpretation" (226).

Dick's *Lies, Inc.* goes even further. The novel resembles Cronenberg's *eXistenZ*, in which various spy organizations conflict each other, but their struggle becomes highly repetitive, thus gaining a comic overtone. In Dick's novel, various industrial and political intelligence agencies are confronted, spies and counterspies betray and save each other, double and triple agents collide, so much so that it becomes impossible to reconstruct a proper, solidified, logical storyline. One virtual reality folds into another so many times that the reader has no chance to arrive at an outside Archimedean point, which would help find the "original" reality and regain a grip on the corporeal world.

The storyline is full of contradictions: events occur without cause and effect, characters who are described dead reappear on a further page. As Andrew Butler argues, these narrative inconsistencies may be explained by extratextual facts: Dick's *Lies, Inc.* was rewritten and republished several times in various forms ("LSD" 271). But it can also be the result of fictional phenomena, since alternate timelines, drug-induced experiences, schizophrenia, telepathic interference modify the perceptions of the characters and disrupt the causal chains of events. Dickian reality, after being altered by drugs, divine characters, conspirators, and paranormal activities, can never be the same again.

Dick's alternate histories with multiple timelines exemplify postmodern theories of historicity. Hayden White, for example, suggests that historical thinking necessarily conceals multiple plots. History writing inevitably comprises various versions of a set of events so that the historian could choose and argue for one particular "storyline": "Unless at least two versions of the same set of events can be imagined, there is no reason for the historian to take upon himself the authority of giving the true account of what really happened"

(23). Based on similar arguments, Hutcheon emphasizes the postmodern urge to rewrite history, the "postmodern concern for the multiplicity and dispersion of truth(s), truth(s) relative to the specificity of place and culture" (*A Poetics* 108). The open-ended nature of postmodernist and science fiction texts contributes to the distrust of any final point in time, questioning singular and teleological interpretations of history.

Language and Narrative Deviations

Dick's fiction, at least in his first and second phase — roughly, in the 1950s and the 1960s — manifests complex fictional worlds, complicated stories, and bifurcating alternate timelines but relatively simple narrative forms.[13]

Dickian characters often realize the artificial, simulated nature of their virtual reality. In his *Eye in the Sky*, the characters go through and finally escape from several dreamworlds. To free themselves from the confinement of the dreamworld, they need to reach an "upper" level, the consciousness of the dreamer. It is, on the one hand, a relatively easy task because the dreamer is always present in the dreamworld; on the other hand, it makes their job highly difficult that the dreamer has an overarching power in his created realm. They have to entrap the dreamer, the creator of the paraspace, by luring him or her into unconsciousness. Eventually, after deactivating several dreamers, the characters manage to break down the dissimulating artifacts and they return to reality. Thus, the storyline of the novel thematizes McHale's ontological metalepses or strange loops when the traditionally asymmetrical construction of embeddedness becomes somewhat symmetrical: the narrated characters realize the presence of the frame world and start to have an impact upon it (*Postmodernist* 35–36, 119–24).

Yet, despite such ontological loops, this text — and several other early novels by Dick — utilizes an extradiegetic, omniscient narrator who uses roughly the same tone throughout the story. Dick's fiction usually presents the events this way, via three or four focal characters, "the focal character being named at the beginning of each narrative segment" (Suvin, "Philip K. Dick's" 9). The complicated, maze-like, metaleptic fabula is narrated with a relatively simple plot: the fabula evokes Ryan's "network" or "maze" model (her types 2a and 3c), while the narrating devices form a much simpler structure, the "plot as interwoven destiny lines" (type 1c; see Ryan, *Avatars* 101–07).

As McHale suggests, this is a distinctive characteristic of many science fiction and cyberpunk texts: "What typically occurs as a configuration of narrative structure or a pattern of language in postmodernist fiction tends to occur as an element of the fictional world in cyberpunk. Cyberpunk, one might say, translates or transcodes postmodernist motifs from the level of form ... to the level of content or 'world'" (*Constructing* 246). Freedman confirms in his essay on Dick that "the great majority of SF inherits certain basic formal properties from the realist, as distinct from the modernist or postmodernist novel: The typical SF text has a smoothly diachronic narrative line" (13).

Nevertheless, as Fludernik argues in her "Scene Shift, Metalepsis, and the Metaleptic Mode" (396), it often becomes difficult to distinguish McHale's "metaphorical" or "ontological" metalepses from the formal, textual-rhetorical ones: one sort of transgression usually implies, in an explicit or implicit manner, the other. Even Dick's early, relatively simple plot structures occasionally surprise the reader with narrative games, which derive from and reflect ontological transgressions. In *Ubik*, for example, each chapter is introduced by alienating mottoes, commercials promoting the life-preserving Ubik. The paratextual elements can be interpreted as metafictional or metaleptic devices, since they "place the reader in a position analogous to [the character] Chip, scanning the advertisements for clues and hidden messages" (Bukatman, *Terminal* 96). The reader is confronted with these strange messages and advertisements in a way similar to the characters, who need to decode messages hidden in television commercials, graffiti, on coins, commodity packaging, and so on.

As I have pointed our before, the ontological games and textual transgressions form mise-an-abyme in *The Man in the High Castle* and *Lies, Inc.* In the latter, the book-within-a-book is a guide towards reality in the rhizomatic maze of alternate timelines. Thus, it *should* tell the truth and provide the ultimate answer to all questions. The problem is that even if it becomes a somewhat reliable source, it does so by using puns, wisecracks, words with multiple and contradictory meanings.

> It seems to me that if you want to catch up on the very vital facts pertaining to Newcolonizedland, you really ought to con [study/swindle] it thoroughly. What you want to learn undoubtedly lies [rests/falsifies] within....
> With dignity, he answered, "I'll read it when I have time."
> "But you'll enjoy it, Mr. ben Applebaum. Not only is the volume educational, but also highly amusing. Let me quote one of Dr. Bloode's quite singular Thingisms."
> "Thingisms?" Rachmael felt baffled — and wary. He had a deep intuition that the Thingism, whatever it was, would not be amusing. Not to him, anyhow, or to any human.
> "I've always enjoyed this one ... since you are about to read the book, here is Thingism Number Twenty, dealing with books.
> Ahem. 'The Book Business is hidebound [conservative/covered with leather]" [149].

The coined terms and puns of Dick's novel are typical devices in cyberpunk and science fiction. (The title is already a pun and a self-reflexive device, as "Inc." is pronounced the same way as "ink," the material of writing). New words are coined to describe non-existing or extrapolated objects, and many of these terms evoke multiple or vague meanings: they "are never fully clarified or translated for the reader" (Bukatman, *Terminal* 54). In Dick's fiction, schizophrenics coin terms such as "kipple" and "gubble" whose denotations are quite broad: they refer to rubbish, gabble, decay, wearing away, existential void, mental crisis, simulacra, and so on (Palmer 226).

Dick's coined terms often evoke multiple meanings. His "mood organs," for example, are devices in the future worlds of *We Can Build You* and *Do Androids Dream of Electric Sheep?*, which can directly manipulate the human brain. Dick's term utilizes the double meaning of the word "organ." On the one hand, it refers to various types of musical instruments, including electronic organs and synthesizers. (In Latin, "organum" refers to musical instruments as such.) On the other hand, it evokes the biological meaning of the word, a part of an organism, especially the brain.

Another possible approach to find the unique narrative traits of cyberpunk and technologized science fiction is to realize that the human perspective often becomes to some extent alienated, embodying the perspective of the machine. As Hayles argues in her *How We Became Posthuman*, "Cyberspace represents a quantum leap forward into the technological construction of vision. Instead of an embodied consciousness looking through the window at a scene, consciousness moves *through* the screen ... leaving behind the body as an unoccupied shell" (38; emphasis in original). Contrasting contemporary science fiction with Henry James's fiction, Hayles stresses that the "crucial difference between Jamesian point-of-view and the cyberspace pov [point-of-view] is that the former implies physical presence, whereas the latter does not" (38). This alienated, artificial perspective results in a technological language, foregrounding metaphors and images that evoke various visual and auditory media.

Gibson's novels, as Easterbrook argues in "The Arc of Our Destruction," utilize "mechanistic metaphor[s]" to describe the human perception, "implicitly positing technology as *primary*, that ground upon which nature is to be understood" (382; emphasis in original).[14] Gibsonian cyberpunk, however, is just one example in contemporary and postmodernist fiction that utilizes filmic and technological metaphors to alienate the human point-of-view. As McHale points out, contemporary fiction often uses cinematic discourse to create self-reflection and metalepsis (*Postmodernist* 128–30).

Dick's novels, especially his later fiction, also provide ample examples of mechanistic metaphors: in *A Scanner Darkly*, drug usage intensifies "the transformation of consciousness into a media technology" (Enn 78). The process is foregrounded by the narrator who describes the memories of the protagonist as a "fantasy film" in his head (18); at the end of the memory, "the rerun of a now gone moment winked out and died forever" (20). Arctor's hallucinations are also described with filmic images: "Great overpowering runs for which there had been no previews. With the audio always up too loud inside his head" (57). The drug-addict's psychedelic coma is described as "an endless horror feature film in his head for the remainder of his life" (86). Therefore, the whole setting, the city of Anaheim, California becomes "a commercial for itself, endlessly replayed" (31).

The cinematic discourse becomes at some point highly alienating for the reader, when the storytelling of the novel is interrupted by dialogues that are written in the form of film scripts. The memories and visions of "fantasy films" that the characters experience are recorded in a way similar to film scripts by the narrator (115–19; 122–23). What is more, the script is also interrupted several times when brief excerpts of a psychiatric article are interjected in order to evoke the defects and perceptual difficulties of brain damage.

Another alienating effect can be found in *Martian Time-Slip*, in the form of strange repetition. The same chain of events (a conversation between the members of a love triangle and an accident with a misplaced music recording) is described successively three times with only slight changes (148–54; 157–61; 194–200). The tautological text, the device of alienating repetition, can of course be explained with various, fictionally acceptable reasons. It is possible that the characters are confronted with alternate timelines or time traveling due to the special, paranormal skills of the autistic child Manfred. Or, possibly, one of the characters experiences a time loop, which is not known for other characters, in a way similar to Harold Ramis's film *Groundhog Day* (1993). Or, one of the focal characters, Steiner or Bohlen loses his sanity and thus time becomes cyclical, repetitive for him: "He had sat, he realized, in Arnie Kott's living room again and again ... [t]he fundamental disturbance in time sense, which Dr. Glaub believed was the basis of schizophrenia, was now harassing him" (206). Yet, it is also possible that the narrator uses a technique well-known in "mainstream," mainly modernist, literature when the same set of events is described with three different perspectives, representing the views of the three focal characters of the conversation.

Whatever explanation is accepted by the reader, it becomes certain that the thematized errors of time flow and perception are manifested with errors in the narration, with disrupted language. The incident evokes de Man's irony, which disrupts regular perception, representation and subjectivity; language becomes "a text-machine" that has gone out-of-hand, and "which undoes any narrative consistency" ("The Concept" 181).

Such examples demonstrate that contemporary (science) fiction, analogously to Gibson's works, "embody within their techniques the assumptions expressed explicitly in the themes" (Hayles, *How We* 39). The unlinear, rhetorically enhanced language "foregrounds the estrangement of technology" (Bukatman, *Terminal* 166): Dickian texts manifest the posthuman experience both in their language and on the thematic level, creating a "cyborg discourse" (Bukatman, *Terminal* 31).

Bukatman traces back the origin of such poetic and "unlinear" science fiction texts to Alfred Bester, who utilized synesthesia and concrete poetry in his novels of the 1950s. Many texts of the New Wave and cyberpunk generations, the works of Bester, Gibson and Delany, employ a unique language to describe paraspace, the world of the matrix, and the experiences of simstim. These authors often utilize typographical devices, for example concrete poetry, when a post-human character "talks": see Gibson's *The Difference Engine* (383), *Neuromancer* (190), and "Johnny Mnemonic" (11–12). Form thus reinforces content: the experimental style coincides with the celebration of technologized, futuristic, and fragmentary neo-avant-garde art.[15]

Another rhetorical-poetic way to distinguish the prose of science fiction from "everyday" language is to utilize synesthesia. In Gibson's cyberpunk and Bester's "Fondly Fahrenheit," sensory experiences (such as those of vision, sound, and temperature) are often interchanged. The same happens in Dick's *Do Androids Dream of Electric Sheep?*, in which the post-apocalyptic future, the alienated, posthuman, existentially barren landscapes are described with synesthetic language. It is not only that the lack of noise becomes tangible and visible for the character, but silence also substitutes and conceals all visible and corporeal objects:

> Silence. It flashed from the woodwork and the walls; it smote him with an awful total power, as if generated by a vast mill.... From the useless pole lamp in the living room it oozed out, meshing with the empty and wordless descent of itself from the fly-specked ceiling. It managed in fact to emerge from every object within his range of vision, as if it — the silence — mean to supplant all things tangible. Hence it assailed not only his ears but his eyes; as he stood by the inert TV set he experienced the silence as visible and, in its own way, alive. Alive! [18].

Dick's latest period (1970–1982) heightens the presence of stylistic deviations in his theological novels, *Valis*, *The Divine Invasion* (1981), *The Transmigration of Timothy Archer* (1982), and *Radio Free Albemuth*. In *Valis*, for example, the storytelling becomes less fluent as the narration includes metafictional and intertextual elements, quoting his other novels, his exegesis, and various philosophical texts. Christopher Palmer argues that "*Valis* is postmodern in form," emphasizing the significance of "metafictionality" and the unusual "presentation of the narrator" in the novel (227). The narrator sometimes calls himself Horselover Fat, other times he is Phil Dick and talks about Fat in third person.

I find Palmer's reading relevant especially concerning the first part of the book, which is basically a collection of mystical contemplations and tragic episodes taking place in the life of the narrator (Phil Dick), who is the same person but a split personality of the central character, Horselover Fat. In this part of the novel, the tragic episodes (the suicide of Fat's friend Gloria, Fat being taken to a mental asylum) and the mystical contemplations are constantly interrupted by the narrator, who blurs the storyline, confronts the other ego and ruins the mystical atmosphere. As the narrator admits, "My God, I'm losing control here, trying to write this down" (100).

The split personalities of the story constantly quarrel with each other. What makes the novel postmodern is that this conflict as a thematic element is manifested and replicated on the level of narration, as well. There is a constant battle between the two selves to gain control over both the content and the tone of the book. Palmer characterizes this latter clash as "a collision between ethical seriousness and a postmodern sense of the textuality of meaning" (237).

On the one hand, sentences inspired by Fat are written in an essayistic style: a religious but confused person discusses his mystical experiences and spiritual world view in a solemn manner. The quotations from the exegesis (printed with bold letters) constantly follow this style. On the other hand, the religious contemplations are occasionally undermined by another language, a Vonnegutian, obscene narration with wisecracks and sardonic remarks on Horselover Fat and his views: "'Smart move, Fat,' I would have told him if I had known what he was planning for his future, during his stay at North Ward. 'You've really scored this time'" (64).

The cynical narrator often lays bare the artifice and addresses the reader, thus questioning the philosophy, belief, and credibility of Horselover Fat: "Did some magic scene lie in the future where Fat would come to his senses, recognize that he was the Savior, and thereby automatically be healed? Don't bet on it. I wouldn't" (121). He tries to find rational justifications for Fat's epiphany, explaining the uncanny events and Fat's exegesis with the character's mental illness and former drug addiction. He says that "If, reading this, you cannot see that Fat is writing about himself, then you understand nothing.... Fat was totally whacked out" (29).

As the novel goes on, the two tones have a mutual impact on each other: Phil Dick gradually loses his sarcasm, while Fat becomes uncertain about his beliefs, often quoting contradictory philosophical sources. Intertextuality both weakens and strengthens Fat's mystical arguments: as Palmer argues, "Outwardly different people echo each other's experiences — or delusions; diverse texts and speculations are found to mean the same thing" (237).

Dick's "How to Build a Universe" (1978) contains similar contents and style to those of *Valis*. The text comprises of a wide range of overtones, presents a scale of styles from playful to solemn, from critical to ironic. Outlining an anecdote about an allegedly misplaced fortune cookie that is later sent to the White House is evidently an ironic technique to argue for a religion and omnipresent God. (The essay writer, in a Chinese restaurant near President Nixon's birthplace, finds a fortune cookie referring to a secret being revealed at the time of Watergate.)

In "How to Build a Universe," like in *Valis*, different philosophies come to the same conclusion and a thinker may have various contradictory arguments. Xenophanes, Heraclitus, and "W. S. Gilbert, of Gilbert and Sullivan," the librettist, indicate analogous ideas (28). Contradicting views by Parmenides and Heraclitus are quoted, and neither argument seems to be rejected (12). The author of the essay appears to be just as much confused as Horselover Fat, who creates and quotes numerous theories every day in *Valis*:

> What Fat claimed was — well, Fat claimed plenty. I must not start any sentence with, "What Fat claimed was." During the years — outright years! — that he labored on his exegesis, Fat must have come up with more theories than there are stars in the universe. Every day he developed a new one, more cunning, more exciting and more fucked [*Valis* 24–25].

The result is a versatile and contradictory text, as "Fat plunges into the flow of theories, terms, citations, accepting, forgetting (never refuting), collaging, stitching" (Palmer 231). Dick also stresses the multiplicity of theories in his essay, claiming that "I have been trying one theory after another: circular time, frozen time, timeless time, what is called 'sacred' as contrasted to 'mundane' time ... I can't count the theories I've tried out" ("How to" 24).

In the end, however, one particular argument overrules the others. Dick's conclusion in the essay is that "if God thinks about Rome circa 50 a.d., then Rome circa 50 a.d. is" (30). Time of consensus reality is an illusion; therefore, consensus reality is only a fake appearance. The form also loses versatility when the mystical language prevails over the sarcastic one in the second part of *Valis*, which ends with the exegesis. The contradictory arguments and the irony disappear, substituted by a theory that assumes the return or eternity of the apostolic age:

> Time is speeding up. And to what end? Maybe we were told that two thousand years ago; maybe it is a delusion that so much time has passed. Maybe it was a week ago, or even earlier today. Perhaps time is not only speeding up; perhaps, in addition, it is going to end.
> And if it does, the rides at Disneyland are never going to be the same again. Because when time ends, the birds and hippos and lions and deer at Disneyland will no longer be simulations, and, for the first time, a real bird will sing [Dick, "How to" 33–34].

Thus, interestingly enough, in *Valis* and "How To Build a Universe" Dick applies a postmodern form of narration, but presents a mythical and quite firmly maintained theory of temporality. His earlier fiction is somewhat conventional in style, but expresses more radical views on time and history.

Conclusion

Mainly based on Bukatman's *Terminal Identity* (157–82) and McHale's *Constructing Postmodernism* (247–53), I argued in this chapter that Dick's proto-cyberpunk fiction highlights the ontological problematics of space and time. The texts reveal the implications of Bukatman's alienated, rhetorically enhanced paraspace and foreshadow cyberspace, a certain manifestation of paraspace first used in literature by Gibson or Vernor Vinge and foregrounded by contemporary social science.

Dick's paraspace is a liminal zone between modernist urban planning and postmodern fluidity, the human and the machine, the real and the virtual. His stories articulate that traditional distinctions and spatial dualities lose their meaning in cyberspace (Whittle 3), or at least they receive new meanings: cyberspace "will not *re*place but *dis*place them" (Benedikt 4; emphasis in original). Such cybernetic liminality, analogously to Turner's liminal and liminoid situations, poses serious problems for the characters: besides its liberating effects, cyberspace also confines the subject. Despite its invigorating possibilities, cyberspace results in "pitfalls for the wired individual" as it can "arouse feelings of fear, concern, and uneasiness — even in those who are experienced with the medium" (Whittle 189, 191). Containment, death, identity crisis, isolation, and the power of the State remain tangible in simulated, virtual realms — perhaps they become even more tangible.

Besides liminality, cyberspace evokes pluralized, unmappable urban architecture, labyrinths and rhizomes, "[the world of] multiforking paths which disqualifies the very concept of mapping" (Cavallaro, *Cyberpunk* 138). Dick's fiction reflects this plurality, foreshadowing the cyberpunk obsession with the multiplicity of cyberspace as it appears, for example, in the filmic images of *eXistenZ*, *The 13th Floor* and *The Matrix Trilogy*. Further, his novels contribute to another trend in science fiction, the conventions of alternate histories, which are, of course, somewhat related to the cyberpunk tradition, the worlds of simulacra; Sterling and Lewis Shiner, for example, wrote the alternate history "Mozart in Mirrorshades" (1985), which was published in the definitive cyberpunk anthology *Mirrorshades* (1986). Dick's oeuvre demonstrates that, as Smethurst observes, novels with "problematic approaches to history and narrative ... at the same time explore the nature of space, and place and placelessness" (15).

Dick extrapolated from his time's technology, foresaw the possibilities of the computer and described certain alternate realities as deriving from computer generated realms. The computer, of course, is not the only instrument that can create liminality and multiplicity — other technological gadgets, machines, traveling, conspiracy theories, hoaxes, books, and drugs can also become McHale's "ontological pluralizers" (*Constructing* 128–34, 178–82), creating alienating effects in the spatiotemporal perception of Dickian characters. Such estranged perception is often indicated by narrative devices. Although Dick's fiction, at first glance, seems less postmodern and playful in form than the texts of following, more conspicuously postmodern and cyberpunk authors, his later, theological novels overtly play with the narration. A careful examination of his earlier texts can also reveal telling examples of disrupted storytelling and estranged narrative perspective.

To summarize, it is a basic assertion of Dick's fiction that the universe is based on liminality, multiplicity and alternate timelines, thus forming the "garden of forking paths," the maze of paraspaces, and exemplifying the structure of rhizomatic models.

Conclusion: Converging and Diverging Manifestations of Liminality and Multiplicity

> Social spaces interpenetrate one another and/or superimpose themselves upon one another. (Henri Lefebvre)
>
> Without space, no multiplicity—without multiplicity, no space. (Doreen Massey)

My book analyzed transformations of liminality, examining how this spatial metaphor shifted in meaning especially after the cultural turn of postmodernism due to the multiplication of space and time. It started by posing theoretical questions based on Turner's liminal and liminoid phenomena. I argued that the spatial, temporal, social and textual connotations of Turner's liminality as well as those of the Bakhtinian carnival might help deconstruct traditional dual oppositions, especially if they are influenced and diversified by Derrida's, de Man's, Foucault's, Bhabha's as well as Deleuze and Guattari's writings. Poststructuralist and postmodern philosophies urge us to redefine the traditional notion of liminality and understand it as a never-ending movement, an oscillation across porous, evanescent boundaries in a multiple universe.

Further, such theories reiterate well-established philosophical and scientific standpoints since Galileo, stressing that space inevitably needs to be conceptualized in connection with time, motion, culture, and social relations (see, for example, Foucault, "Of Other" 23, 26). Contemporary critics of culture stress that space is not a static and empty frame, but "an inherently dynamic simultaneity" and "an ever-shifting social geometry of power and signification" (Massey 3), the product of social and capitalistic flows with "Great movements, vast rhythms, immense waves — these all collide and 'interfere,' with one another; lesser movements ... interpenetrate" (Lefebvre 87).

Michel de Certeau's approach to urban and liminal space interweaves social science and theories of rhetorics, articulating "the acts of ... stylistic metamorphosis of space" (102). Especially urban space develops "the site(s) for chaotic, deregulated, and unregulatable forms" (Grosz 107), philosophically connecting with Deleuze and Guattari's schizophrenic flux and fluidity.

My book rests on the hypothesis that unique spatial formations such as Foucault's heterotopias, liminal places and multiple spaces, rhizomatic assemblages reveal even more tangibly such dynamism, flux and relativity, inherently implying poststructuralist interpretations of time, narrative, the body, social relations, and so on.

Furthermore, analyzing spatial patterns is useful for the literary critic because distinctive fictional spaces reveal a great deal about genres, subgenres, literary trends, and narratives. As Franco Moretti argues, space in literature can highlight the "place-bound nature of literary forms: each of them with its peculiar geometry, its boundaries, its spatial taboos and favorite roots ... [which] bring[s] to light the *internal* logic of narrative: the semiotic domain around which a plot coalesces and self-organizes" (*Atlas* 5; emphasis in original). Liminality thus can be interpreted as spatial formation that can be found in various genres in various modes, manifesting diverse narrative configurations.

My analysis of detective fiction pointed out somewhat covert examples of liminality in the genre. I found in Christie's texts mainly the traditional understanding of liminality: Turner's liminal, temporarily unstructured social formations. Gaiman's fiction provides telling examples of formal, narrative liminality, when the ironic narrative perspective engenders oscillations between narrative perspectives. His fantasy, of course, is liminal concerning its thematic zones, as well: the fantastic nature of his fictional realms is never definite enough to solidify, leaving the reader with Todorov's hesitation. His fiction exemplifies the contemporary trend of Slipstream, New Weird and Interstitial Art, "21st Century Stories," in which "the fictive worlds themselves are inherently unstable" (Wolfe and Beamer 24). Thus, the liminality of ontological worlds is reflected on the formal level, demonstrating McHale's narrative theory (*Postmodernist* 164–75). Furthermore, the fantastic realm becomes a liminal space and simultaneously a site including multiple zones in his *Neverwhere* and *The Graveyard Book*.

I interpreted Lem's fiction as a mixture of (anti-)detective fiction and (meta-)science fiction, which recapitulates Nietzsche's and Foucault's arguments about the relativity and contingency of the human disciplines. Lem's subject, evoking the conventions of detective fiction and Kafka's writings, searches for an all-encompassing unity, a grand narrative, and an Archimedean point outside the labyrinthine discourse, but only ends up playing with the limits of the inside and outside. His novels embody the oscillation of liminality, demonstrating the way it manifests itself by means of the "revenge of the mirror," Derrida's play, and the Freudian and Lacanian "fort-da" movement. The texts demonstrate that the limit, the threshold that gives a name to liminality, becomes endlessly multiplied and abyssal. As Derrida argues, instead of effacing the limit, one needs "to multiply its figures, to complicate, thicken, delinearize, fold, and divide the line precisely by making it increase and multiply" ("The Animal" 398).

Yet, the toughest conundrum of my theoretical and textual analyses was evoked in my analysis of Dick's oeuvre, posing the question how liminality is to be understood, if the notion can be used at all, when dualistic realities open up towards pluralized universes, turning binary spatial formations into rhizomatic spaces. By analyzing postmodern urbanity, cyberspace and paraspace in his fiction, I intended to demonstrate that fictional spaces and places, his virtual cities, engender both a liminal zone between the human and the computer, and a zone of multiplicity.

A liminal space can open up gates to multiple worlds, like in C. S Lewis's *The Magician's Nephew* (1955), in which magic rings bring the children protagonists to a forest that serves as an intermediary realm, a junction between various fantastic universes. Analogously, in science fiction and cyberpunk, the interface as a liminal phenomenon may lead the computer users into the multiplicity of virtual domains, into forking paths and multiply embedded realms. Nevertheless, virtual reality as such is a liminal space, which mediates between the realm of the humans and that of the machines. In such a space, traditional dual distinctions erode or become reinterpreted, and hierarchies collapse. Cyberspace evokes the carnival, "the world where anything may happen, where identities and roles are subverted and where … reality and fiction are extremely difficult to separate" (Cavallaro, *Cyberpunk* 150). The limit, the threshold remains crucial, but it becomes hidden and undetectable in this space: "Such a place is therefore all frontier zone" (Miller 154). Thus, cyberspace can simultaneously be conceived of both as a labyrinthine, rhizomatic organism, and as a liminal space, the spatial extension of the computer, which manifests itself as a liminal object between the human and mechanical terrain.

The manifold loops between liminal plateaus transform virtual realities into rhizomatic paraspaces, embodying various, simultaneously coexisting spatial and temporal formations. Foucault's heterotopia, liminal and multiplied spaces and time-structures, juxtaposed and embedded realms, (pseudo-) labyrinths and rhizomatic organisms, cyclical, oscillating and nomadic movements strengthen, interact with and obliterate each other. My interpretations of liminality and multiplicity in popular fiction embrace, or at least link to all these spatial and theoretical models. As Doreen Massey argues, conceptualizing contemporary space "inherently implies the existence in the lived world of a simultaneous multiplicity of spaces: [viewpoints] cross-cutting, intersecting, aligning with one another, or existing in relations of paradox or antagonism" (3). The *multiplicity of spaces,* in fact, needs to be interpreted with *the multiplicity of theories and theoretical models*—hence originates the heterogeneous nature of my work.

In the introductory chapter, I outlined four possible modes of liminality, four manifestations of the phenomenon that I recurrently drew on. I finish my work by opening, restructuring and diversifying these four modes, describing their implications. I outline a short summary on how Christie's, Gaiman's, Lem's and Dick's fictional and narrative spaces pose the problematics of liminality and those of multiplicity. The most important characteristics of their texts, as concerning liminality and multiplicity in space, time, narrative and social structures, are the following:

First, the analyzed texts articulate theories that state that liminal and multiple space is often approached by aimless wandering, instead of a purposeful, linear, teleological movement. The digressive wanderings of Benjamin's urban flaneur, Bauman's vagabond, de Certeau's walker, Derrida's errant, and Deleuze and Guattari's nomads, the schizophrenic stroll, all reveal a passage outside and between limits, playing with limits, with the inside and outside. Such wanderings are often prohibited by the Establishment and thus take place "underground," in either or both meanings of the word — enough to mention Gaiman's underworld in *Neverwhere* and *The Graveyard Book*, or the drug users in Dick's *A Scanner Darkly*.[1]

The nomadic roving of urban vagabonds is also related to tourism, legalized traveling, and traveling by a vehicle; therefore, the train and the space ship gain crucial significance as liminal places in detective stories and science fiction. Even such forms of mobility, however, are often devoid of linear movement and so they differ from de Certeau's organized, orderly train journey, the "perfect actualization of the rational utopia" (111). Instead, traveling turns into a journey with "a series of failures and malfunctions," aimless, cyclic, meaningless loops, infinite, "sterile repetition" (Palmer 21, 29), or evokes the situation of being obstructed, lost and stranded. We can find examples for such ill-fated journeys in Christie's *Murder on the Orient Express, And Then There Were None*, Lem's *Return from the Stars, The Chain of Chance*, Dick's "The Commuter," *A Maze of Death*, "I Hope I Shall Arrive Soon," and so on.

Second, liminality and multiplied worlds foreground and intensify the crisis of the subject in the modern and postmodern condition: the itinerant, schizophrenic subject becomes lost or fragmented in liminality. Christie's works (*Crooked House, The Mousetrap, Ordeal by Innocence*) suggest that characters wear masks and find only an unstable, provisional self during the investigation. The investigation manifests a period of social liminality when transgression, doubling, and reversals saturate the characters' lives, creating an enforced, unpleasant carnivalistic experience. Science fiction stresses that the human self becomes suspended or simulated in liminal worlds and multiple universes: Lem's protagonists do not find but lose their identity in the uncanny, abyssal mirrors that they are confronted with, as it happens literally to the characters who go through a complete amnesia in *The Invincible*.

Lem's and Dick's fiction indicates that the self and the Other, human and machine cannot be distinguished and so the human subject's independence, precession and dominance is always questioned by the Other, the machine. As Deleuze and Guattari argue, "The subject spreads itself out along the entire circumference of the circle, the center of which has been abandoned by the ego. At the center is the desiring machine" (*Anti* 21). This often leads to epistemological problematics, linguistic and discursive dilemmas (mainly in Lem), and foregrounds ontological crises (in Dick).

Third, the human control over subjective phenomena and one's objective environment frequently vanishes in paraspace. Most protagonists try to obtain the freedom to move between the universes, to control the liminality and multiplicity of spaces, but the success is many times dubious. Neither the characters, nor the reader is capable of navigating among the multiplicity of universes. As Smethurst points out, postmodern characters often "seek some form of grounding" (21), but in vain, because "shelters from the chaos become more artificial, virtual and bizarre" (272). One never really knows where he or she is: simulated and fantastic realms as well as fake humans, Doubles deceive the characters both in detective fiction (such as Christie's *At Bertram's Hotel, The Thirteen Problems*) and in science fiction (Lem's *Solaris*, Dick's *The Three Stigmata of Palmer Eldritch*, and so on).

Since humans lose the ability to control space, it becomes an outer force that prevails over, moves and confines them. The surrounding space becomes a semi-living, usually malevolent, or at least threatening force, for example the planet in Lem's *Solaris* and the horrifying house in Dick's *Eye in the Sky* (207–08). Thus, fictional characters often experience Roger Caillois's psychological compulsion of mimicry, which states that the subject is overwhelmed by a wish to become similar to its neighborhood without any practical reason. Mimicry, turning into an automatism, leads to a schizophrenic situation when the individual intends to project itself into the nearby space:

> To these dispossessed souls, space seems to be a devouring force. Space pursues them, encircles them, digests them in a gigantic phagocytosis. It ends by replacing them. Then the body separates itself from thought, the individual breaks the boundary of his skin and occupies the other side of his senses. He tries to look at *himself from* any point whatever in space [30; emphasis in original].

The schizophrenic self constructs an outer perspective that eliminates his own: the viewpoint of an ultimate, superior power associated with space. Such an eye and face is frequently experienced literally in science fiction, for example in Dick's *Eye in the Sky* (94–95) and "I Hope I Shall Arrive Soon" (364).[2] Thus, instead of man mapping and controlling space, space dominates the characters.

Fourth, the novels portray the complex space-time experience of the subject, and the angst, the existential crisis, the problematic nature of nothingness and being, when one realizes that the subject is not at home in the world. Thus, although I have not analyzed the question from this angle in my work, I would like to emphasize here that the impact of phenomenology, existentialism and hermeneutics may become crucial for the theory of liminality. The problematics of the inside and outside world as well as the intersections between are to be understood not only as technological problems, but also as phenomenological questions. Phenomenology stresses that we do not live in an empty space; our consciousness defines our environment, as deeply as our environment defines our consciousness. Gaston Bachelard, for example, argues that "man is half-open being" (222), since we exist on the surface, on the borderline between the reversible inside and outside, terrorized simultaneously by agoraphobia and claustrophobia (218–22). Or, as Heidegger stresses in *Being and Time*, a "basic state" of our existence forms existential spatiality, "Being-in-the-world" (169). Just as spatiality needs an entity that makes a disclosure of space, our inner world and thoughts are always infiltrated by the experience of space and time (171). In his relatively late essay "Building, Dwelling, Thinking," Heidegger foregrounds a typically liminal formation, the bridge. His description demonstrates that it is our perception of the bridge that gives meaning to the limits and to dualities such as A and B, which are connected and formed by the bridge. Thus, the bridge "*gathers* to itself" entities such as earth and sky, divinities and mortals, revealing that "the boundary is not that at which something stops but, as the Greeks recognized, the boundary is that from which something *begins its essential unfolding*" (331, 332; emphasis in original).

Fifth, after experimenting with and traveling into liminal zones and alternate realms, often there is no return to a natural, authentic world. As Gaiman's *Neverwhere* indicates, certain fantasy characters decide on their own accord to stay in the fantasy world. Lem's characters frequently do not leave liminal space because they cannot abandon the play with boundaries. His astronauts neither simply stay at home nor, in fact, arrive *properly* on the alien planet, but remain suspended in limbo, orbiting around the alien planet (in *The Chain of Chance,* and most parts of *Fiasco* and *Solaris*). In Dick's fiction, the lack of escape is often tragic for the characters who are compelled to stay in paraspace. Virtuality many times obliterates quotidian reality, creating an irrevocable synthesis of nature and technology: "The action of his novels takes place in a time when there can no longer be any talk of returning to nature or of turning away from the 'artificial,' since the fusion of the natural with the artificial has long since become an accomplished fact" (Lem, "Philip K. Dick" 127).

Dickian worlds are similar to Baudrillard's vision of our contemporary universe, the space of simulation where reality is saturated by media. Under this condition, people only recycle, recreate the "natural," embodying media images, photographs, and commercials; as Dick's character states, "It's the result of mass communication ... People model themselves after ads" (*Eye in the Sky* 32). The character's claim coincides with well-known ideas of media and cultural studies, such as Barthes arguments in his book on photography, according to which the overflow of images "completely re-realizes the human world of conflicts and desires, under cover of illustrating it.... Nowadays the images are livelier than people" (118).

Sixth, texts with liminal spaces and alternate realities may be interpreted as metafictional or self-reflexive texts, since they overtly manifest the artificiality of a fictional world, thus indicating their own constructed nature. The seemingly traditional prose in Lem's fiction integrates, in fact, a dual self-reflection: one that can be identified with Lem's awareness of literary and science fiction traditions, a "metageneric" self-consciousness, and the other that derives from consciously and openly utilizing scientific models, cultural and philosophical theories, thus engendering Csicsery-Ronay's "metacommentary."

Dick's ontological science fiction, his alternate histories make it clear that *the* fifties do not exist. There is *a* fifties that is the result of (re)construction: not something that is existent in its own right, but a man-made structure created by authority figures and maintained by fantasies and narratives. As Jameson observes, Dick's novels reveal that "the fifties is a thing, but a thing that we can build, just as the science fiction writer builds his own small-scale model" (*Postmodernism* 285). McHale also argues that a major issue in science fiction and postmodern texts is metafictional "world-construction," the "paraspace motif," various "ways of world-making," that is, "strategies for staging confrontations among two or more worlds, thus laying bare the plurality of worlds ... and focusing attention on the boundary or interface between worlds" (*Constructing* 151, 247–53).

Such thematic, epistemological and ontological self-reflection is often indicated by narrative means. Irony and narrative self-reflection are highly tangible in the oeuvre of Gaiman, and occasionally present in the fiction of Christie, Lem, and Dick. The narrative games in Gaiman's fiction indicate that the transference between reality and the fantastic world may be covert and unnoticed. His fiction also highlights the importance of multiple perspectives in literature, theory, and our quotidian reality. Dick's mise-en-abymes and occasionally alienated prose indicate the unreliable nature of perception due to the presence of alternate realities and that of simulacra. The fictional multiplication and alienation of the universe is often represented by an estranged experimental prose in science fiction, for example when the text "creates a defamiliarising horizon" that imitates the point-of-view of a machine, cyborg, schizophrenic person or an alien creature (Bényei 64; see also Hayles, *How We* 38). Such defamiliarized horizons can be detected in Lem's "The Mask," Dick's *A Scanner Darkly, Martian Time-Slip, Valis,* and so on.

Seventh, the narrative games, self-reflexive episodes and intertextual allusions in Christie's, Gaiman's and Lem's oeuvre reveal the overarching and tangible presence of parodying imitation and *genre bending* in literature. Their texts often manifest a highly playful attitude towards genre conventions, drawing on but at the same time subverting and digressing from the norms. They repeatedly blend traditional detective fiction with fantasy, horror, postmodern anti-detective stories, and science fiction, thus crossing the boundaries between McHale's epistemological and ontological dominant. One can consequently detect a *generic liminality* in these texts, which evokes the poststructuralist understanding of spatial liminality. Derrida's "law" of the genre is fairly similar to Foucault's arguments on limit and transgression; Derrida stresses that the unavoidable presence of generic "re-marking" traits, in every text, defines, demarcates and "gathers together the corpus and, at the same time, in the same blinking of an eye, keeps it from closing … [The] floodgate of genre declasses what it allows to be classed … Putting to death the very thing that it engenders" (Derrida, "The Law" 64, 65). Genre traits, elements of the generic pact between author and reader, constantly undermine and question the evoked genre: they form a non-definitive meaning, a center that is not the center, supplement, a boundary that does not (only) delimit. Such generic elements are simultaneously inside and outside the text, detained at its threshold, "within and without the work, along its boundary" (Derrida, "The Law" 65).

My analysis of liminal and multiple space, time, thematic and narrative structures in certain genres of popular fiction is in many ways a preliminary work, which paves the way for future research. I selected well-known authors whose fiction provides highly illustrative examples — a more thorough genre analysis of detective fiction, fantasy and science fiction would be worthwhile to be conducted. I mentioned a few films that significantly buttressed my arguments — the visual study of liminality and multiplicity in science fiction and fantasy would be extremely fruitful. A detailed survey of postmodernist liminality in feminist and postcolonial literature would also open up new perspectives. A phenomenological approach to liminal and multiple space could be the object of another study.

Hopefully I have managed to demonstrate that McHale's "ontological dominant," the plurality of fluid, unhierarchized liminal spaces, and the multiplicity of epistemological and fictional perspectives, are highly tangible in detective fiction, fantasy and science fiction. These phenomena also resonate with the cultural and theoretical turns of postmodernism, poststructuralism and deconstruction, discourses that intend to avoid the construction of hierarchies and dichotomies.

The tendency to undermine and evade dichotomies is, of course, an age-old inclination of religious and mythical thinking. As Yuri Lotman and Boris Uspensky point out, certain doctrines of (Western) Christianity always permitted a "neutral zone" and a "subjective continuum" between polarities such as present and future, holy and sinful (4–5), creating liminal sites such as limbo and purgatory. Angels may also be interpreted as intermediary characters between the mundane and sacred, earthly and heavenly realms. Further, since at least Nietzsche's philosophy the problematic nature of duality and that of clear-cut distinctions has been stressed repeatedly by various philosophical theories, disciplines of science, cultural studies, literary criticism, and other cultural discourses.

Nevertheless, liminality and multiplicity still remain relevant, timely, contemporary issues. Turner's anthropological essays, poststructuralist and postmodern theories emphasize that transgression and liminality only temporarily undermine borderlines, and they somewhat even confirm distinctions. As Smethurst observes, although postmodernism "puts borders under erasure, their traces remain, and sometimes the attention given them causes such a reaction that they are, for a time, reinforced" (13). Our living space is still "divided by boundaries of class, race, ethnicity, and gender" (Smethurst 34), and the differences between fiction and history, real and representational, local and global, the self and the Other, remain palpable to some extent in our social and cultural life.

Analogously, McHale warns us that despite the numerous forms of interaction, intertextual allusions and common themes between popular and mainstream literature in postmodernism, the institutions of high culture and those of low culture do not necessarily mingle: "the myth of the collapse of hierarchical distinctions in postmodern culture is just that, a myth, and the institutions for the production, distribution and consumption of high culture continue to be distinct from those for popular culture" (*Constructing* 226). His caveat somewhat questions the prominent view, which has been present in criticism since at least Jameson's "Postmodernism and Consumer Society," and which stresses "the erosion of the older distinction between high culture and so-called mass or popular culture" (14). The influence of popular art and its growing interrelatedness with high art have raised overarching cultural debates since at least the avant-garde movements, the theories of Benjamin and Theodor Adorno, as, for example, Andreas Huyssen's *After the Great Divide* demonstrates. Nevertheless, extensive interpretive works and institutions which would explicitly blend genre criticism with mainstream criticism could be more common.

Critics have to maintain a broad perspective and work through difficulties if they want to be the catalysts to the erosion of cultural borderlines. Exploring narrative, thematic, and generic manifestations of liminality might be a possible approach for such an attempt. Consequently, critics can, with the help of postmodern philosophy (for example, semiotics, psychoanalysis, poststructuralism, feminism, narratology, post-colonialism) and contemporary mainstream and popular fiction, foreground the importance of liminality and multiplicity in space, time, social formations, and textual constructions.

Liminoid and pluralized perspectives, places, social and narrative structures will probably become more and more widespread in everyday life, human interactions, cultural discourses, and literary criticism. Whether we experience the increase of liminal situations and multiplied time-space with pleasure or anxiety remains a crucial question; this work, analyzing the consequences and implications of such spatial models in fiction and criticism, intended to provide guidelines for understanding this ambiguous experience.

Notes

Introduction

1. The play of liminality is often associated with the ambiguity of the center. Turner finds the elusive nature of the center crucial in liminality when he argues that the community — or "communitas"— resulting from liminality "with its unstructured character ... might as well be represented by the 'emptiness at the center,' which is nevertheless indispensable to the functioning of the structure" (*The Ritual* 127). Analogously, Derrida argues that the appearance and disappearance of a center, its interiority and exteriority, create a constant game in the structures of human reasoning: "The center is at the center of totality, and yet, since the center does not belong to the totality, (is not part of the totality), the totality *has its center elsewhere*. The center is not the center.... The concept of centered structure is in fact the concept of play" ("Structure, Sign and Play" 352; emphasis in original). Liminality demonstrates that center and marginality, structure and anti-structure, play and work are seemingly opposite but actually interdependent phenomena.

2. Derrida, referring to other controversial episodes in Carroll's novels, says that "I no longer know who I am (following) or who it is I am chasing, who is following me or hunting me. Who comes before and who is after whom? I no longer know where my head is. Madness: 'We're all mad here. I'm mad. You're mad'" ("The Animal" 379). Deleuze also discusses the paradoxical reversals of the Alice novels in his *The Logic of Sense*.

3. This second trait evokes the experience of the "Frontier" in American culture: it is the civilizing process, not the result, which is the topic in many western films, literature, and so on. As McHale observes, even though the actual Frontier has vanished, its influence on fictional world-construction remains tangible even during postmodernism. The image of the Frontier still provides a fuzzy borderline zone, a space of interior liminality when texts intend to reopen and "recover the frontier, sometimes nostalgically or elegiacally, sometimes in an ironic mode" (*Postmodernist* 50). Arpad Szakolczai also argues that the Frontier, "moving always further to the West," makes America "the case of permanent liminality *par excellence*" (215; emphasis in original). Thus, I disagree with Fludernik when she contrasts the contemporary interpretations and manifestations of liminality with the never-ending frontier, stressing the distinction between "a boundary that can be transgressed in either direction" and "a boundary that is to be extended to infinity — the typical scenario of the frontier image" ("Carceral" 47).

4. The entire question of liminality, especially the problematics of reversals, porous and evasive borderlines could be analyzed from the perspective of phenomenology. Gaston Bachelard, for example, argues that "Outside and inside ... are always ready to be reversed, to exchange their hostility" (218). The far-reaching theoretical ramifications of phenomenology, however, would exceed the capacities of this work — my analysis remains basically a poststructuralist endeavor.

5. The relationship between the various framing models and the labyrinthine-rhizomatic

structures cannot be purely oppositional, exactly because such models blur the borderlines between oppositions and question antithesis as such. The relationship between my models of 1.a, 1.b and 2 should therefore be imagined as an interwoven grid. As Miller argues, the ambiguity of liminality and multiplicity often makes it "impossible to decide which element ... commands or encloses the other. It is impossible to decide whether the series should be thought of as a sequence of elements each external to the next or according to some model of enclosure like that of the Chinese boxes" (155).

6. The antagonism of mass culture and high culture, however, when it comes to the institutional differences between genre and "mainstream" criticism, consumerist and elite audience, fandom and academia, has still not been dissolved (see McHale, *Constructing* 225–27). Matt Hills, for example, observes that institutional oppositions "cannot be reduced to points of 'modernist' or 'postmodernist' logic" (*Fan Cultures* 12): in spite of the "liminal" (19) identities of the fan-scholars and scholar-fans, different discourses, contexts and expectations characterize fan culture and academia, and "while *differential institutional constraints* act on fan and academic cultural practices ... fans and academics will remain opposed" (20; emphasis in original). The question of canonization results in further distinctions: genre critics tend to demarcate themselves by refusing the official canon and canonization as such. Peter Stockwell, for example, stresses that "One of the attractions of academic work in the science fiction genre is the resistance to the idea of establishing a 'canon' of approved texts" (8). Analogously, Brian Attebery argues that the criticism of fantasy texts possesses an open-mindedness that "high culture" lacks, creating "a place to stand and judge the canon itself. Readers of fantasy have a certain freedom which is denied to readers within the pale" (4).

7. Although there are minor differences between the contemporary trends of Slipstream and New Weird, the fiction of the New Wave Fabulists and that of the Interstitial Arts Foundation, they all "freely draw on the furniture of horror, fantasy, or science fiction, as well as the conventions of domestic realism, memoir, surrealism, even nonfiction" (Wolfe and Beamer 21). Further, unruly narrative structure, experimental style, "shifts in point of view," disrupted chronology, metafiction, embedded tales characterize such fiction (Wolfe and Beamer 26–32; Mendlesohn, "Conjunctions" 238). For further clarification on these literary trends, see my analysis of Gaiman's and Kelly Link's narrative techniques in Chapter 2.

8. Gaiman's *Interworld* ([2007]; co-authored with Michael Reaves) exemplifies and overtly manifests the overlapping, as well as the rivalry between science fiction and fantasy. In the novel, the plurality of possible universes, the multiverse, is an extensive continuum and a battle field between two worlds: the "Binary," that is, technologized, science fiction and cyberpunk inspired realm and the "HEX," a fantastic, magic society. Millions of possible universes take place somewhere between the two poles, influenced, attacked, but not completely conquered by the empires.

9. I agree with Swirski that certain works by Lem, such as *The Futurological Congress* (1971) and "Tale of the Three Storytelling Machines of King Genius" (1967), evoke the "Chinese box" ontology of postmodernist fiction (Swirski, "Playing a Game" 38). But the novels that I focus on (*Solaris, Return from the Stars, His Master's Voice, Fiasco, The Investigation, The Chain of Chance*) feature relatively simple narrative structures and display rather modernist traits: they thematize the subject trapped in the Kafkaesque world of bureaucracy, anxiety and absurd illogic, depicting the protagonist's struggle with this chaos and thus demonstrating the limits of human science and philosophy. Epistemological concerns occasionally evoke ontological dilemmas, illustrating McHale's argument that "push epistemological questions far enough and they 'tip over' into ontological questions" (*Postmodernist* 11). Postmodern philosophies are highly detectable in Lem's novels—I utilize them myself in my analysis. Nevertheless, in my interpretations the modernist writing style and world view remains dominant in Lem's oeuvre.

Chapter 1

1. The correlation between the simple, abstract formulas in detective fiction and the complex analyses they evoke can be exemplified also by Lacan's, Derrida's, and Barbara Johnson's

theoretical interpretations of Poe's "The Purloined Letter" (1844) in *The Purloined Poe: Lacan, Derrida and Psychoanalytic Reading*.

   2. Poe's "The Murders in the Rue Morgue" (1841) is a highly analytical mystery story — in which, however, the culprit is not human. Superficial, formulaized psychology manifests itself in his "The Purloined Letter," while the detective becomes a meticulous *reader* in order to find clues in "The Mystery of Marie Roget" (1842), where Dupin analyzes newspaper articles and identifies their contradictions to solve the puzzle.

   3. Nevertheless, detective fiction is far from being a realistic genre. Poe's narrator points out in "The Mystery of Marie Roget" that although the flow of mysterious events can be explained rationally by the analytical mind, less able thinkers have "occasionally been startled into a vague yet thrilling half-credence in the supernatural" (199). Conan Doyle's detective stories, in spite of their stress on scientific reasoning, also utilize thematic elements of adventure and fantastic stories. The novels draw attention to these problematics when, for example, Holmes condemns Watson's narrative style, which dilutes the story of rationalistic detection "with romanticism" (*Sign of the Four* 6), thus becoming "meretricious" ("The Adventure of the Crooked" 378).

   4. The crime scene is also used for narrative purposes, featuring Barthes's proairetic code. The spatial lexia form proairetic code when the detective finds a hidden element, an essential clue in the house, which will have a crucial effect on the plot. In Conan Doyle's "The Adventure of the Norwood Builder" (1903), for example, the discovery of a secret room leads to the assumption that the "victim" is in fact alive, and that his scam can be revealed by a false fire alarm.

   5. Poirot seems to both reject and emphasize the significance of clues. In *Cards on the Table*, for example, Poirot denies that he has deployed any clues when solving the mystery: "There was *nothing*, you see, to go upon.... There were no tangible clues — no fingerprints — no incriminating papers or documents. There were only — the people themselves.'" Quite contradictorily, however, his next sentence cancels out his speech: "'And one tangible clue — the bridge scores'" (186; emphasis in original). In *Murder on the Orient Express*, Poirot is *compelled* to deal with the abundance of clues and red herrings, although "It is the psychology" that he would like to seek, "not the fingerprint or the cigarette ash" (89).

   6. Thus, Christie reveals ideas overtly that are covertly present in Conan Doyle's and Poe's detective fiction. Moretti argues in his essay on Conan Doyle's detective stories that the duality of innocence and guilt correlates with the duality of conformity and individuality. The crowd is featureless, uniform, and so it is "something irreducibly personal that betrays the criminal ... The perfect crime — the nightmare of detective fiction — is the featureless, disindividualized crime that anyone could have committed" ("Clues" 135).

   7. As Shaw and Vanacker point out, Christie categorically rejects Freudian psychology. First, because the genre intends to defend "its own territory of the logical game against the influence of Freudian theories of the irrational and the unconscious." Second, "because such theories tend to deny evil and excuse the criminal," also presuming that "people can no longer be categorized" (77).

   8. The narrator Charles Hayward follows a long-established convention of detective stories when he reveals a contradiction between the seemingly impartial, distant intellect of the sleuth and the covert, but almost inevitable, financial benefits of the investigation. Although Watson emphasizes that Sherlock Holmes always considers his cases as intellectual puzzles and he is not affected by personal or financial concerns, in "The Adventure at the Priory School" (1904) the detective accepts a reward by an extremely rich nobleman who is an accomplice in the case and so his behavior becomes slightly similar to that of a blackmailer. Poe's Dupin also reveals his partiality, admitting in "The Mystery of Marie Roget" that "For our own purpose, therefore, if not for the purpose of justice, it is indispensable that our first step should be the determination of the identity of the corpse with the Marie Roget who is missing" (214), since otherwise the reward would not be obtainable.

   9. As I have mentioned before, these references often attack the predecessors on basis of the order-chaos dichotomy. The criticized novels are either too messy, not as rational, orderly and intellectual as the conventions require, or quite the opposite: from the perspective of a

hard-boiled narrator, the predecessors are too intellectual, abstract and orderly. "They are too contrived," argues Chandler about the Golden Age writers ("The Simple Art" 10); their novels have "the austere simplicity of fiction, rather than the tangled woof of facts" (*The Big Sleep* 103). Chandler admittedly was more interested in the description of immoral city life than in the flawless, well-made storylines of the traditional whodunit: "The technical basis of the *Black Mask* type of story ... was that the scene outranked the plot" (Introduction viii).

Chapter 2

1. Nevertheless, it is possible to emphasize "socio-political dimensions" in Tolkien's oeuvre, arguing, as Zipes does, that Tolkien's fantasies "presented solutions and answers to the problems confronting mankind" (*Breaking the Magic* 158). Unlike Tolkien, contemporary criticism frequently foregrounds social contexts that relate fairy tales and fantastic literature to reality.

2. Although Tolkien's novels, at first glance, seem to fit into the immersive fantasy category, taking place exclusively in Faerie, Mendlesohn argues that they are portal-quest fantasies, due to the process whereby "the protagonist goes from a mundane life, in which the fantastic, if he or she is aware of it, is very distant and unknown ... into direct contact with the fantastic" ("Toward a Taxonomy" 174). Analogously, in *The Graveyard Book*, the fantastic world is tangible from the beginning—the special skills of "the man Jack" indicate the presence of the supernatural—and so the text *could* be classified as an immersive fantasy. Yet, as the novel describes the maturation of the protagonist who becomes more and more familiar with the rules of the Underworld, the text should rather be interpreted as a portal-quest fantasy.

3. Unfortunately, Booth's theory of irony often interweaves the implied author with the actual, historical writer: "We are often dependent on the assumption that in *that* time and *that* place, this author most probably new or intended such-and-such, in contrast to what the surface says" (133; emphasis in original). Booth's assumption about the fixed and univocal interpretations of "stable irony" (2–6) is also problematic and so his theory has become the target of criticism in several poststructuralist and deconstructionist arguments (see Fish 344–48; de Man, "The Concept" 165–67; Miller 143).

4. Many other critics argue that the distinctions between the detective and the perpetrator, which are notably undermined in hard-boiled and metaphysical detective stories, have always been somewhat illusionary. Moretti, for example, finds opposition not so much between the murderer and the detective, but between the perpetrator and the innocent majority. Sin represents isolation, individuality and uniqueness, while innocence stands for stereotypical behavior and conformity. The detective possesses individuality, although sacrifices it for the sake of the society: "For this reason, he can 'understand' the criminal (and, when necessary, enact criminal deeds): potentially, he too was a criminal" (Moretti, "Clues" 142). Accordingly, Holmes commits larceny and becomes an accomplice in murder in "The Adventure of Charles Augustus Milverton."

5. The story, similarly to Douglas Adams's *The Restaurant at the End of the Universe* (1980) and Neil Gaiman and Terry Pratchett's *Good Omens: The Nice and Accurate Prophecies of Agnes Nutter, Witch* (1990), illustrates McHale's argument in *Constructing Postmodernism* that "realistic representations of ... [the] apocalypse, however thoughtful and earnest ... can only be inadequate" (160), but ironic representations can renew the genre.

6. Although it is seldom indicated overtly in the narration that the events are perceived by Mrs. Whitaker, the external focalizer often "looks over the shoulder" of the protagonist, demonstrating Bal's "ambiguous," "free indirect" or "double focalization" (*Narratology* 159).

7. Although there are analogies between Traill's and Mendlesohn's system, the differences, perhaps, are more tangible. Traill outlines five categories. Mendlesohn's intrusion and portal-quest fantasies would both fall in the first subtype in Traill's system, in "the disjunctive mode," where "The characters of both [the supernatural and the natural] domain are able to coexist and interact, but each recognizes that the other is alien" (11). Traill's second category, "the fantasy mode," more or less coincides with Mendlesohn's immersive fantasies, as in these texts "the entire fictional world is composed of the supernatural domain" (Traill 12). Traill's third category

(ambiguous mode) resembles Mendlesohn's liminal fantasy, but Traill stresses the unreliable instead of the estranged narration, and she does not discuss the lack of surprise. Traill's fourth category, "the supernatural naturalized," is entirely missing in Mendlesohn's system, but it draws on Todorov's definition of the "uncanny," as "the narrator imparts a natural explanation for the strange events" (Traill 16). Traill's fifth category, the paranormal mode, resembles science fiction texts that explain seemingly fantastic phenomena by rational, scientific means, and so supernatural events "are reinterpreted and brought within the paradigm of the natural" (Traill 17–18).

8. The "actual reader" is also an artificial construction, a role "constructed from social and historical knowledge of the time" of the book (Iser, *The Act of Reading* 28).

9. Interestingly enough, Lovecraft's story "The Outsider" (1926) is also written from the perspective of the monster, although this story lacks parodying humor, maintaining the serious elements of the horror genre. Furthermore, Lem's "The Mask" (1976), a curious hybrid of chivalrous love story, horror and detective fiction, is also written from the point-of-view of a monster-robot. (See my analysis of the story in Chapter 3).

10. The significance of fairy tales in Gaiman's oeuvre is also underlined by the acknowledgments in *Anansi Boys*, which refer to two major artists of the fairy tale tradition, Zora Neale Hurston and Frederick "Tex" Avery. Avery was a cartoonist who created animated films based on traditional fairy tales, often in a sarcastic and humorous form. Hurston, a novelist and an anthropologist of Caribbean folklore, collected and adapted tales that gave voice to the previously silent social groups, creating tales with the female African American point-of-view (see Barr 28).

11. Ryan stresses that both cases allow narrative games, transgressions, the contamination of levels ("Stacks" 890–892), which, as I have indicated before, are privileged characteristics in the contemporary fantasy of the New Wave Fabulists, including Gaiman's oeuvre (see, for example, my analysis on "Murder Mysteries").

12. In "The Modal Structure of Narrative Universes," when Ryan describes the first two cases, she argues that the texts form "relative worlds" (722), "alternate universes" (730). The third mode is defined by a different term, "layers of reality," when the "domain of the actual in a narrative universe ... [is] split into two or more autonomous spheres, each governed by its own laws" (721). (See also Ryan, "Possible Worlds" 568.)

13. Furthermore, there is a god who is imperceptible for the human characters: people cannot see, hear, or remember him, as he can totally fade out of perception. This is the moment when the largely straightforward narration of *American Gods* becomes somewhat subversive: the omniscient narrator is replaced by a narrator with limited knowledge, who, in a way similar to its human characters, is unable to hear and remember what the god says (285).

14. Thus, Mayhew becomes an extremely privileged character, as the novel emphasizes that people should occupy only one of the worlds. The marquis warns the protagonist that only a "few individuals manage a kind of half-life ... and it isn't a good life" (340). It is usually the rats, a highly despised species, and the "Rat-speakers"— homeless citizens who serve and communicate with the rats — that mediate between London Above and London Below.

15. Another text which plays the same intertextual game by referring both to a canonical and a subcultural convention via Sherlock Holmes is Nicholas Meyer's *The Seven Per Cent Solution* (1974). The novel rewrites the figure of the detective as a patient of Sigmund Freud, thus portraying both a culturally honored historical figure (Freud) and a subculturally celebrated hero (Holmes).

Chapter 3

1. Hayles refers to the double-edged meaning of the monk's statement, although she understands the conflicting implications figuratively: "she is his sister because she counts as a human person. She also may be like him because he operates according to biocultural programs that dictate his actions" ("Unmasking" 40). The fact that a certain "skillful master craftsman,"

a machinist, serves as a physician in the monastery (Lem, "The Mask" 228) casts further doubts on the human body of the monk.

2. Lem divides his own writings into three groups and periods in "Reflections on My Life" (1984). His early novels "are devoid of any value" (13). In his middle period, into which he assigns *Eden* (1959), *Solaris* and *Return from the Stars*, he wrote books which "do not oversimplify the world" (16), but which are nonetheless quite traditional in form. In his third period, when he wrote, for example, reviews of and introductions to non-existent books, his form became highly unconventional: "I left the fields already exploited and broke new ground" (19).

3. In other words, naming and taxonomy form a subject-object, master-servant relationship: "Finding oneself deprived of language, one loses the power to name, to name oneself" (Derrida, "The Animal" 388). The subversion of hierarchy, therefore, often involves "misnaming," that is, to rewrite and "violate the system of naming" (Bhabha 225).

4. Unlike Yossef, Freedman considers Kelvin a relatively skillful psychologist in his *Critical Theory and Science Fiction*, arguing that "Kelvin (a Solaristic *psychologist*, it should be remembered) achieves what degree of contact he can with the ocean mainly through a painful psychic agon that involves the unconscious itself. His is a struggle that may produce a certain degree of knowledge and self-knowledge" (108; emphasis in original).

5. Scientific and emotional puzzles are intertwined in both novels, but *Solaris* focuses on the former, while *Return from the Stars* on the latter. This might be one of the reasons why Lem was dissatisfied with the latter novel: "I gave birth to *Solaris* and *Return from the Stars* in a similar manner, but I think that *Solaris* is a good book and *Return from the Stars* is a poor one, because in the latter the underlying problems of social evil and its elimination are treated in a manner that is too primitive, too unlikely, and perhaps even false" ("Reflections" 21).

6. The wooden reel and the piece of string, and the resulting game, can also be interpreted as liminal objects and activities based on D. W. Winnicott's theory on playing and transitional phenomena. His "transitional objects" are neither external, nor internal objects; playing belongs neither to the self, nor to the (m)other, but it occupies an in-between space between them (59–60). Several of his case studies focus on string, describing a little boy who is "dealing with a fear of separation [from the mother], attempting to deny the separation by his use of string [in various activities and games]" (20). The string in these cases becomes "simultaneously a symbol of separateness and of union" (50).

7. As Hayles points out, the neutral gender of the protagonist is expressed subtly by the (nonexistent) past tense verb form at the beginning of the Polish text. This is followed by a "liminal moment," when "the narrator moves from an 'it' ... into a linguistically enculturated 'she'" ("Unmasking" 29, 30).

8. Exaggerated mirror images, of course, are not always uncanny and realistic: they can also turn into parodying caricatures. Freud indicates that the problematic incidents of "involuntary repetition," the "unintended recurrence of the same situation" ("The Uncanny" 237) can also lead to parody. Besides the "visitors," exaggerated mirror images are manifested in the oceanic formations of the planet when the "mimoids" generate caricatures (113). Several similar incidents are described with sarcasm in *The Star Diaries* and *Peace on Earth*. Lem unmasks the image of the Double as a cliché in science fiction, including his own works, when Ijon Tichy has to face and bicker with his multiplied personalities due to high velocity space-traveling, time-warps, the echo of his radio signals, his severed corpus callosum, and so on.

9. As Csicsery-Ronay speculates, it remains unanswered whether "Andre Berton [is] a distorted allusion to the manifester of Surrealism" ("The Book is" 20). Most names in the novel are telling names. In the original Polish version, as well as in the French and Hungarian translation, Kelvin's wife is called "Harey." The English translators changed the name into "Rheya," thus making an overt reference to the Earth goddess. "Harey," however, may also evoke the name "Harry," which might be an allusion to "Old Harry," the devil. The translators also mitigated the reference in Snaut's name to snout, abating the pig-like traits of the character and changing his name to "Snow." While Csicsery-Ronay finds the altered English names somewhat adequate, Abraham Yossef condemns the translation, arguing that the "translators into English acted in an incomprehensible way" (54).

Chapter 4

1. It is also important to emphasize that not only postmodern or present day environments can be interpreted as fluid spaces or networks of communication. As Henri Lefebvre argues, from an economic-historical perspective, capitalist social spaces and marketplaces always existed "by virtue of networks and pathways, by virtue of bunches or clusters of relationships" (86). Thus, even places which are conventionally considered separate and immobile, such as a regular house, are in fact "permeated from every direction by streams of energy ... [becoming the] convergence of waves and currents ... [and] an information-based machine with low energy requirements" (93). An early prototype of "the space of flows" may be Venice, a most historic city that appears in Gibson's *Idoru*. Naturally, it is neither a postmodern megacity, nor a representative of Castells's global cities. Yet, built on water and founded on fluidity, Venice is a city that resisted order, mapping, and planning throughout its history (Cavallaro, *Cyberpunk* 146–48).

2. Avant-garde artifacts and outdated analogue technology may be interpreted as "fashionably archaic" phenomena in the dystopian wastelands of the "Sprawl" stories, since they provide essential means for the characters to survive and remain "hip." In Gibson's later works, however, avant-garde art becomes a consciously palpable quotation. Eventually, the post-9/11 novels, especially *Spook Country* (2007), add up to burlesque travesties, and the avant-garde cultural phenomena and the up-to-date technology appear in a parodying manner.

3. *Metropolis*, like *Blade Runner*, envisions an ambiguous, double-edged city: on the one hand, it provides an early example of a dark city, foreshadowing Film Noir and cyberpunk cities (Bukatman, *Blade Runner* 63). On the other hand, *Metropolis* also has a utopian side and so Gibson's "The Gernsback Continuum" criticizes the film when a book of utopian architecture "contained sketches of an idealized city that drew on *Metropolis*" (31).

4. Barlow's arguments, which might seem naïve to the contemporary reader, coincide with early cyberpunk's enthusiasm for cyberspace. Authors and critics believed that cyberspace would reduce social distinctions and eliminate racial and gender prejudices, providing a utopian liminal zone (Haraway 35). Cyberpunk was initially viewed as a subculture that embodied a revolt against the mainstream, the "straight world": their mirrored sunglasses and other symbols represented a struggle for an alternate discourse (Hebdige 5–10). Like many other subcultures, however, they eventually became commercialized and institutionalized, losing some of their subversive power.

5. Analogously, in Gibson's *Neuromancer* whenever the AI hijacks Case's consciousness in cyberspace, his body becomes temporarily dead, his heart rate flatlines and so he arrives "literally, at death's threshold" (Swanstrom 23).

6. Dick's empathic and masochistic characters evoke a short story by Lem, in which a special drug evokes utmost empathy in humans, and results in escalating aggression and shared physical pain in the community (Lem, "Altruizine" 275–79).

7. The highly similar but somewhat different, confusing surnames in Dick's fiction evoke the narratological phenomenon of "transworld identity," when characters migrate "across the semi-permeable membrane" that divides fictional worlds, contributing to "the penetration of one world by another, the violation, in some sense, of an ontological boundary" (McHale, *Postmodernist* 35 and *Constructing* 153).

8. Such odd incidents, misspelled or forgotten proper names, unexpected memories, slips of the tongue evoke Freud's signs of repressed experiences as he describes them, for example, in *The Psychopathology of Everyday Life*. Dick openly reveals the Freudian influence of his novels when a character explains these incidents by using "Freudian jargon" in *Time Out of Joint* (24).

9. Umberto Rossi, in his thoughtful essay on media in Philip K. Dick's works, argues that "the idea that the radio is a good medium, as opposed to lying newspapers and manipulative TV, can be found in several works by Dick" ("Radio Free" 22). Thus, Rossi's reading of the role of the radio in *Dr. Bloodmoney* and *Radio Free Albemuth* is somewhat different from mine.

10. My interpretation of Dick's alternate histories rests on contemporary social science, physics, culture studies and philosophy, for example Doreen Massey's arguments, which call for

the disruption of the strict dual distinction between space and time. As Massey stresses, space-time should rather be understood as dynamism between inextricably interwoven elements (261). Smethurst's postmodern chronotope also demonstrates that "in cultural and scientific theory, space and time are increasingly dealt with as a single property, or as two aspects of the same thing" (38).

11. The "Nelsons" also appear as "plain, quite commonplace people" in Dick's "What the Dead Men Say" (287).

12. The novel foreshadows Douglas Adams's humorous *Mostly Harmless*, in which the consequences of alternate timelines and time traveling irrevocably disrupt history. The end of traditional temporality and historicity, which is foregrounded by Dick and Jameson, is described with irony by Adams: "The great history faculty of the University of Maximegalon finally gave up, closed itself down and surrendered its buildings to the rapidly growing joint faculty of Divinity and Water Polo, which had been after them for years" (2).

13. Darko Suvin argues that Dick's central period lasts only for a couple of years between 1962 and 1965, followed by a period of "falling off" after 1966 (Suvin, "P. K. Dick's" 12). I rather apply Andrew Butler's classification in *The Pocket Essential Philip K. Dick* (59), which argues for a longer peak period between 1961 and 1969.

14. In *Neuromancer*, the protagonist's recollection is described with images of photography, film, and computer technology. Further, when the AI creates a virtual universe for Case, a scarf is described by the narrator with images of computer circuitry. The episode is highly self-reflexive, as it foreshadows *on the narrative level* that the virtual reality will unmask itself *on the thematic level*. As Swanstrom observes, "The circuit on the scarf acts as a gateway between the distinct orders of narrative and description ... [serving as] an aperture between differing ontologies" (21–22).

15. Yet *Neuromancer* is basically the only novel (in addition to a few short stories) in which the unusual and nonlinear language dominates: Gibson's later works comprise mainly straightforward narration, losing the avant-garde edge. Dick's fiction is quite the opposite: his early works comprise relatively simple narrative techniques, while the later novels become more complex and ambiguous in form.

Conclusion

1. The correlation between nomadic roving and underground, holey space is articulated not only in Deleuze and Guattari's *Thousand Plateaus* (413), but also in Nietzsche's preface to his *Daybreak*. Nietzsche's "'subterranean man' ... who tunnels and mines and undermines" is engaged in a seemingly aimless wandering: "His friends are unable to divine where he is or whither he is going, that they will sometimes ask themselves: 'what? is he going at all? Does he still have — a path?'" (1). De Certeau's walkers also follow "the subterranean passages of the city ... accompanied by the rumble of subway trains" (102).

2. Dick's "Notes" implies that envisioning such an overpowering eye or face in the sky, as it is manifested in his works, is related to his own psychological problems, such as his buried, infantile memories of his father's gas mask, and to his alienation from the public. He writes: "I looked up at the sky and saw a face. I didn't really see it, but the face was there, and it was not a human face; it was a vast visage of perfect evil. I realize now (and I think I dimly realized at the time) what caused me to see it: the months of isolation, of deprivation of human contact, in fact sensory deprivation as such ... It was immense; it filled the quarter of the sky. It had empty slots for eyes — it was metal and cruel and, worst of all, it was God" (377).

Bibliography

Nonfiction (Print)

Aldiss, Brian W. *Billion Year Spree: The True History of Science Fiction.* London: Corgi, 1973.
Alexander, Bethany. "No Need to Choose: A Magnificent Anarchy of Belief." *The Neil Gaiman Reader.* Ed. Darrell Schweitzer. Rockville: Wildside, 2007. 135–40.
Attebery, Brian. *Strategies of Fantasy.* Bloomington: Indiana University Press, 1992.
Bacchilega, Christina. *Postmodern Fairy Tales: Gender and Narrative Strategies.* Philadelphia: University of Pennsylvania Press, 1997.
Bachelard, Gaston. *The Poetics of Space.* Trans. Maria Jolas. Boston: Beacon Press, 1994.
Bakhtin, Mikhail. *The Dialogic Imagination.* Ed. Michael Holquist, trans. Caryl Emerson and Michael Holquist. Austin: University of Texas Press, 1981.
———. "Discourse in the Novel." *The Dialogic Imagination,* 259–422.
———. "Forms of Time and of the Chronotope in the Novel." *The Dialogic Imagination,* 84–259.
———. *Rabelais and His World.* Trans. Helene Iswolsky. Bloomington: Indiana University Press, 1984.
Bal, Mieke. "His Master's Eye." *Modernity and the Hegemony of Vision.* Ed. David Michael Levin. Berkeley: University of California Press, 1993. 379–404.
———. *Narratology: Introduction to the Theory of Narrative.* Toronto: University of Toronto Press, 1994.
Barnard, Robert. *A Talent to Deceive: An Appreciation of Agatha Christie.* London: Collins, 1980.
Barr, Marleen S. *Feminist Fabulation: Space/Postmodern Fiction.* Iowa City: University of Iowa, 1992.
Barthes, Roland. *Camera Lucida: Reflections on Photography.* Trans. Richard Howard. New York: Noonday Press, 1991.
———. "Paris not Flooded." *The Eiffel Tower and Other Mythologies.* Trans. Richard Howard. Berkeley: University of California Press, 1997. 31–34.
———. *S/Z: An Essay.* Trans. Richard Miller. New York: Hill and Wang, 1993.
———. "The Structural Analysis of Narrative: Apropos of Acts 10–11." *The Semiotic Challenge.* Trans. Richard Howard. New York: Hill and Wang, 1988. 217–45.
Baudrillard, Jean. "The Ecstasy of Communication." Trans. John Johnston. *Postmodern Culture.* Ed. Hal Foster. London: Pluto, 1985. 126–34.
———. "The Masses: The Implosion of the Social in the Media." *Selected Writings.* Ed. Mark Poster. Cambridge: Polity Press, 1988. 207–19.
———. *Simulacra and Simulation.* Trans. Sheila Faria Glaser. Ann Arbor: University of Michigan Press, 2000.
Bauman, Zygmunt. *Globalization: The Human Consequences.* Cambridge: Polity, 2006.
Belsey, Catherine. "Deconstructing the Text: Sherlock Holmes." Bennett 277–85.

Benedikt, Michael. Introduction. *Cyberspace: First Steps.* Cambridge: MIT Press, 1994. 1–27.
Benjamin, Walter. *Charles Baudelaire: A Lyric Poet in the Era of High Capitalism.* Trans. Harry Zohn. London: Verso, 1992.
_____. "The Work of Art in the Age of Mechanical Reproduction." *Illuminations.* Ed. Hannah Arendt, trans. Harry Zohn. New York: Shocken Books, 1969. 217–51.
Bennett, Tony, ed. *Popular Fiction: Technology, Ideology, Production, Reading.* London: Routledge, 1990.
Bényei, Tamás. "Leakings: Reappropriating Science Fiction — the Case of Kurt Vonnegut." *Anatomy of Science Fiction.* Ed. Donald E. Morse. Newcastle: Cambridge Scholars Press, 2006. 41–69.
Bhabha, Homi K. *The Location of Culture.* London: Routledge, 1994.
Bogen, Joseph E. "The Other Side of the Brain II: An Appositional Mind." *Bulletin of the Los Angeles Neurological Society* 34.3. (1969): 135–62.
Booth, Wayne C. *A Rhetoric of Irony.* Chicago: University of Chicago Press, 1974.
Boym, Svetlana. *The Future of Nostalgia.* New York: Basic Books, 2001.
Brand, Dana. "From the *Flaneur* to the Detective: Interpreting the City of Poe." Bennett 220–37.
Bukatman, Scott. *Blade Runner.* London: BFI, 2000.
_____. "Gibson's Typewriter." *Flame Wars: The Discourse of Cyberculture.* Ed. Mark Dery. Durham: Duke University Press, 1994. 71–90.
_____. *Terminal Identity: The Virtual Subject in Postmodern Science Fiction.* Durham: Duke University Press, 1993.
Bürger, Peter. *The Decline of Modernism.* Trans. Nicholas Walker. University Park: Pennsylvania State University Press, 1992.
Burleson, Donald R. *H. P. Lovecraft: A Critical Study.* Westport: Greenwood Press, 1983.
Butler, Andrew M. "Between the 'Deaths' of Science Fiction: A Skeptical View of the Possibility for Anti-Genres." *Journal of the Fantastic in the Arts* 15.3 (2005): 208–16.
_____. "LSD, Lying Ink, and Lies, Inc." *Science Fiction Studies* 32.96 (2005): 265–80.
_____. *The Pocket Essential Cyberpunk.* Harpenden: Pocket Essentials, 2000.
_____. *The Pocket Essential Philip K. Dick.* Harpenden: Pocket Essentials, 2000.
Butler, Judith. *Gender Trouble: Feminism and the Subversion of Identity.* London: Routledge, 1990.
Caillois, Roger. "Mimicry and Legendary Psychasthenia." Trans. John Shepley. *October* 31 (1984): 17–32.
Campbell, Laura. "Dickian Time in *The Man in the High Castle.*" *Extrapolation* 33.3 (1992): 190–201.
Canary, Robert H. "Science Fiction as Fictive History." *Extrapolation* 16.1 (1974): 81–95.
Carlson, Marvin. "Is There a Real Inspector Hound? Mousetraps, Deathtraps, and the Disappearing Detective." *Modern Drama* 36.3 (1993): 431–42.
Carroll, Noël. *The Philosophy of Horror or Paradoxes of the Heart.* New York: Routledge, 1990.
Castells, Manuel. *The Information Age: Economy, Society and Culture. Volume I. The Rise of the Network Society.* Malden: Blackwell, 1996.
Cavallaro, Dani. *Cyberpunk and Cyberculture: Science Fiction and the Work of William Gibson.* London and New Brunswick: Athlone Press, 2000.
_____. *The Gothic Vision: Three Centuries of Horror, Terror and Fear.* London: Continuum, 2002.
Chandler, Raymond. Introduction. *Trouble Is My Business.* New York: Vintage Crime, 1992. vii–x.
_____. "The Simple Art of Murder." *The Second Chandler Omnibus.* London: Hamilton, 1979. 3–15
Clute, John. "Beyond the Pale." *Conjunctions 39: The New Wave Fabulists.* Ed. Bradford Morrow and Peter Straub. Annandale-on-Hudson: Bard College, 2003. 420–33.
_____. "Canary Fever." *Journal of the Fantastic in the Arts* 15.3 (2005): 217–27.
Constable, Catherine. "Baudrillard Reloaded: Interrelating Philosophy and Film via *The Matrix Trilogy.*" *Screen* 47.2 (2006): 233–49.

Cook, Guy. *Discourse and Literature—The Interplay of Form and Mind*. Oxford: Oxford University Press, 1994.
Csicsery-Ronay, Istvan. "The Book is the Alien: On Certain and Uncertain Readings of Lem's *Solaris*." *Science Fiction Studies* 12.1 (1985): 6–21.
———. "How Not to Write a Book on Lem." *Science Fiction Studies* 13.3 (1986): 387–91.
———. "The Sentimental Futurist: Cybernetics and Art in William Gibson's *Neuromancer*." *Spring* 33.3 (1992): 221–40.
Davies, Eric. "Technognosis, Magic, Memory, and the Angels of Information." *Flame Wars: The Discourse of Cyberculture*. Ed. Mark Dery. Durham: Duke University Press, 1994. 29–60.
Day, Gary. "Ordeal by Analysis: Agatha Christie's *The Thirteen Problems*." *Twentieth Century Suspense: The Thriller Comes of Age*. Ed. Clive Bloom. New York: St. Martin's Press, 1990. 80–96.
de Certeau, Michel. *The Practice of Everyday Life*. Trans. Steven Randall. Berkeley: University of California Press, 1988.
Deleuze, Gilles. *The Logic of Sense*. Trans. Mark Lester and Charles Stivale, ed. Constantin V. Boundas. London: Athlone Press, 1990.
Deleuze, Gilles, and Felix Guattari. *Anti-Oedipus: Capitalism and Schizophrenia*. Trans. Robert Hurley, Mark Seem and Helen R. Lane. Minneapolis: University of Minnesota Press, 1985.
———. *A Thousand Plateaus: Capitalism and Schizophrenia*. Trans. Brian Massumi. London: Athlone Press, 1988.
de Man, Paul. *Allegories of Reading: Figural Language in Rousseau, Nietzsche, Rilke, and Proust*. New Haven: Yale University Press, 1979.
———. "The Concept of Irony." *Aesthetic Ideology*. Minneapolis: University of Minnesota Press, 1996. 163–84.
Derrida, Jacques. "The Animal That Therefore I Am (More to Follow)." Trans. David Wills. *Critical Inquiry* 28.2 (2002): 369–418.
———. "Différance." *The Margins of Philosophy*. Trans. Alan Bass. London: Prentice Hall, 1982. 1–27.
———. *Dissemination*. Trans. Barbara Johnson. London: Athlone Press, 1981.
———. "The Law of Genre." Trans. Avital Ronell. *Critical Inquiry* 7.1 (1980): 55–81.
———. *Of Grammatology*. Trans. Gayatri Chakravorty Spivak. Baltimore: Johns Hopkins University Press, 1976.
———. *Positions*. Trans. Alan Bass. London: Athlone Press, 1987.
———. *Spurs: Nietzsche's Styles*. Trans. Barbara Harlow. Chicago: University of Chicago Press, 1979.
———. "Structure, Sign and Play in the Discourse of the Human Sciences." *Writing and Difference*. Trans. Alan Bass. London: Routledge, 2004.
Dery, Mark. *Escape Velocity: Cyberculture at the End of the Century*. New York: Grove Press, 1996.
Devas, Angela. "Murder, Mass Culture, and the Feminine: A View from the *4.50 from Paddington*." *Feminist Media Studies* 2.2 (2002): 251–65.
Dolezel, Lubomir. "Truth and Authenticity in Narrative." *Poetics Today* 1.3 (1980): 7–25.
Dowd, Chris. "An Autopsy of Storytelling. Metafiction and Neil Gaiman." *The Neil Gaiman Reader*. Ed. Darrell Schweitzer. Rockville: Wildside, 2007. 103–20.
Duff, David. Introduction. *Modern Genre Theory*. Harlow: Longman, 2000. 1–23.
Duncan, Andy. "Alternate History." *The Cambridge Companion to Science Fiction*. Ed. Edward James and Farah Mendlesohn. Cambridge: Cambridge University Press, 2003. 209–18.
Easterbrook, Neil. "The Arc of Our Destruction: Reversal and Erasure in Cyberpunk." *Science Fiction Studies* 19.3 (1992): 378–94.
———. "The Sublime Simulacra: Repetition, Reversal, and Re-covery in Lem's *Solaris*." *Critique* 36.3 (1995): 177–94.
Eco, Umberto. *The Role of The Reader: Explorations in the Semiotics of Texts*. Bloomington: Indiana University Press, 1979.

———. *Semiotics and the Philosophy of Language*. London: Macmillan, 1984.
Eco, Umberto, and Thomas A. Sebeok, ed. *The Sign of Three. Dupin, Holmes, Peirce*. Bloomington: Indiana University Press, 1983.
Ekman, Stefan. "Down, Out and Invisible in London and Seattle." *Foundation. The International Review of Science Fiction* 34.94 (2005): 64–74.
Enns, Anthony. "Media, Drugs and Schizophrenia in the Works of Philip K. Dick." *Science Fiction Studies* 33.1 (2006): 68–88.
Fenkl, Heinz Insu. Introduction. *Interfictions: An Anthology of Interstitial Writing*. Ed. Delia Sherman and Theodora Goss. Boston: Interstitial Arts Foundation, 2007. i–viii.
Fish, Stanley Eugene. *Is There a Text in This Class?* Cambridge: Harvard University Press, 1994.
Fitting, Peter. "Reality as Ideological Construct: A Reading of Five Novels by Philip K. Dick." *Science Fiction Studies* 10.2 (1983): 219–36.
Fludernik, Monika. "Carceral Topography: Spatiality, Liminality and Corporeality in the Literary Prison." *Textual Practice* 13.1 (1999): 43–77.
———. "Scene Shift, Metalepsis, and the Metaleptic Mode." *Style* 37.4 (2003): 382–400.
Foster, John Burt. Rev. of *The Future of Nostalgia*, by Svetlana Boym. *Modern Language Quarterly* 64.4 (2003): 513–17.
Foucault, Michel. "Confinement, Psychiatry, Prison." *Politics, Philosophy, Culture. Interviews and Other Writings 1977–1984*. Ed. Lawrence D. Kritzman, trans. Alan Sheridan, et al. New York: Routledge, 1988. 178–210.
———. "The Father's 'No.'" *Language, Counter-Memory, Practice*, 68–86.
———. *Language, Counter-Memory, Practice: Selected Essays and Interviews*. Trans. Donald F. Bouchard and Sherry Simon. Ithaca: Cornell University Press, 1996.
———. "Of Other Spaces." Trans. Jay Miskowiec. *Diacritics* 16 (Spring 1986): 22–27.
———. "The Order of Discourse." Trans. Ian McLeod. *Untying the Text: A Poststructuralist Reader*. Ed. R. Young. Boston: Routledge and Kegan Paul, 1981. 48–78.
———. "Power and Strategies." *Power/Knowledge: Selected Interviews and Other Writings 1972–1977*. Ed. Colin Gordon, trans. Colin Gordon, et al. Pantheon: New York, 1980. 134–45.
———. "A Preface to Transgression." *Language, Counter-Memory, Practice*, 29–52.
Foucault, Michel, and Gilles Deleuze. "Intellectuals and Power." Foucault, *Language, Counter-Memory, Practice*, 205–17.
Frank, Lawrence. *Victorian Detective Fiction and the Nature of Evidence: The Scientific Investigations of Poe, Dickens and Doyle*. Gordonsville: Palgrave Macmillan, 2003.
Freedman, Carl. *Critical Theory and Science Fiction*. Hanover: University Press of New England, 2000.
———. "Towards a Theory of Paranoia: The Science Fiction of Philip K. Dick." Umland 7–17.
Freud, Sigmund. "Beyond the Pleasure Principle." *The Standard Edition of the Complete Psychological Works of Sigmund Freud. Volume XVIII. (1920–1922)*. Trans. J. Strachey. London: Hogarth Press, Institute of Psycho-analysis, 1981. 7–64.
———. *The Psychopathology of Everyday Life*. *The Standard Edition of the Complete Psychological Works of Sigmund Freud. Volume VI. (1901)*. Trans. J. Strachey. London: Hogarth Press, Institute of Psycho-analysis, 1981.
———. "The Uncanny." *The Standard Edition of the Complete Psychological Works of Sigmund Freud. Volume XVII. (1917–1919)*. Trans. J. Strachey. London: Hogarth Press, Institute of Psycho-analysis, 1975. 217–52.
Frye, Northrop. *Anatomy of Criticism. Four Essays*. Princeton: Princeton University Press, 1973.
Genette, Gérard. *Palimpsests: Literature in the Second Degree*. Trans. Channa Newman and Claude Doubinsky. Lincoln: University of Nebraska Press, 1997.
Gilbert, Sandra M., and Susan Gubar. *The Madwoman in the Attic. The Woman Writer and the Nineteenth-Century Literary Imagination*. New Haven: Yale University Press, 1979.
Gill, Gillian. *Agatha Christie: The Woman and Her Mysteries*. New York: Free Press, 1990.
Ginzburg, Carlo. "Morelli, Freud and Sherlock Holmes: Clues and Scientific Method." Bennett 252–76.

Grant, Glenn. "Transcendence Through Detournement in William Gibson's *Neuromancer*." *Science Fiction Studies* 17.1 (1990): 41–49.

Grosz, Elizabeth. *Space, Time and Perversion. Essays on the Politics of Bodies*. New York: Routledge, 1995.

Haraway, Donna. "A Manifesto for Cyborgs: Science, Technology, and Socialist Feminism in the 1980s." *The Haraway Reader*. Ed. Donna Haraway. New York: Routledge, 2004. 7–46.

Harries, Karsten. "Nietzsche's Labyrinths: Variations on an Ancient Theme." *Nietzsche and "An Architecture of Our Minds."* Ed. Alexandra Kostka and Irving Wohlfarth. Los Angeles: Getty Research Institute for the History of Art and the Humanities, 1999. 35–52.

Harvey, David. *The Condition of Postmodernity: An Enquiry into the Origins of Cultural Change*. Cambridge: Blackwell, 1997.

Hayles, N. Katherine. *Chaos Bound. Orderly Disorder in Contemporary Literature and Science*. Ithaca: Cornell University Press, 1991.

———. *How We Became Posthuman: Virtual Bodies in Cybernetics, Literature and Informatics*. Chicago: University of Chicago Press, 1999.

———. "(Un)masking the Agent: Stanislaw Lem's 'The Mask.'" *The Art and Science of Stanislaw Lem*. Ed. Peter Swirski. Montreal: McGill-Queen's University Press, 2006. 22–46.

Heidegger, Martin. *Being and Time*. Trans. John Macquarrie and Edward Robinson. Malden: Blackwell, 2008.

———. "Building, Dwelling, Thinking." *Basic Writings from "Being and Time" (1927) to "The Task of Thinking" (1964)*. Ed. David Farrel Krell. London: Routledge and Kegan Paul, 1978. 319–39.

Helford, Elyce Rae. "'We are only seeking Man': Gender, Psychoanalysis, and Stanislaw Lem's *Solaris*." *Science Fiction Studies* 19.2 (1992): 167–77.

Hemmingson, Michael. "The Canon Is Not Sacred: Public Domain and *The League of Extraordinary Gentlemen*." *Science Fiction Studies* 36.2 (2009): 375–78.

Hidalgo-Downing, Laura. *Negation, Text Worlds, and Discourse: The Pragmatics of Fiction. Advances in Discourse Processes. Vol. LXVI*. Stamford: Ablex, 2000.

Hills, Matt. *Fan Cultures*. London: Routledge, 2004.

———. "Mapping Fantasy's Narrative Spaces." *Terry Pratchett: Guilty of Literature*. Ed. Andrew M. Butler, Edward James and Farah Mendlesohn. Baltimore: Old Earth Books, 2004. 217–37.

———. *The Pleasures of Horror*. London: Continuum, 2005.

Holland, Norman. "Text — Unity — Identity — Self." *Reader-Response Criticism: From Formalism to Poststructuralism*. Ed. Jane P. Tompkins. Baltimore: Johns Hopkins University Press, 1988. 118–34.

Holquist, Michael. *Dialogism: Bakhtin and His World*. London: Routledge, 1991.

Hühn, Peter. "The Detective as Reader: Narrativity and Reading Concepts in Detective Fiction." *Modern Fiction Studies* 33.3 (1987): 451–66.

Hume, Kathryn. *Fantasy and Mimesis: Responses to Reality in Western Literature*. New York: Methuen, 1984.

Hutcheon, Linda. *Irony's Edge: The Theory and Politics of Irony*. London: Routledge, 1995.

———. *Narcissistic Narrative: The Metafictional Paradox*. Waterloo: Wilfried Laurier University Press, 1980.

———. *A Poetics of Postmodernism: History, Theory, Fiction*. London: Routledge, 1992.

———. *A Theory of Parody: The Teachings of Twentieth-Century Art Forms*. New York: Methuen, 1985.

Huyssen, Andreas. *After the Great Divide. Modernism, Mass Culture, Postmodernism*. London: Macmillan, 1988.

Irigaray, Luce. *Speculum of the Other Woman*. Trans. Gillian C. Gill. Ithaca: Cornell University Press, 1992.

Iser, Wolfgang. *The Act of Reading: A Theory of Aesthetic Response*. Baltimore: Johns Hopkins University Press, 1978.

_____. *The Fictive and the Imaginary: Charting Literary Anthropology*. Baltimore: Johns Hopkins University Press, 1993.
_____. *Prospecting: From Reader Response to Literary Anthropology*. Baltimore: Johns Hopkins University Press, 1989.
Jackson, Rosemary. *Fantasy: the Literature of Subversion*. London: Routledge, 1986.
Jameson, Fredric. "Postmodernism and Consumer Society." *Postmodernism and Its Discontents. Theories, Practices*. Ed. E. Ann Kaplan. London: Verso, 1988. 13–29.
_____. *Postmodernism, or, The Cultural Logic of Late Capitalism*. London: Verso, 1996.
_____. "Progress Versus Utopia; or, Can We Imagine the Future?" *Science Fiction Studies* 9.2 (1982): 147–58.
Jarzebski, Jerzy. "Stanislaw Lem's 'Star Diaries.'" Trans. Franz Rottensteiner and Istvan Csicsery-Ronay, Jr. *Science Fiction Studies* 13.3 (1986): 361–73.
_____. "The World as Code and Labyrinth: Stanislaw Lem's *Memoirs Found in a Bathtub*." Trans. Franz Rottensteiner. *Science Fiction Roots and Branches*. Ed. Rhys Garnett and R. J. Ellis. London: Macmillan, 1990. 79–87.
Jencks, Charles. *The New Paradigm in Architecture: The Language of Postmodernism*. New Haven: Yale University Press, 2002.
Jenkins, Alice. "Tunnel Visions and Underground Geography in Fantasy." *Foundation: The International Review of Science Fiction* 35.98 (2006): 28–43.
Jenkins, Henry. "Introduction: On the Pleasures of *Not* Belonging." *Interfictions 2: An Anthology of Interstitial Writing*. Ed. Delia Sherman and Christopher Barzak. Boston: Interstitial Arts Foundation, 2009. v–xvi.
Kafalenos, Emma. "The Power of Double Coding to Represent New Forms of Representation: *The Truman Show, Dorian Gray*, "Blow-Up," and Whistler's *Caprice in Purple and Gold*." *Poetics Today* 24.1 (2003): 1–33.
Kandel, Michael. "Two Meditations on Stanislaw Lem." *Science Fiction Studies* 13.3 (1986): 374–81.
Kanner, Leo. "Autistic Disturbances of Affective Contact." *Nervous Child* 2 (1943): 217–250.
Kittler, Friedrich A. *Discourse Networks 1800–1900*. Trans. Michael Metteer and Chris Cullens. Stanford: Stanford University Press, 1990.
Knight, Stephen. *Crime Fiction, 1800–1900: Detection, Death, Diversity*. New York: Palgrave Macmillan, 2004.
Kuhn, Thomas S. *The Structure of Scientific Revolutions*. Chicago: University of Chicago Press, 1962.
Lacan, Jacques. *Ecrits: A Selection*. Trans. Alan Sheridan. London: Routledge, 1989.
_____. *The Four Fundamental Concepts of Psycho-analysis*. Ed. Jacques-Alain Miller, trans. Alan Sheridan. London: Hogarth, 1977.
_____. "The Mirror Stage as Formative of the Function of the I as Revealed in Psychoanalytic Experience." *Ecrits: A Selection*, 1–7.
_____. "The Signification of the Phallus." *Ecrits: A Selection*, 281–91.
Lefebvre, Henri. *The Production of Space*. Trans. Donald Nicholson-Smith. Malden: Blackwell, 2009.
Lejeune, Philippe. "The Autobiographical Pact." *On Autobiography*. Ed. Paul John Eakin, trans. Katherine Leary. Minneapolis: University of Minnesota Press, 1989. 3–30.
Lem, Stanislaw. *Microworlds. Writings on Science Fiction and Fantasy*. Ed. Franz Rottensteiner. New York: Harcourt Brace Jovanovich, 1984.
_____. "Philip K. Dick: A Visionary Among the Charlatans." Trans. Robert Abernathy. *Microworlds*, 106–135.
_____. "Reflections on My Life." Trans. Franz Rottensteiner. *Microworlds*, 1–30.
_____. "Robots in Science Fiction." *SF: The Other Side of Realism. Essays on Modern Fantasy and Science Fiction*. Ed. Thomas D. Clareson. Bowling Green: Bowling Green University Press, 1971. 307–25.
Lotman, Jurij M., and B. A. Uspenskij. *The Semiotics of Russian Culture*. Ed. Ann Shukman. Ann Arbor: Dept. of Slavic Languages and Literatures, University of Michigan, 1984.

Luckhurst, Roger. *Science Fiction.* Cambridge: Polity, 2005.
Lugones, Maria. "On Complex Communication." *Hypatia* 21.3 (2006): 75–85.
Lyotard, Jean-François. *The Postmodern Condition: A Report on Knowledge.* Trans. Geoff Bennington. Minneapolis: University of Minnesota Press, 1984.
Malmgren, Carl. *Anatomy of Murder: Mystery, Detective, and Crime Fiction.* Bowling Green: Bowling Green State University Popular Press, 2001.
_____. *Worlds Apart: Narratology of Science Fiction.* Bloomington: Indiana University Press, 1991.
Marx, Karl. *Capital: A Critique of Political Economy.* Trans. Samuel Moore and Edward Aveling, ed. Friedrich Engels. New York: The Modern Library, 1906.
Massey, Doreen. *Space, Place and Gender.* Cambridge: Polity Press, 1996.
McCaffery, Larry. "Introduction: The Desert of the Real." *Storming the Reality Studio. A Casebook of Cyberpunk and Postmodern Science Fiction.* Ed. Larry McCaffery. Durham: Duke University Press, 1991. 1–16.
McHale, Brian. *Constructing Postmodernism.* London: Routledge, 1992.
_____. *Postmodernist Fiction.* London: Routledge, 1987.
McLuhan, Marshall. *Understanding Media: The Extensions of Man.* London: Ark Paperbacks, 1987.
Mendlesohn, Farah. "*Conjunctions 39* and Liminal Fantasy." *Journal of the Fantastic in the Arts* 15.3 (2005): 228–39.
_____. *Rhetorics of Fantasy.* Middletown: Wesleyan University Press, 2008.
_____. "Toward a Taxonomy of Fantasy." *Journal of the Fantastic in the Arts* 13.2 (2002): 169–83.
Merivale, Patricia, and Susan Elisabeth Sweeney. "The Game's Afoot. On the Trail of The Metaphysical Detective Story." *Detecting Texts: The Metaphysical Detective Story from Poe to Postmodernism.* Philadelphia: University of Pennsylvania Press, 1999. 1–24.
Merrill, Robert. "Christie's Narrative Games." *Theory and Practice of Classic Detective Fiction.* Ed. Jerome H. Delamater and Ruth Prigozy. Westport: Greenwood Press, 1997. 87–101.
Metz, Christian. *The Imaginary Signifier: Psychoanalysis and the Cinema.* Ed. Celia Britton, et al. Bloomington: Indiana University Press, 1982.
Mezei, Kathy. "Spinsters, Surveillance and Speech: The Case of Miss Marple, Miss Mole, and Miss Jekyll." *Journal of Modern Literature* 30.2 (2007): 103–20.
Miller, J. Hillis. "The Critic as Host." *Theory Now and Then.* New York: Harvester, 1991. 143–70.
Minkowski, Eugene. "Findings in a Case of Schizophrenic Depression." *Existence: A New Dimension in Psychiatry and Psychology.* Ed. Rolly May et al. New York: Basic Books, 1959. 127–138.
Mitchell, William J. *City of Bits: Space, Place and the Infobahn.* Cambridge: MIT Press, 1995.
Moretti, Franco. *Atlas of the European Novel.* London: Verso, 2007.
_____. "Clues." *Signs Taken for Wonders: Essays in the Sociology of Literary Forms.* London: Verso, 1983. 130–56.
Moskowitz, Sam. *Explorers of the Infinite: Shapers of Science Fiction.* Westport: Hyperion Press, 1974.
Mulvey, Laura. "Visual Pleasure and Narrative Cinema." *Narrative, Apparatus, Ideology: A Film Theory Reader.* Ed. Philip Rosen. New York: Columbia University Press, 1986. 198–209.
Nicholls, Peter. "*Solaris* by Stanislaw Lem." *Foundation. The International Review of Science Fiction* 1.1 (1972): 60–65.
Nietzsche, Friedrich. *Daybreak: Thoughts on the Prejudices of Morality.* Trans. R. J. Hollingdale. Cambridge: Cambridge University Press, 2005.
_____. *Human, All Too Human.* Trans. R. J. Hollingdale. Cambridge: Cambridge University Press, 2005.
_____. *On the Genealogy of Morals.* Trans. Walter Kaufman and R. J. Hollingdale. New York: Vintage, 1989.
_____. "On Truth and Lying in an Extra-Moral Sense." *Friedrich Nietzsche on Rhetoric and*

Language. Ed. and trans. Sander L. Gilman, Carole Blair and David J. Parent. New York: Oxford University Press, 1989. 246–57.

———. *Twilight of the Idols, or How to Philosophize with a Hammer: The Anti-Christ, Ecce Homo, Twilight of the Idols, and Other Writings*. Ed. Aaron Ridley, trans. Judith Norman. Cambridge: Cambridge University Press, 2005. 153–230.

———. *The Will to Power. A New Translation*. Ed. Walter Kaufman, trans. Walter Kaufman and R. J. Hollingdale. New York: Vintage Books, 1968.

Nikolajeva, Maria. *The Magic Code: The Use of Magical Patterns in Fantasy for Children*. Stockholm : Almqvist & Wiksell International, 1988.

Nudelman, Rafail. "Labyrinth, Double and Mask in the Science Fiction of Stanislaw Lem." *Learning from Other Worlds: Estrangement, Cognition, and the Politics of Science Fiction and Utopia*. Ed. Patrick Parrinder. Liverpool: Liverpool University Press, 2000. 178–92.

O'Farrell, Clare. *Michel Foucault*. London: Sage, 2005.

Palmer, Christopher. *Philip K. Dick: Exhilaration and Terror of the Postmodern*. Liverpool: Liverpool University Press, 2003.

Panek, LeRoy. *An Introduction to the Detective Story*. Bowling Green: Popular Press, 1987.

Pavel, Thomas. "Narrative Domains." *Poetics Today* 1.4 (1980): 105–14.

Penfield, Wilder. "The Interpretive Cortex." *Science* 129 (1959): 1719–25.

Philmus, Robert M. "Stanislaw Lem's Futurological Congress as a Metageneric Text." *Visions and Re-visions: (Re)constructing Science Fiction*. Liverpool: Liverpool University Press, 2005. 66–78.

Pierce, Hazel Beasley. *A Literary Symbiosis: Science Fiction/Fantasy Mystery*. Westport: Greenwood Press, 1983.

Pratchett, Terry, Ian Stewart, and Jack Cohen. *The Science of Discworld*. London: Ebury Press, 2000.

Rajchman, John. "Foucault's Art of Seeing." *October* 44 (1988): 88–117.

Rattray, R. S. *Akan-Ashanti Folk-tales: Collected and Translated by Capt. R. S. Rattray and Illustrated by Africans of the Gold Coast Colony*. Oxford: Clarendon, 1930.

Revzin, I. I. "Notes on the Semiotic Analysis of Detective Novels: With Examples from the Novels of Agatha Christie." Trans. Julian Graffy. *New Literary History* 9.2 (1978): 385–88.

Ricoeur, Paul. "Life in Quest of a Narrative." *On Paul Ricoeur: Narrative and Interpretation*. Ed. David Wood. London: Routledge, 1991. 20–33.

Rimmon-Kenan, Shlomith. *Narrative Fiction: Contemporary Poetics*. London: Routledge, 1983.

Rose, Mark. *Alien Encounters: Anatomy of Science Fiction*. Cambridge: Harvard University Press, 1981.

Rossi, Umberto. "Just a Bunch of Words: The Image of the Secluded Family and the Problem of Logos in P. K. Dick's *Time Out of Joint*." *Extrapolation* 37.3 (1996): 195–211.

———. "Radio Free PKD." *Foundation: The International Review of Science Fiction* 37.106 (2009): 10–28.

Rust, Richard Dilworth. "Liminality in *The Turn of The Screw*." *Studies in Short Fiction* 25 (1988): 441–46.

Ryan, Marie-Laure. *Avatars of Story*. Minneapolis: University of Minnesota Press, 2006.

———. "The Modal Structure of Narrative Universes." *Poetics Today* 6.4 (1985): 717–65.

———. "Possible Worlds and Accessibility Relations: A Semantic Typology of Fiction." *Poetics Today* 12.3 (1990): 553–76.

———. "Stacks, Frames and Boundaries, or Narrative as Computer Language." *Poetics Today* 11.4 (1990): 873–99.

Saler, Michael. "'Clap If You Believe in Sherlock Holmes': Mass Culture and the Re-Enchantment of Modernity." *The Historical Journal* 46.3 (2003): 599–622.

Sawyer, Andy. "Narrativum and Lies-to-Children: 'Palatable Instruction' in *The Science of Discworld*." *HJEAS: Hungarian Journal of English and American Studies* 6.1 (2000): 155–78.

Schweitzer, Darrell. "Tapdancing on the Shoulders of Giants: Neil Gaiman's *Stardust* and its Antecedents." *The Neil Gaiman Reader*. Ed. Darrell Schweitzer. Rockville: Wildside, 2007. 115–21.

Sebeok, Thomas A., and Jean Umiker-Sebeok. "'You Know My Method': A Juxtaposition of Charles S. Peirce and Sherlock Holmes." Eco and Sebeok, *The Sign of Three*, 11–54.
Shapiro, Gary. *Nietzschean Narratives*. Bloomington: Indiana University Press, 1989.
Shaw, Marion, and Sabine Vanacker. *Reflecting on Miss Marple*. New York: Routledge, 1991.
Shklovsky, Viktor. "Sherlock Holmes and the Mystery Story." *Theory of Prose*. Trans. Benjamin Sher. Urbana: Dalkey Archive Press, 1998. 101–16.
Silverman, Kaja. *The Subject of Semiotics*. New York: Oxford University Press, 1983.
Smethurst, Paul. *The Postmodern Chronotope: Reading Space and Time in Contemporary Fiction*. Amsterdam: Rodopi, 2000.
Soja, Edward W. *Postmodern Geographies: The Reassertion of Space in Critical Social Theory*. London: Verso, 1990.
Spanos, William J. "The Detective and the Boundary. Some Notes on the Postmodern Literary Imagination." *Repetitions: The Postmodern Occasion in Literature and Culture*. Baton Rouge: Louisiana State University Press, 1987. 13–49.
Stallybrass, Peter, and Allon White. *The Politics and Poetics of Transgression*. London: Methuen, 1986.
Steiner, T. R. "Stanislaw Lem's Detective Stories: A Genre Extended." *Modern Fiction Studies* 29.3 (1983): 451–62.
Sterling, Bruce. "Preface from *Mirrorshades*." *Storming the Reality Studio: A Casebook of Cyberpunk and Postmodern Science Fiction*. Ed. Larry McCaffery. Durham: Duke University Press, 1991. 343–48.
Stockwell, Peter. *The Poetics of Science Fiction*. Harlow: Longman, 2000.
Suvin, Darko. "The Open-Ended Parables of Stanislaw Lem and *Solaris*." *Solaris; Translated from the French by Joanna Kilmartin and Steve Cox; Afterword by Darko Suvin*. New York: Berkley, 1972. 212–23.
———. "P. K. Dick's Opus: Artifice as Refuge and World View (Introductory Reflections)." *Science Fiction Studies* 2.1 (1975): 9–22.
Swanstrom, Linda. "Landscapes and Locodescription in William Gibson's *Neuromancer*." *Foundation: The International Review of Science Fiction* 35.98 (2006): 16–27
Swirski, Peter. *Between Literature and Science: Poe, Lem and Explorations in Aesthetics, Cognitive Science and Literary Knowledge*. Montreal: McGill-Queen's University Press, 2000.
———. *From Lowbrow to Nobrow*. Montreal: McGill-Queen's University Press, 2005.
———. "Playing a Game of Ontology: A Postmodern Reading of *The Futurological Congress*." *Extrapolation* 33.1 (1992): 32–40.
Symons, Julian. *Bloody Murder. From the Detective Story to the Crime Novel: A History*. London: Faber and Faber, 1972.
Szakolczai, Arpad. *Reflexive Historical Sociology: Routledge Studies in Social and Political Thought*. London: Routledge, 2000.
Thomsen, Christian W. "Robot Ethics and Robot Parody: Remarks on Isaac Asimov's *I, Robot* and Some Critical Essays and Short Stories by Stanislaw Lem." *The Mechanical God. Machines in Science Fiction*. Ed. Thomas P. Dunn and Richard D. Erlich. Westport: Greenwood Press, 1982. 27–39.
Todorov, Tzvetan. *The Fantastic. A Structural Approach to a Literary Genre*. Trans. Richard Howard. Cleveland: Press of Case Western Reserve University, 1975.
———. *Introduction to Poetics*. Trans. Richard Howard. Minneapolis: University of Minnesota Press, 1981.
———. "The Limits of Edgar Poe." *Genres in Discourse*. Trans. Catherine Porter. Cambridge: Cambridge University Press, 1990. 93–102.
———. "The Typology of Detective Fiction." *The Poetics of Prose*. Trans. Richard Howard. Ithaca: Cornell University Press, 1977. 42–52.
Tolkien, J. R. R. "On Fairy-Stories." *Tree and Leaf*. London: HarperCollins, 2001. 3–81.
Tomas, David. "Old Rituals for New Space: *Rites de Passage* and William Gibson's Cultural Model of Cyberspace." *Cyberspace: First Steps*. Ed. Michael Benedikt. Cambridge: MIT Press, 1994. 31–48.

Traill, Nancy H. *Possible Worlds of the Fantastic: The Rise of the Paranormal Fiction.* Toronto: University of Toronto Press, 1996.
Truzzi, Marcello. "Sherlock Holmes. Applied Social Psychologist." Eco and Sebeok, *The Sign of Three*, 55–80.
Turner, Victor. "Liminal to Liminoid, in Play, Flow, Ritual: An Essay in Comparative Symbology." *From Ritual to Theatre. The Human Seriousness of Play.* New York: PAJ Publications, 1982. 20–60.
_____. *The Ritual Process: Structure and Antistructure.* Ithaca: Cornell University Press, 1977.
Umland, Samuel J., ed. *Philip K. Dick: Contemporary Critical Interpretations.* Westport: Greenwood Press, 1995.
Virilio, Paul. *The Information Bomb.* Trans. Chris Turner. London: Verso, 2000.
von Franz, Marie-Louise. "The Process of Individuation." *Man and His Symbols.* Ed. Carl G. Jung, et al. New York: Dell-Bantam, 1964. 159–254.
Walker, Daniel. "Going After Scientism Through Science Fiction." *Extrapolation* 48.1 (2007): 152–68.
Watson, Ian. "Le Guin's *Lathe of Heaven* and the Role of Dick: The False Reality as Mediator." *Science Fiction Studies* 2.1 (1975): 67–76.
Weinstone, Ann. "Resisting Monsters: Notes on *Solaris*." *Science Fiction Studies* 21.2 (1994): 173–90.
Werth, Paul. *Text Worlds: Representing Conceptual Space in Discourse.* Harlow: Longman, 1999.
Westfahl, Gary. "'The Gernsback Continuum': William Gibson in the Context of Science Fiction." *Fiction 2000. Cyberpunk and the Future of Narrative.* Ed. George Slusser and Tom Shippey. Athens: University of Georgia Press, 1992. 88–108.
White, Hayden. "The Value of Narrativity in the Representation of Reality." *Critical Inquiry* 7.1 (1980): 5–27.
Whittle, David B. *Cyberspace: The Human Dimension.* New York: W. H. Freeman, 1997.
Winnicott, D. W. *Playing and Reality.* Harmondsworth: Penguin Books, 1982.
Wolfe, Gary K. *The Known and the Unknown: The Iconography of Science Fiction.* Kent: Kent State University Press, 1979.
_____. "Locus Looks at Books: Gary K. Wolfe." Rev. of *Anansi Boys*, by Neil Gaiman. *Locus* 538 (November 2005): 15+.
_____. "Locus Looks at Books: Gary K. Wolfe." Rev. of *The Graveyard Book,* by Neil Gaiman. *Locus* 570 (July 2008): 19.
Wolfe, Gary K., and Amelia Beamer. "21st Century Stories." *Foundation: The International Review of Science Fiction* 37.103 (2008): 16–37.
Wolk, Anthony. "The Swiss Connection: Psychological Systems in the Novels of Philip K. Dick." Umland 101–26.
Wollen, Peter. "'Ridleyville' and Los Angeles." *The Hieroglyphics of Space: Reading and Experiencing the Modern Metropolis.* Ed. Neil Leach. New York: Routledge, 2002. 236–43.
Yossef, Abraham "Understanding Lem: 'Solaris' Revisited." *Foundation. The International Review of Science Fiction* 18.46 (1989): 51–58.
Zipes, Jack. *Breaking the Magic Spell: Radical Theories of Folk and Fairy Tales.* Austin: University of Texas, 1979.
_____. "Cross-Cultural Connections and the Contamination of the Classical Fairy Tale." *The Great Fairy Tale Tradition*, 845–69.
_____, ed. *The Great Fairy Tale Tradition: From Straparola and Basile to the Brothers Grimm. Selected, Translated and Edited by Jack Zipes.* New York: W.W. Norton, 2001.
Zukin, Sharon. *Landscapes of Power: From Detroit to Disney World.* Berkeley: University of California Press, 1991.

Fiction (Print)

Adams, Douglas. *The Hitch Hiker's Guide to the Galaxy*. London: Pan Books, 1980.
———. *Mostly Harmless*. London: Pan Books, 1992.
———. *The Restaurant at the End of the Universe*. London: Pan Books, 1980.
Aiken, Joan. *All You've Ever Wanted, and Other Stories*. London: Cape, 1953.
Bester, Alfred. *The Demolished Man*. London: Millennium, 1999.
———. "Fondly Fahrenheit." *The Ultimate Cyberpunk*. Ed. Pat Cadigan. New York: Ibooks, 2002. 1–26.
Borges, Jorge Luis. "The Circular Ruins." Trans. James E. Irby. *Labyrinths*, 72–77.
———. "The Garden of Forking Paths." Trans. Donald A. Yates. *Labyrinths*, 44–54.
———. *Labyrinths. Selected Stories and Other Writings*. Ed. Donald A. Yates and James E. Irby. Harmondsworth: King Penguin, 1981.
———. "The Two Kings and the Two Labyrinths." *Collected Fictions*. Trans. Andrew Hurley. London: Penguin Books, 1999. 263–64.
———. "'There Are More Things.'" Trans. Norman Thomas di Giovanni. *The Book of Sand*. Harmondsworth: Penguin, 1979. 35–42.
Cadigan, Pat. *Tea from an Empty Cup*. New York: Tor, 1998.
Calamai, Peter. "The Steamship Friesland." Campbell and Prepolec, *Gaslight Grimoire*, 159–86.
Campbell, J. R., and Charles Prepolec, ed. *Gaslight Grimoire. Fantastic Tales of Sherlock Holmes*. Calgary: Edge Science Fiction and Fantasy, 2008.
Carroll, Lewis. *Through the Looking Glass*. London: Penguin Books, 1994.
Carter, Angela. "The Snow Child." *The Bloody Chamber, And Other Stories*. New York: Penguin, 1993. 91–92.
Chandler, Raymond. *The Big Sleep*. New York: Vintage, 1988.
Christie, Agatha. *4.50 from Paddington*. London: HarperCollins, 1993.
———. *Appointment with Death*. London: HarperCollins, 2001.
———. *At Bertram's Hotel*. London: HarperCollins, 2002.
———. "The Bloodstained Pavement." *The Thirteen Problems*, 44–53.
———. "The Blue Geranium." *The Thirteen Problems*, 78–94.
———. *The Body in the Library*. London: HarperCollins, 2005.
———. *Cards on the Table*. London: Pan Books, 1973.
———. *Crooked House*. London: HarperCollins, 2008.
———. *Five Little Pigs*. London: HarperCollins, 2001.
———. Foreword. *The Mysterious Mr. Quin*. n. pag.
———. "The Four Suspects." *The Thirteen Problems*, 111–126.
———. "Four-and-Twenty Blackbirds." *The Adventure of the Christmas Pudding and a Selection of Entrees*. London: HarperCollins, 1994.
———. "Harlequin's Lane." *The Mysterious Mr. Quin*, 361–96.
———. "The Idol House of Astarte." *The Thirteen Problems*, 18–32.
———. "Ingots of Gold." *The Thirteen Problems*, 32–44.
———. "The Man from the Sea." *The Mysterious Mr. Quin*, 155–97.
———. *The Murder of Roger Ackroyd*. New York: Pocket Books, 1975.
———. *Murder on the Orient Express*. London: HarperCollins, 2001.
———. *The Mysterious Affair at Styles*. London: HarperCollins, 2001.
———. *The Mysterious Mr. Quin*. London: HarperCollins, 2003.
———. *Ordeal by Innocence*. Glasgow: Fontana Books, 1963.
———. "Strange Jest." *Miss Marple's Final Cases and Two Other Stories*. London: Collins, 1979. 31–44.
———. *The Thirteen Problems*. London: Collins, 1981.
———. "The Tuesday Night Club." *The Thirteen Problems*, 7–18.
Conan Doyle, Arthur. "The Adventure of Charles Augustus Milverton." *The Original Illustrated*, 645–56.

———. "The Adventure of the Crooked Man." *The Original Illustrated*, 377–87.
———. "The Adventure of the Dying Detective." *The Original Illustrated*, 827–37.
———. "The Adventure of the Empty House." *The Original Illustrated*, 554–68.
———. "The Adventure of the Norwood Builder." *The Original Illustrated*, 569–82.
———. "The Adventure of the Priory School." *The Original Illustrated*, 613–30.
———. "The Adventure of the Six Napoleons." *The Original Illustrated*, 657–69.
———. *The Adventures of Sherlock Holmes*. Harmondsworth: Penguin, 1985.
———. "The Blue Carbuncle." *The Adventures of Sherlock Holmes*, 144–64.
———. "The Five Orange Pips." *The Adventures of Sherlock Holmes*, 100–19.
———. *The Hound of the Baskervilles. The Original Illustrated*, 449–551.
———. *The Land of Mist. The Lost World*, 239–419.
———. *The Lost World and Other Stories*. Ware: Wordsworth Classics, 1995.
———. *The Original Illustrated "Strand" Sherlock Holmes. The Complete Facsimile Edition*. Ware: Wordsworth Edition, 1996.
———. "The Poison Belt." *The Lost World*, 171–238.
———. "A Scandal in Bohemia." *The Adventures of Sherlock Holmes*, 9–32.
———. *The Sign of the Four. The Sign of the Four, A Scandal in Bohemia and Other Stories*. New York: A. L. Burt, 1920. 1–165.
———. *A Study in Scarlet. The Original Illustrated*, 11–63.
———. "When the World Screamed." *The Lost World*, 437–61.
Coover, Robert. "The Dead Queen." *Quarterly Review of Literature* 18 (1973): 304–13.
Dick, Philip K. "Adjustment Team." *The Second Variety*, 269–87.
———. "The Commuter." *The Second Variety*, 129–39.
———. *The Cosmic Puppets*. London: HarperCollins, 1998.
———. *Counter-clock World*. London: Hodder and Stoughton, 1977.
———. *Do Androids Dream of Electric Sheep? Filmed as* Blade Runner. London: Gollancz, 2004.
———. *Dr. Bloodmoney*. London: Gollancz, 2004.
———. "The Electric Ant." *We Can Remember It for You*, 225–39.
———. *Eye in the Sky*. New York: Ace Books, 1957.
———. "Faith of Our Fathers." *We Can Remember It for You*, 197–222.
———. "I Hope I Shall Arrive Soon." *We Can Remember It For You*, 359–73.
———. "Introduction: How to Build a Universe that Doesn't Fall Apart Two Days Later." *I Hope I Shall Arrive Soon*. Ed. Mark Hurst and Paul Williams. London: Grafton, 1988. 7–34.
———. *Lies, Inc.* London: Panther Books, 1985.
———. "The Little Black Box." *We Can Remember It for You*, 1–21.
———. *The Man in the High Castle*. Harmondsworth: Penguin, 1976.
———. *Martian Time-Slip*. New York: Vintage, 1995.
———. *A Maze of Death*. London: Panther, 1984.
———. "The Minority Report." *Minority Report*, 71–102.
———. *Minority Report: The Collected Short Stories of Philip K. Dick. Volume Four*. London: Millennium, 2000.
———. "Notes." *Minority Report*, 375–80.
———. *Radio Free Albemuth*. New York: Avon Books, 1985.
———. *A Scanner Darkly*. New York: Vintage Books, 1991.
———. "Second Variety." *The Second Variety*, 15–52.
———. *The Second Variety. The Collected Short Stories of Philip K. Dick. Volume Two*. London: Millennium, 1999.
———. "Small Town." *The Second Variety*, 341–53.
———. *The Three Stigmata of Palmer Eldritch*. London: Triad, 1978.
———. *Time Out of Joint*. Harmondsworth: Penguin, 1984.
———. *Ubik*. New York: Bantam, 1977.
———. *We Can Build You*. London: HarperCollins, 1997.
———. *We Can Remember It for You Wholesale: The Collected Short Stories of Philip K. Dick. Volume Five*. London: Millennium, 2000.

―――. "What the Dead Men Say." *Minority Report*, 245–88.
Doctorow, Cory. *Someone Comes to Town, Someone Leaves Town*. New York: Tor Books, 2005.
Ellison, Ralph. *Invisible Man*. London: Penguin Books, 2001.
Gaiman, Neil. *American Gods*. New York: HarperTorch, 2002.
―――. "An Introduction." *Smoke and Mirrors*. 35–48.
―――. *Anansi Boys*. New York: HarperTorch, 2006.
―――. "Chivalry." *Smoke and Mirrors*. 35–48.
―――. Foreword. *Lud-in-the-Mist*. By Hope Mirrlees. Cold Spring Harbor: Cold Spring Press, 2005. 7–8.
―――. *Fragile Things. Short Fictions and Wonders*. London: Headline 2007.
―――. *The Graveyard Book*. London: Bloomsbury, 2008
―――. "How to Talk to Girls at Parties." *Fragile Things*, 309–328.
―――. "Murder Mysteries." *Smoke and Mirrors*. 339–370.
―――. *Neverwhere*. New York: HarperTorch, 2001.
―――. "Only the End of the World Again." *Smoke and Mirrors*. 201–218.
―――. *The Sandman: The Doll's House*. New York: DC Comics, 1995.
―――. "Shoggoth's Old Peculiar." *Smoke and Mirrors*. 173–84.
―――. *Smoke and Mirrors: Short Fictions and Illusions*. London: Headline, 1999.
―――. "Snow, Glass, Apples." *Smoke and Mirrors*. 371–79.
―――. "A Study in Emerald." *Fragile Things*, 25–56.
Gaiman, Neil, and Michael Reaves. *Interworld*. New York: HarperCollins, 2007.
Gibson, William. *Burning Chrome*. New York: Ace Books, 1986.
―――. *Count Zero*. New York: Ace Books, 1987.
―――. "The Gernsback Continuum." *Burning Chrome*, 23–35.
―――. *Idoru*. London: Penguin, 1997.
―――. "Johnny Mnemonic." *Burning Chrome*, 1–22.
―――. *Mona Lisa Overdrive*. London: Victor Gollancz, 1988.
―――. *Neuromancer*. New York: Ace Books, 1984.
―――. *Spook Country*. New York: G. P. Putnam's Sons, 2007
Gibson, William, and Bruce Sterling. *The Difference Engine*. London: Victor Gollancz, 1990.
Heinlein, Robert. *The Puppet Masters*. New York: Ballantine, 1990.
Hessel, Franz. "The Seventh Dwarf." *The Penguin Book of Western Fairy Tales*. Ed. Jack Zipes. London: Penguin Books, 1993. 613–14.
James, Henry. *The Turn of the Screw. A Casebook on Henry James's "The Turn of the Screw."* Ed. Gerald Willen. New York: Thomas Y. Crowell, 1961. 3–94.
Kafka, Franz. "In the Penal Settlement." *Metamorphosis and Other Stories*. Trans. Willa and Edward Muir. London: Vintage, 1999. 167–99.
Kelly, James Patrick, and John Kessel, ed. *Rewired: The Post-Cyberpunk Anthology*. San Francisco: Tachyon, 2007.
Lee, Tanith. "Red as Blood." *Red as Blood: Tales from the Sisters Grimmer*. New York: Wollheim, 1983. 18–27.
Lem, Stanislaw. "Altruizine, or a True Account of How Bonhomius the Hermetic Hermit Tried to Bring about Happiness, and What Came of It." *The Cyberiad*, 249–79.
―――. *The Chain of Chance*. Trans. Louis Iribarne. New York: Harcourt Brace Jovanovich, 1978.
―――. *The Cyberiad. Fables for the Cybernetic Age*. Trans. Michael Kandel. San Diego: Harvest, 1985.
―――. *Fiasco*. Trans. Michael Kandel. London: Futura Publications, 1989.
―――. "Further Reminiscences of Ijon Tichy." *Memoirs of a Space Traveller*. Trans. Joel Stern and Maria Swiecicka-Ziemianek. London: Mandarin, 35–110.
―――. *The Futurological Congress*. Trans. Michael Kandel. New York: Avon, 1976.
―――. *His Master's Voice*. Trans. Michael Kandel. Evanston: Northwestern University Press, 1999.
―――. "The Inquest." Trans. Louis Iribarne and Magdalena Majcherczyk. *More Tales of Pirx the Pilot*, 90–161.
―――. *The Investigation*. Trans. Adele Milch. London: Andre Deutsch, 1992.

_____. *The Invincible*. Trans. Wendayne Ackerman. *Tales of Pirx the Pilot—Return from the Stars—The Invincible*. Harmondsworth: King Penguin, 1982. 413–590.
_____. "The Mask." *Mortal Engines*. Trans. Michael Kandel. Orlando: Harvest, 1992. 181–239.
_____. *Memoirs Found in a Bathtub*. Trans. Michael Kandel and Christine Rose. New York: Avon, 1976.
_____. *More Tales of Pirx the Pilot*. London: Mandarin, 1990.
_____. *Peace on Earth*. Trans. Elinor Ford and Michael Kandel. San Diego: Harvest, 1994.
_____. "Pirx's Tale." Trans. Louis Iribarne and Magdalena Majcherczyk. *More Tales of Pirx the Pilot*, 3–20.
_____. *Return from the Stars*. Trans. Barbara Marszal and Frank Simpson. New York: Harcourt Brace Jovanovich, 1980.
_____. "The Seventh Sally, Or How Trurl's Own Perfection Led to No Good." *The Cyberiad*, 161–71.
_____. *Solaris*. Trans. Joanna Kilmartin and Steve Cox. London: Faber and Faber, 1991.
_____. *The Star Diaries*. Trans. Michael Kandel. London: Futura Publications, 1978.
_____. "Tale of the Three Storytelling Machines of King Genius." *The Cyberiad*, 173–248.
Lewis, C. S. *The Lion, The Witch and the Wardrobe*. London: HarperCollins, 2004.
_____. *The Magician's Nephew*. London: HarperCollins Children's Books, 1998.
Link, Kelly. "Lull." *Conjunctions 39: The New Wave Fabulists*. Ed. Bradford Morrow and Peter Straub. Annandale-on-Hudson: Bard College, 2003. 53–83.
_____. "Magic for Beginners." *Magic for Beginners*. Orlando: Harcourt, 2006. 203–57.
Lovecraft, H. P. "The Outsider." *Tales*. Ed. Peter Straub. New York: The Library of America, 2005. 8–14.
Meyer, Nicholas. *The Seven Per Cent Solution: Being a Reprint from the Reminiscences of John H. Watson, M.D.* London: Coronet Books, 1976.
Mirrlees, Hope. *Lud-in-the-Mist*. Cold Spring Harbor: Cold Spring Press, 2005.
Newman, Kim. "The Red Planet League." Campbell and Prepolec, *Gaslight Grimoire*, 273–317.
Noon, Jeff. *Vurt*. London: Pan Publications, 2001.
Poe, Edgar Allan. "The Murders in the Rue Morgue." *Poe's Tales*, 378–410.
_____. "The Mystery of Marie Roget." *Poe's Tales*, 410–54.
_____. *Poe's Tales of Mystery and Imagination*. London: J. M. Dent & Sons, 1959.
_____. "The Purloined Letter." *Poe's Tales*, 454–71.
_____. "Thou Art the Man." *Poe's Tales*, 471–84.
Pratchett, Terry, and Neil Gaiman. *Good Omens. The Nice and Accurate Prophecies of Agnes Nutter, Witch*. London: Corgi, 1991.
Reaves, Michael, and John Pelan. *Shadows over Baker Street*. New York: Ballantine Books, 2003.
Rice, Anne. *The Vampire Lestat. The Second Book in the Chronicles of the Vampires*. London: Futura Books, 1996.
Sayers, Dorothy. *Five Red Herrings*. New York: HarperTorch, 1995.
Shelley, Mary. *Frankenstein, or The Modern Prometheus*. Ware: Wordsworth Classics, 1999.
Sterling, Bruce, and Lewis Shiner. "Mozart in Mirrorshades." *Mirrorshades: The Cyberpunk Anthology*. Ed. Bruce Sterling. New York: Arbor House, 1986. 223–39.
Stross, Charles. *The Atrocity Archives*. Urbana: Golden Gryphon Press, 2004.
Vonnegut, Kurt. *Slaughterhouse-Five, or the Children's Crusade. A Duty-Dance with Death*. London: Vintage, 2000.
Wellman, Manly Wade, and Wade Wellman. *The Further Adventures of Sherlock Holmes: War of the Worlds*. London: Titan Books, 2009.

Online Sources

Barlow, John Perry. "Crime and Puzzlement." *Electronic Frontier Foundation*. Accessed 30.1.2010. <http://w2.eff.org/Misc/Publications/John_Perry_Barlow/HTML/crime_and_puzzlement_1.html>

Gaiman, Neil. "'I Cthulhu,' or What's A Tentacle-Faced Thing Like Me Doing In A Sunken City Like This (Latitude 47° 9' S, Longitude 126° 43' W)?" *Neil Gaiman.* Harper Collins ublishers. Accessed 30.1.2010 <http://www.neilgaiman.com/p/Cool_Stuff/Short_Stories/I_Cthulhu>

Person, Lawrence. "Notes Toward a Postcyberpunk Manifesto." *Information DataBase The Cyberpunk Project.* Accessed 30.1.2010. <http://project.cyberpunk.ru/idb/notes_toward_a_post cyberpunk_manifesto.html>

Rose, Frank. "Philip K. Dick Goes Legit With Library of America Canon." *Wired* 15.06 (2007): n.p. Accessed 30.1.2010. <http://www.wired.com/culture/culturereviews/magazine/15-06/pl_print>

Play (Print)

Christie, Agatha. *The Mousetrap. The Mousetrap and Other Plays.* New York: Bantam, 1981. 279–358.

Films

The 13th Floor. Dir. Josef Rusnak. Columbia and TriStar, 1999.
Aliens. Dir. James Cameron. Twentieth Century–Fox, 1986.
Animatrix. Dir. Andy Jones et al. Warner, 2003.
Blade Runner. Dir. Ridley Scott. Warner, 1982.
Dark City. Dir. Alex Proyas. New Line Cinema, 1998.
eXistenZ. Dir. David Cronenberg. Alliance Atlantis, 1999.
Groundhog Day. Dir. Harold Ramis. Columbia Pictures, 1993.
Johnny Mnemonic. Dir. Robert Longo. Sony, 1995.
The Matrix. Dir. Andy Wachowski and Larry Wachowski. Warner, 1999.
The Matrix Reloaded. Dir. Andy Wachowski and Larry Wachowski. Warner, 2003.
The Matrix Revolutions. Dir. Andy Wachowski and Larry Wachowski. Warner, 2003.
Metropolis. Dir. Fritz Lang. UFA, 1927.
Modern Times. Dir. Charlie Chaplin. United Artists, 1936.
Murder, She Said. Dir. George Pollock. George H. Brown Productions, 1961.
Pan's Labyrinth. Dir. Guillermo del Toro. Tequila Gang, 2006.
Scream. Dir. Wes Craven. Dimension Films, 1996.
Videodrome. Dir. David Cronenberg. Canadian Film Development Corporation, 1983.

Index

Adams, Douglas 7, 16, 17, 74, 84, 121, 176, 180; *Hitchhiker's Guide...* 84; *Mostly Harmless* 16, 84, 180
"Adjustment Team" 125, 135
Adorno, Theodor 172
Aiken, Joan 83
Aldiss, Brian W. 22
Alexander, Bethany 62, 65
Aliens (film) 117
alternate history 4, 20, 29, 64, 123, 150–154, 161, 169, 179
"Altruizine" 114, 179
American Gods 54, 75, 80, 177
Amis, Martin 4
Anansi Boys 54, 56, 69–70, 71, 74, 177
android 90, 128, 141, 142, 145; *see also* schizoid android
Animatrix (film) 144
anthropology 1, 171, 177
anthropomorphism 93, 95, 99, 104, 118
anti-detective fiction 25, 38, 92, 170; *see also* metaphysical detective fiction
anti-utopia *see* dystopia
Appointment with Death 40, 45
arcade 19, 102, 110, 112
architecture 2, 3, 15, 23, 29, 40, 107, 110, 121, 122, 123–128, 130, 131, 161, 179
ars poetica 63
Art Deco 123, 125, 128
astrology 87, 98
astronaut 90, 92, 99, 101, 103, 115, 116, 118, 139, 144, 168
astronomy 87, 97, 98
At Bertram's Hotel 26, 43, 48, 167
Attebery, Brian 55, 56, 174
Auster, Paul 4
automaton 90, 92, 116, 144; *see also* robot
automobile 126, 128, 132

avant-garde 20, 23, 125, 126, 158, 172, 179, 180

Bacchilega, Christina 68, 70, 112
Bachelard, Gaston 168, 173
Bakhtin, Mikhail 9, 24, 34–39, 44, 46, 54, 74–75, 116, 163; *see also* carnival; chronotope; grotesque body; heteroglossia
Bal, Mieke 56, 65, 71, 72, 75, 83, 176
Ballard, J.G. 22, 126
Barlow, John Perry 133, 179
Barnard, Robert 35, 36, 40, 43, 45, 49
Barr, Marleen S. 70, 177
Barthes, Roland 31, 34, 37, 128–129, 169, 175
Baudrillard 1, 21, 23, 27, 28, 107, 111–113, 123, 124, 134, 136–137, 142, 169
Bauman, Zygmunt 122, 123, 131–132, 166
Beckett, Samuel 27
Belsey, Catherine 32
Benedikt, Michael 125, 161
Benjamin, Walter 19, 26, 38, 51, 110, 126, 131–132, 144–145, 166, 172; *see also* flaneur
Bényei Tamás 170
Bester, Alfred 22, 133, 158
Bhabha, Homi 12–13, 18, 19, 24, 27, 29, 112, 121, 163, 178; *see also* mimicry
binary opposition 3, 9, 10, 11–13, 143, 165, 174; *see also* duality
Blade Runner (film) 90, 124, 128, 129, 179
"The Bloodstained Pavement" 48, 50
"The Blue Geranium" 49
body 9, 63, 91, 100, 106, 111, 112, 116–117, 138, 140–144, 156, 164, 167, 178, 179; *see also* grotesque body
The Body in the Library 40
Booth, Wayne C. 58–59, 81, 176
border (borderline) 1, 3, 5, 13, 14, 24, 55,

77, 79, 98, 119, 121, 122, 131, 149, 168, 171, 172, 173, 174; *see also* boundary; frontier

Borges, Jorge Luis 4, 15, 16, 20, 25, 82, 108, 109, 119, 130; "The Circular Ruins" 15, 130; "The Garden of Forking Paths" 16; "The Two Kings" 109; "There Are More Things" 82, 119

boundary 2, 3, 7, 12, 14, 15, 19, 21, 24, 26, 27, 56, 57, 61, 66, 67, 72, 76, 77, 81, 113, 117, 118, 122, 140–142, 163–171, 173, 179; *see also* border; frontier

Boym, Svetlana 128, 141, 148
brand 147, 148
Brand, Dana 32, 38, 39
bridge (game) 37, 175
bridge (large structure) 14, 71, 110, 168, 175
Bukatman, Scott 4, 17, 20, 28, 121–122, 126, 128, 130, 133, 135, 137, 143
Bulgakov, Mikhail 5
Bürger, Peter 32
Burleson, Donald R. 97
butler 47
Butler, Andrew 23, 24, 151, 153, 180
Butler, Judith 27, 112

Caillois, Roger 167
Calamai, Peter 89
Calvino, Italo 4, 108
Canary, Robert H. 152
canon 20, 22, 57, 70, 76, 81–82, 97, 174, 177
car *see* automobile
Cards on the Table 36, 37, 40, 42, 51, 175
Carlson, Marvin 47, 64
carnival 9, 44, 46, 52, 77, 12, 163, 165, 167
Carpentier, Alejo 9
Carroll, Lewis 9, 151, 173
Carroll, Noël 114
Carter, Angela 4, 70
Castells, Manuel 23, 124, 179
causal reversal 9–10
causality 10–11, 35, 87
Cavallaro, Dani 70, 125, 161, 165, 179
center 56, 79, 106, 108, 109, 152, 167, 170, 173; *see also* city center
The Chain of Chance 27, 92–93, 98, 99, 101–103, 110, 118, 119, 166, 168, 174
Challenger, Professor 88–89, 117–118; *see also* Conan Doyle, Arthur; Holmes, Sherlock
Chandler, Raymond 33, 65, 176
"Chivalry" 66–68, 81
Christie, Agatha 5, 19–21, 25–26, 31–53, 54, 55, 61, 64, 65, 85, 92, 140, 164, 166, 167, 169, 170, 175; *Appointment with Death* 40, 45; *At Bertram's Hotel* 26, 43, 48, 167; "The Bloodstained Pavement" 48, 50; "The Blue Geranium" 49; *The Body in the Library* 40; *Cards on the Table* 36, 37, 40, 42, 51, 175; *Crooked House* 26, 40, 44–45, 52, 166, 175; *Five Little Pigs* 42; "Four-and-Twenty Blackbirds" 65; *4.50 from Paddington* 38, 41, 44, 45, 49; "The Four Suspects." 42; "Harlequin's Lane" 39; "The Idol House of Astarte" 48, 49; "Ingots of Gold" 42; "The Man from the Sea" 48; *The Mousetrap* 41, 43, 64, 166; *The Murder of Roger Ackroyd* 40, 61; *Murder on the Orient Express* 26, 40, 44, 51, 166, 175; *The Mysterious Affair at Styles* 36, 38, 41; *The Mysterious Mr. Quin* 44, 49, 50; *Ordeal by Innocence* 26, 40, 45–47, 48, 52, 166; "Strange Jest" 42; *The Thirteen Problems* 26, 38, 42, 48, 49, 50, 167; "The Tuesday Night Club" 47, 49; *see also* Marple, Jane; Poirot, Hercule

chronotope 2, 9, 21, 34–39, 55, 78, 124, 180
"The Circular Ruins" 15, 130
city 59, 76, 92, 99, 107, 109, 110, 122–132, 137, 140–141, 144, 149, 157, 176, 179, 180; *see also* metropolis; urbanity; virtual city
city center 141
Clute, John 2, 24, 56, 58, 60
code 34, 37, 60, 86, 95, 96, 109, 118, 134, 137, 175; *see also* metacode
"The Commuter" 125, 132, 141, 166
computer 28, 90, 95, 122, 124, 125, 126, 137, 138–139, 142–143, 145, 149, 162, 165, 180
Conan Doyle, Arthur 26, 33, 34, 39, 41, 48, 63–64, 86–89, 92, 93, 98, 117, 118, 175; *see also* Challenger, Professor; Holmes, Sherlock; Watson, Doctor
Constable, Catherine 28
Cook, Guy 10
Coover, Robert 4, 70
Cortazar, Julio 4, 41
The Cosmic Puppets 131
Count Zero 28
Counter-clock World 9, 151
counterculture 133, 148
Craven, Wes 41
Cronenberg, David 28, 153
Crooked House 26, 40, 44–45, 52, 166, 175
Csicsery-Ronay, Istvan, Jr. 94, 100, 105–106, 126, 169, 178
Cthulhu (mythos) 73, 82, 89

Index

cultural liminality *see* institutional liminality
The Cyberiad 28, 114, 119
cyberpunk 5, 16, 20, 21, 22–23, 25, 28, 121–123, 125–128, 140, 142, 154–155, 156, 158, 161, 162, 165, 174, 179; *see also* proto-cyberpunk
cyberspace 20, 28–29, 121–126, 133, 137–140, 156, 161, 165, 179; *see also* virtual reality
cyborg 4, 21, 91, 114, 142, 146, 158, 170

Dadaism 126
danse macabre 77
Dark City (film) 125
D'Aulnoy, Madame 23, 83, 133
Day, Gary 42, 50
Debord, Guy 23, 133
De Certeau, Michel 2, 14, 19, 29, 54, 123, 164, 166, 180; see *also* walker
deconstruction 1, 3, 9–12, 24, 171, 176
Delany, Samuel 17, 22, 158
Deleuze, Gilles 1, 10, 16, 17–19, 21, 28, 29, 82, 121, 131, 133, 134–135, 137, 143, 163, 164, 166, 167, 173, 180
Del Toro, Guillermo 107
de Man, Paul 9, 11, 18, 67, 87, 150–151, 157, 163, 176
Derrida, Jacques 1, 9, 11–12, 13–14, 18, 23, 24, 29, 105, 106, 109, 114, 138, 163, 165, 166, 170, 173, 174, 175, 178; *see also* center; hymen; supplement
Dery, Mark 126
Detection Club 33
detective 26, 27, 32, 35–40, 42, 43, 45, 48, 49, 51, 52, 61, 63–64, 86–89, 90, 91, 93, 101, 103, 111, 117, 133, 175, 176, 177
detective writer 33, 36, 40, 42, 50
Dick, Philip K. 4, 5, 9, 16, 19–22, 28–29, 64, 90, 108, 118, 121–162, 165, 166, 167, 168, 169, 170, 179–180; "Adjustment Team" 125, 135; "The Commuter" 125, 132, 141, 166; *The Cosmic Puppets* 131; *Counter-clock World* 9, 151; *Do Androids...?* 29, 90, 126–127, 128, 133, 138, 146–147, 156; *Dr. Bloodmoney* 142, 144, 179; "The Electric Ant" 141, 142; *Eye in the Sky* 138, 140, 145, 148, 154, 167–168, 169; "Faith of Our Fathers" 149–150; "How to Build a Universe..." 136, 160–161; "I Hope I Shall Arrive Soon" 16, 138, 140, 141, 166, 168; *Lies, Inc.* 143, 151, 153, 155; "The Little Black Box" 138; *The Man in the High Castle* 29, 149–150;

Martian Time-Slip 29, 130, 136, 137, 142, 146, 157, 170; *A Maze of Death* 138, 139, 140, 166; "The Minority Report" 133; "Notes" 136, 180; *Radio Free Albemuth* 126, 142, 144, 158, 179; *A Scanner Darkly* 29, 133, 137, 142, 144, 146, 166, 170; "Second Variety" 90; "Small Town" 130; *The Three Stigmata of Palmer Eldritch* 16, 140, 141, 152–153, 167; *Time Out of Joint* 29, 134–135, 140, 141, 147–149, 179; *Ubik* 9, 29, 135, 137, 139, 141, 151, 153, 155; *We Can Build You* 29, 142, 145–146, 156; "What the Dead Men Say" 144, 145, 180
Do Androids...? 29, 90, 126–127, 128, 133, 138, 146–147, 156
Dr. Bloodmoney 142, 144, 179
Doctorow, Cory 23
Doctorow, E.L. 4
Dolezel, Lubomir 15, 74
doll 15, 111, 116–117
the Double 48, 111, 115–116, 118, 167, 178
Dostoyevsky, Fyodor 4–5
Dowd, Chris 58, 67, 69
dream 10, 17, 41, 58, 73, 77, 87, 98, 108, 115, 116, 122, 125, 129, 130–131, 132, 139, 142, 145, 148, 149,
dreamer 154
dreamworld 134–135, 138, 154
duality 11, 14, 28, 72, 171, 175; *see also* binary opposition
Duchamp, Marcel 126
Duff, David 24,
Duncan, Andy 152
dystopia 92, 134, 138, 150, 179

Easterbrook, Neil 94, 104, 105, 156
Eco, Umberto 25, 74, 82, 108, 109
Egan, Greg 23
Ekman, Stefan 72, 76, 77
"The Electric Ant" 141, 142
elevator 110, 124
Ellison, Ralph 76
Enns, Anthony 139
errant 138, 166
escalator 110
eXistenZ (film) 28, 153, 161
Eye in the Sky 138, 140, 145, 148, 154, 167–168, 169

fabula (fable) 33, 62, 64, 154
Faerie 56, 57, 75, 82, 176
fairy tales 20, 24, 46, 54, 57, 62, 68–71, 74, 80, 83, 140, 176, 177
"Faith of Our Fathers" 149–150

Faulkner, William 27
feminism 1, 3, 37, 42, 70, 99, 101, 104, 109, 111, 119, 171, 172
Fenkl, Heinz Insu 2, 24
Fiasco 91, 98–99, 106, 107, 108, 112, 117, 118–119, 168, 174
film noir 23, 128, 179
Fish, Stanley Eugene 10, 176
Fitting, Peter 135, 153
Five Little Pigs 42
flaneur 19, 26, 32, 38, 39, 51, 131, 132, 166
Fludernik, Monika 121, 155, 173
focal character 80, 154, 157
focalization 26, 40, 56, 66, 75, 81, 176
focalizer 66, 75, 78, 176
forking paths 3, 16, 17, 161, 162, 165
fort-da play 3, 104–106, 165
Foucault, Michel 1, 2, 13, 14, 16, 21, 27, 29, 56, 72, 75, 76, 94, 96, 97, 104–106, 133, 163, 164, 165, 170; *see also* heterotopia; panopticon; transgression
"Four-and-Twenty Blackbirds" 65
4.50 from Paddington 38, 41, 44, 45, 49
"The Four Suspects" 42
Fowles, John 4
Frank, Lawrence 86, 89
Freedman, Carl 23, 27, 100, 155, 178
Freud, Sigmund 81, 95, 104, 105, 113, 115–116, 118, 139, 140–141, 165, 175, 177, 178, 179; *see also* the Double; psychoanalysis; uncanny (Freud)
Freudian slip 140, 141
the Frontier (edge of civilization) 122, 133, 148, 173
frontier (borderline) 2, 13, 14, 24, 105, 109; *see also* border; boundary
Frye, Northrop 45, 53
"Further Reminiscences of Ijon Tichy" 119
The Futurological Congress 95, 174

Gaiman, Neil 4, 5, 19–21, 26, 54–83, 85, 164, 166, 168, 169, 170, 174, 176–177; *American Gods* 54, 75, 80, 177; *Anansi Boys* 54, 56, 69–70, 71, 74, 177; "Chivalry" 66–68, 81; *The Graveyard Book* 56, 74–80, 81, 82, 164, 166, 176; "How to Talk to Girls at Parties" 65, 66; "I, Cthulhu" 68, 81; "Murder Mysteries" 55, 59–61, 73, 80, 177; *Neverwhere* 56, 74–80, 81, 164, 166, 168; "Only the End of the World Again" 65, 73; *The Sandman* 69; "Shoggoth's Old Peculiar" 62, 73; "Snow, Glass, Apples" 62, 70–71, 81; "A Study in Emerald" 55, 61–64, 80, 82

garden of forking paths *see* forking paths
"The Garden of Forking Paths" 16
generic liminality 20, 55, 82, 90–94, 117, 170
Genette, Gerard 62–63, 64
genre 54–56, 57, 59, 61, 62, 64, 80–83, 85–86, 90, 92, 93, 99, 111, 114, 117, 118, 119, 164, 170, 172, 174, 175, 176, 177; *see also* subgenre
geography 2, 8, 23, 37, 76, 121, 125, 131, 141, 147
"The Gernsback Continuum" 126, 179
Gibson, William 28, 125–126, 128, 140, 143, 156, 158, 161, 179, 180; *Count Zero* 28; "The Gernsback Continuum" 126, 179; *Idoru* 125, 179; "Johnny Mnemonic" 158; *Mona Lisa Overdrive* 28, 125; *Neuromancer* 125, 140, 158, 179, 180; *Spook Country* 179
Gilbert, Sandra M. 70
Gill, Gillian 35, 37, 38, 41, 47
Gilman, Charlotte Perkins 5
Ginzburg, Carlo 34, 87
global village 124
Godwin, William 48, 64
Gogol, Nikolai V. 4
Golden Age (in detective fiction) 33, 39, 64, 176
Gothic 4, 26, 48, 49, 86
Grant, Glenn 126
The Graveyard Book 56, 74–80, 81, 82, 164, 166, 176
Grosz, Elisabeth 14, 121, 137, 164
grotesque body 9, 116–117
Groundhog Day (film) 157
Guattari, Felix 16, 17–19, 21, 29, 82, 121, 131, 133, 134, 135, 137, 143, 163, 164, 166, 167, 180; *see also* Deleuze, Gilles
Gubar, Susan 70

hacker 130, 133
hallucination 17, 108, 122, 135, 139, 141, 144, 146, 148, 150, 157
Hammett, Dashiel 33
Haraway, Donna 122, 142, 179
hard-boiled detective fiction 23, 33, 52, 53, 38, 65, 92, 101, 103, 176
"Harlequin's Lane" 39
Harries, Karsten 108
Harvey, David 110, 123–124, 125, 128–129, 130, 131, 133, 134, 147
Hayles, N. Katherine 108, 109, 114, 145, 156
Heidegger, Martin 168
Heinlein, Robert 90

Helford, Elyce Rae 99–100
Hemmingson, Michael 89
Hessel, Franz 70
heteroglossia 74
heterotopia 13, 16, 21, 74, 75–76, 164, 165
Hidalgo-Downing, Laura 74
hierarchy 3, 8, 9, 11, 12, 13, 15–16, 37, 43, 44, 46–47, 52, 53, 60, 77, 116, 122, 149, 165, 171, 178
Hills, Matt 6, 41, 76, 82, 174
His Master's Voice 95, 96, 98, 104, 109, 120, 174; "The Inquest" 90
historicity 4, 29, 147–148, 153, 180
historiographic metafiction 21, 152
Hitchhiker's Guide... 84
Hoffmann, E.T.A. 4, 116, 118
holey space 17, 180
Holland, Norman 42–43
Holmes, Sherlock 62–64, 82, 86–89, 91, 117, 175, 176, 177; *see also* Conan Doyle, Arthur; Watson, Doctor
Holquist, Michael 36
horror (genre) 54, 41, 48, 49, 50, 54, 59, 61, 64, 80, 81, 82, 97, 114, 157, 170, 174, 177
hotel 43, 102
house 5, 19, 34, 36, 37, 39, 42, 45, 46, 47, 48, 70, 78, 102, 130, 132, 138, 139, 140, 141, 167, 175, 179
house of mirrors 111
housewife 42, 134, 141
"How to Build a Universe..." 136, 160–161
"How to Talk to Girls at Parties" 65, 66
Hutcheon, Linda 21, 33, 50, 56, 62, 68, 81, 83, 152, 154; *see also* historiographic metafiction
Huyssen, Andreas 172
hybridity 3, 4, 11, 12–13, 19, 23, 24, 84, 86, 114, 121, 142, 177
hymen 12
hypertextuality 2, 62, 64, 80; *see also* Genette, Gerard; intertextuality

"I, Cthulhu" 68, 81
"I Hope I Shall Arrive Soon" 16, 138, 140, 141, 166, 168
"The Idol House of Astarte" 48, 49
Idoru 125, 179
immersive fantasy 57, 176; *see also* intrusion fantasy; liminal fantasy; Mendlesohn, Farah; portal-quest fantasy
immigrant 13, 18–19, 121
"Ingots of Gold" 42
insect 99, 118

institution 3, 22, 34, 81, 133, 137, 171–172, 174, 179
institutional liminality 20, 82
interstitial being 114
Interstitial Writing 24, 81, 164, 174
intertextuality 2, 21, 26, 59, 62–63, 72, 81–82, 158, 159, 170, 171, 177; *see also* hypertextuality
intrusion fantasy 57, 59, 61, 176; *see also* immersive fantasy; liminal fantasy; Mendlesohn, Farah; portal-quest fantasy
The Investigation 27, 92, 93, 110, 112, 119, 174
The Invincible 118, 167
invisibility 49, 72, 76–80, 114, 122, 146
Irigaray, Luce 27, 111, 112
irony 2, 9, 21, 28, 50, 55–59, 61, 62, 66–68, 72, 74, 80–81, 89, 98–104, 108, 118, 120, 128, 145, 148, 150–151, 152, 157, 160, 164, 169, 173, 176, 180
Irving, Washington 4
Iser, Wolfgang 55, 56, 67–68, 72, 177
island 46, 107

Jackson, Rosemary 2, 27
James, Henry 5, 58, 156
Jameson, Fredric 4, 20, 22, 23, 66, 110, 124, 125, 126, 128, 140, 147–149, 152, 169, 172, 180
Jarzebski, Jerzy 92, 106, 107, 119
Jencks, Charles 3, 13, 110, 122, 123, 125
Jenkins, Alice 75
Jenkins, Henry 24
"Johnny Mnemonic" 158
Johnny Mnemonic (film) 128
jouissance 129
Joyce, James 62
Jung, C.G. 107

Kafalenos, Emma 2
Kafka, Franz 5, 20, 57, 92, 105–106, 143, 164, 174
Kandel, Michael 90,
Kipling, Rudyard 82
Kittler, Friedrich 143–144
Klee, Paul 126
Knight, Stephen 40, 42
Knights of the Holy Contact 101, 102, 111
Knox, Ronald 33
Kuhn, Thomas S. 31, 89, 94

labyrinth 3, 13, 14, 17–19, 28, 79, 87, 99, 107–111, 112, 118, 123, 140, 141, 152, 161, 164, 165, 173; *see also* maze

Lacan, Jacques 1, 3, 27, 85, 99, 100, 104–105, 113, 118, 165, 174
Lang, Fritz 128
Lee, Taniath 70
Le Fanu, Sheridan 4
Lefebvre, Henri 2, 3, 7, 76, 163, 179
Le Guin, Ursula K. 22
Lejeune, Philippe 24, 55
Lem, Stanisław 4, 5, 19, 19–21, 25, 27–28, 84–120, 164, 166, 167, 168, 169, 170, 174, 177–178; "Altruizine" 114, 179; *The Chain of Chance* 27, 92–93, 98, 99, 101–103, 110, 118, 119, 166, 168, 174; *The Cyberiad* 28, 114, 119; *Fiasco* 91, 98–99, 106, 107, 108, 112, 117, 118–119, 168, 174; "Further Reminiscences of Ijon Tichy" 119; *The Futurological Congress* 95, 174; *His Master's Voice* 95, 96, 98, 104, 109, 120, 174; "The Inquest" 90; *The Investigation* 27, 92, 93, 110, 112, 119, 174; *The Invincible* 118, 167; "The Mask" 91, 114, 170, 177, 178; *Memoirs Found in a Bathtub* 94, 105–106, 109; *Peace on Earth* 90, 178; "Pirx's Tale" 98, 99; *Return from the Stars* 27, 93, 98–104, 109, 110, 112, 113, 115, 166, 174, 178; "The Seventh Sally..." 119; *Solaris* 20, 27, 85, 93, 94–100, 101, 103, 104–106, 107, 111, 112, 114, 115, 116, 118, 120, 167, 168, 174, 178; *The Star Diaries* 28, 102, 119, 178; "Tale of the Three Storytelling..." 95–96, 108, 114, 120, 174
Lewis, C.S. 57, 165
Lies, Inc. 143, 151, 153, 155
limbo 2, 7, 168, 171
liminal fantasy 21, 26, 54, 56–59, 65–68, 81, 83, 177; *see also* immersive fantasy; intrusion fantasy; Mendlesohn, Farah; portal-quest fantasy
Link, Kelly 60, 174
"The Little Black Box" 138
London (city) 36, 39, 44, 63, 64, 75–79, 92, 110, 177
Lotman, Jurij M. 171
Lovecraft, H.P. 23, 61, 62–63, 64–65, 68, 73, 81, 82, 97, 177
Luckhurst, Roger 125, 126
Lyotard, Jean François 23, 26

Machine Age 126
magic realism 57
mainstream criticism 23, 172, 174
mainstream literature 3, 4, 5, 20, 22, 26, 82, 110, 171, 172
Malmgren, Carl 2, 27, 33, 40, 52, 55, 118

"The Man from the Sea" 48
The Man in the High Castle 29, 149–150
map 2, 64, 123, 130–131, 132
mapping 28, 123, 128–131, 140, 161, 168, 179
Marple, Jane 35, 38, 42, 44, 48–50
Martian Time-Slip 29, 130, 136, 137, 142, 146, 157, 170
Marx, Karl 131, 144
mask 22, 44, 46, 52, 117, 166, 180
"The Mask" 91, 114, 170, 177, 178
Massey, Doreen 163, 165, 179–180
mathematics 100, 101, 125, 145
matrix 28, 122, 124, 125, 158
The Matrix (film) 119, 144
The Matrix Revolutions (film) 117
The Matrix Trilogy 28, 161
maze 16, 107–11, 123, 138, 139, 140, 141, 154, 155, 162, 166; *see also* labyrinth
A Maze of Death 138, 139, 140, 166
McCaffery, Larry 23, 126
McHale, Brian 2, 4, 6, 15–17, 21, 22, 25, 27, 28, 57, 60, 67, 74, 81, 85, 110, 122, 140, 154, 155, 156, 161, 162, 164, 169, 170, 171, 173, 174, 176, 179
McLuhan, Marshall 23, 124, 145
Melville, Herman 118
Memoirs Found in a Bathtub 94, 105–106, 109
Mendlesohn, Farah 2, 21, 26, 56, 57–60, 65, 66–67, 75, 81, 83, 174, 176–177; *see also* immersive fantasy; intrusion fantasy; liminal fantasy; portal-quest fantasy
Merrill, Robert 39, 40, 48–49
metacode 89
metafiction 2, 21, 40, 41, 56, 60, 67, 68, 72, 75, 80, 152, 155, 158, 169, 174
metalepsis 2, 15, 60, 72, 108, 154, 156,
metaphysical detective fiction 5, 25, 27, 29, 84, 90–91, 108, 110, 118, 176
metropolis 92, 125
Metropolis (film) 128, 144, 179
Metz, Christian 146
Meyer Nicholas 88, 177
Mezei, Kathy 37, 38, 40, 44, 47
Miller, Arthur 130
Miller, J. Hillis 1–2, 3, 12, 14, 21, 109, 165, 174, 176; *see also* parasite
mimicry 12–13, 112, 167
Minkowski, Eugene 147
"The Minority Report" 133
Mirrlees, Hope 5, 83
mirror 3, 27–28, 58, 67, 85, 94, 104, 107, 108, 111–117, 118
mirror stage 27, 85

Index

mirroring with a rupture *see* revenge of the mirror
Mirrorshades 161
mise-en-abyme 41, 60, 72, 98, 150, 155, 170
Mitchell, William J. 124, 142
Modern Times (film) 144
modernity (modernism) 2, 4, 8, 13, 20, 22, 25, 46, 56, 62, 85, 122, 123–130, 132, 147–148, 166
Mona Lisa Overdrive 28, 125
monster 4, 31, 32, 64, 70–71, 111, 114–115, 118, 119, 139, 177
monstrosity 70, 78, 114–115
Moore, Charles 125
Moretti, Franco 39, 44, 86, 164, 175, 176
Moskowitz, Sam 26, 88
Mostly Harmless 16, 84, 180
The Mousetrap 41, 43, 64, 166
multiplicity 3, 4, 14–16, 28–29, 51, 94, 121, 147, 154, 160–172
Mulvey, Laura 3, 27, 113
"Murder Mysteries" 55, 59–61, 73, 80, 177
The Murder of Roger Ackroyd 40, 61
Murder on the Orient Express 26, 40, 44, 51, 166, 175
Murder, She Said (film) 41
"The Murders in the Rue Morgue" 36, 175
The Mysterious Affair at Styles 36, 38, 41
The Mysterious Mr. Quin 44, 49, 50
"The Mystery of Marie Roget" 175

Nabokov, Vladimir 25
narrative liminality 4, 21, 55, 82, 121, 164
narrative perspective *see* focalization; perspective (in storytelling); voice (in storytelling)
narratology 1, 2, 15, 33, 65, 172, 179
network 28, 122, 124, 142, 144, 152, 154, 179
Neuromancer 125, 140, 158, 179, 180
Neverwhere 56, 74–80, 81, 164, 166, 168
New Wave Fabulists 20, 24, 26, 55, 60, 81, 174, 177
New Wave movement 20, 22, 158
New Weird 24, 164, 174
New York (city) 127, 128
Newman, Kim 82
Nicholls, Peter 97
Nietzsche, Friedrich 9, 10, 11, 18, 84, 87, 95, 97, 107, 108–109, 143, 164, 171, 180
Nikolajeva, Maria 77, 78, 79
1950s 24, 92, 134, 148–149, 152, 154, 158, 169
1960s 22, 23, 35, 128, 149, 152, 154
1970s 22

1980s 22
nomad 18–19, 131, 134, 139, 165, 166, 180
nomadism 134
nomadology 121
Noon, Jeff 133
nostalgia 3, 43, 66, 123–128, 134, 148, 173
"Notes" 136, 180
novice 8, 78, 80, 107
Nudelman, Rafail 107, 115

ocean 73, 93, 96, 99, 100, 106, 107, 116, 178
O'Farrell, Clare 1
"Only the End of the World Again" 65, 73
Ordeal by Innocence 26, 40, 45–47, 48, 52, 166
oscillation 2, 3, 13, 14, 21, 54, 68, 81, 85, 86, 100, 104, 114, 163, 164, 165
the Other 2, 21, 27, 43, 71, 85, 96, 99, 104–106, 111, 113, 114, 118, 144, 167, 171
other spaces *see* heterotopia
otherness 12, 99

pact autobiographical 24, 55; detective fiction 55; fantastic 55; generic (genre) 24, 170; narrative 54–55
Palmer, Christopher 156, 158–160, 166
Panek, LeRoy 26, 48, 50
panopticon 19, 133
Pan's Labyrinth (film) 107
paradigm 1, 4, 5, 24, 25, 31, 85, 88, 94–98, 106, 128, 177
parasite 2, 12
paraspace 17, 20, 29, 121–122, 133, 137, 139, 140, 141, 151–154, 158, 161, 162, 165, 167, 169,
Paris (city) 98, 128–30
pastiche 2, 62, 82, 89
Pavel, Thomas 15, 74–75
Peace on Earth 90, 178
Peirce, Charles S. 87
Pelan, John 82
Penfield, Wilder 146–147
permanent liminality 8, 173
permanent parabasis 67
Perrault, Charles 83
Person, Lawrence 23
perspective (in storytelling) 2, 3, 4, 21, 26, 38, 55, 56–59, 66, 67–72, 75, 81, 83, 156–157, 162, 164, 168, 170, 171, 177; *see also* focalization; voice (in storytelling)
pharmakos 45, 52; *see also* scapegoat
Philmus, Robert M. 94
photograph 65, 67, 169

photography 126, 146, 169, 180
Picabia, Francis 126
Pierce, Hazel Beasley 26, 47, 48, 85, 86
"Pirx's Tale" 98, 99
Plato 134
play (activity) 3, 8–9, 23, 26, 52, 62, 94, 100, 105–106, 118, 129, 139, 165, 168, 173, 178
play (genre) 41, 53
pleasure center 146
Poe, Edgar Allan 4, 26, 33, 34, 36, 41, 48, 58, 64, 81, 89, 91, 175; "The Murders in the Rue Morgue" 36, 175; "The Mystery of Marie Roget" 175; "The Purloined Letter" 175; "Thou Art the Man" 91
poet 150
poet laureate 148
poetics 3, 25
poetry 95, 158
point-of-view *see* focalization; perspective (in storytelling); voice (in storytelling)
Poirot, Hercule 35, 36, 38, 40, 41, 42, 48–49, 175
Pollock, Georges 41
portal 21, 44, 107, 142
portal-quest fantasy 57–58, 59, 60, 75, 176; *see also* immersive fantasy; intrusion fantasy; liminal fantasy; Mendlesohn, Farah
possible worlds 15, 26, 66, 72–75
Pratchett, Terry 76, 89, 176
programmer 122
proto-cyberpunk 20, 29, 123, 126, 161
proto-science fiction 26, 48
psychoanalysis 1, 3, 27, 95, 104, 107, 118, 119, 172
psychology 7, 20, 23, 27, 29, 39, 41–43, 51, 56, 71, 88, 90, 93, 97, 98, 100, 104, 139, 147, 167, 175, 178, 180
"The Purloined Letter" 175
puzzle 31, 33, 36, 39, 40, 42, 43, 49, 85, 89, 90–93, 118, 134, 150, 175, 178

quantum physics 122

Radcliffe, Ann 48
Radio Free Albemuth 126, 142, 144, 158, 179
Rajchman, John 72
rationalism 31–32, 50, 85–86, 117
Rattray, R.S. 69
realism 1, 20, 72, 85, 148, 174
Reaves, Michael 82, 174
remembering 61, 131, 139
remembrance *see* remembering

Return from the Stars 27, 93, 98–104, 109, 110, 112, 113, 115, 166, 174, 178
revenge of the mirror 85, 111–117, 118, 165, 167, 178, 179
Revzin, I.I. 33, 48
rhizome 3, 17–19, 21, 28, 109, 121, 155, 161, 162, 164, 165, 173; *see also* Deleuze, Gilles; Guattari, Felix; labyrinth
Rice, Anne 71
Ricoeur, Paul 33
Rimmon-Kenan, Shlomith 65, 75
rite-of-passage 14, 104, 107, 122
Robbe-Grillet, Alain 27
robot 90–91, 93, 95–96, 102, 114, 115, 116, 119, 120, 142, 145, 146, 147, 177; *see also* automaton
rocket 99; *see also* space ship
Rose, Frank 20
Rose, Mark 99, 118
Rossi, Umberto 135, 148, 179
Rust, Richard Dilworth 58, 60
Ryan, Marie-Laure 2, 15, 16, 72, 73, 154, 177

Saler, Michael 86, 88, 89
The Sandman 69
Sawyer, Andy 6, 31, 85
Sayers, Dorothy 33, 50
A Scanner Darkly 29, 133, 137, 142, 144, 146, 166, 170
scapegoat 44, 45, 52; *see also* pharmakos
schizoid android 145–146
schizophrenia 21, 134, 136–137, 139, 142, 145, 146, 153, 156, 157, 164, 166, 167–168, 170
Schweitzer, Darrell 62
sci-fi 22, 98, 99
science 12, 31, 84, 85, 86–89, 92, 93, 94–98, 100, 108, 113, 117, 142, 171, 174
Scream (film) 41
"Second Variety" 90
semiotics 34, 42, 81, 87, 164, 172
"The Seventh Sally..." 119
Shadowrun 23
Shakespeare, William 95, 117, 118
Shapiro, Gary 87
Shaw, Marion 35, 38, 42, 43, 44, 47, 49, 50, 52, 175
Shelley, Mary 4, 115
Shklovsky, Viktor 32, 37, 39, 50, 64
"Shoggoth's Old Peculiar" 62, 73
Silverman, Kaja 105
simulacrum 43, 21, 23, 28, 43, 107, 122, 123, 131, 133–141, 148–149, 150, 156, 161, 170
sjuzet (plot) 33

skyscraper 125, 128
slip of the tongue 95, 179; see also Freudian slip
Slipstream 24, 164, 174
"Small Town" 130
Smethurst, Paul 1, 9, 124, 147, 161, 167, 171, 180
"Snow, Glass, Apples" 62, 70–71, 81
social criticism 23, 76, 148
social science 161, 164, 179
Soja, Edward J. 2
Solaris 20, 27, 85, 93, 94–100, 101, 103, 104–106, 107, 111, 112, 114, 115, 116, 118, 120, 167, 168, 174, 178
Solaristics 96–97, 108
space opera 111
space ship 91, 99, 101, 102, 138, 166
Spanos, William J. 25
spectacle 23, 66, 102, 126, 128–130, 133, 137, 148
Spook Country 179
Stallybrass, Peter 9
The Star Diaries 28, 102, 119, 178
steampunk 126
Steiner, T.R. 92, 101, 103
Stephenson, Neal 23
Sterling, Bruce 121, 142, 161
Sterne, Laurence 4
Stockwell, Peter 174
"Strange Jest" 42
strange loops *see* metalepsis
Stross, Charles 23
structuralism 3, 33, 34, 53
"A Study in Emerald" 55, 61–64, 80, 82
subculture 82, 177, 179
subgenre 40, 57, 59, 64, 107, 111, 152, 164
subject (in philosophy) 2, 3, 4, 7, 8, 12, 27, 47, 85, 87, 104–105, 111, 116, 121, 137, 140, 142–145, 161, 164, 166–168, 174, 178
suburb 121, 124, 132, 134, 141, 148
subway 77, 180; *see also* underworld
supplement 12, 34, 170
Surrealism 174, 178
Suvin, Darko 93, 97, 115, 154, 180
Swanstrom, Linda 21, 122, 179, 180
Sweeney, Susan Elisabeth 91, 25, 91, 108, 110, 118
Swirski, Peter 20, 23, 92, 93, 94, 102, 120, 174
Symons, Julian 33, 39, 64
Szakolczai, Arpad 8, 173

"Tale of the Three Storytelling..." 95–96, 108, 114, 120, 174

teleology 13, 18, 108, 151, 154, 166
television 126, 134, 144, 145, 146, 148, 155, 158
terminal identity 20, 29
thematic liminality 4, 21, 55, 56, 82, 117
"There Are More Things" 82, 119
The Thirteen Problems 26, 38, 42, 48, 49, 50, 167
The 13th Floor (film) 15, 28, 128, 161
Thomsen, Christian W. 90, 119
"Thou Art the Man" 91
The Three Stigmata of Palmer Eldritch 16, 140, 141, 152–153, 167
threshold 7, 8, 12, 57, 115, 165, 170, 179
Todorov 2, 21, 24, 26, 32–33, 34, 35, 40, 56, 58, 60, 61, 66, 71, 164, 177
Tolkien, J.R.R. 55, 56–58, 81, 82, 176; *see also* Faerie
Tomas, David 21, 122
tourism 93, 102, 131–132, 166
Traill, Nancy H. 55, 66, 67, 72, 176–177
train 36, 41, 44, 77–78, 124, 126, 130, 132, 141, 166, 180
transgression 2, 3, 7, 12–15, 24–25, 34, 40–41, 48, 51, 54, 60, 61, 66, 72, 85, 94, 105, 114, 116, 122, 155, 167, 170, 171, 173, 177
translation 12, 95, 97, 120, 156, 178
traveler 38, 122, 131–132, 134, 137–140
traveller-flaneur 131, 132
Truzzi, Marcello 34, 87
"The Tuesday Night Club" 47, 49
Turner, Victor 1, 2, 7–9, 13, 14, 24, 44, 45–46, 53, 78, 81, 161, 163, 164, 171, 173
twilight zone 77, 132
"The Two Kings" 109
typewriter 126, 143

Ubik 9, 29, 135, 137, 139, 141, 151, 153, 155
uncanny (Freud) 27, 28, 81, 109, 113, 115–116, 167, 178
uncanny (Todorov) 24, 26, 61, 177
underground 17, 23, 75, 101, 109, 166, 180; *see also* subway
underworld 46, 75–80, 166, 176; *see also* subway
urban fantasy 23
urbanity 2, 3, 13, 19, 28, 29, 39, 110, 121–128, 130–131, 133, 144, 161, 164, 165, 166
Uspenskij, B.A. (Uspensky) 171
utopia 57, 107, 109, 123, 125, 129, 130, 132, 134, 135, 138, 140, 148–149, 166, 179

V (television series) 90
vagabond 119, 131–132, 166

Vanacker, Sabine 35, 38, 42, 43, 44, 47, 49, 50, 52, 175
Van Dine, S.S. 33, 34
Van Gennep, Arnold 7, 46
Verne, Jules 118
Videodrome (film) 28
Vidocq, François 64
Vinge, Vernor 161
Virilio, Paul 23, 122, 131, 133, 138, 140, 141, 142
virtual city 128, 130, 165
virtual reality 28, 119, 122, 130, 131, 137, 138, 141–142, 153, 154 161, 165, 180; *see also* cyberspace
visibility 14, 56, 71, 109, 143, 158; *see also* invisibility
voice (in storytelling) 21, 26, 56, 58, 65, 66, 67, 71, 73, 74, 81, 177; *see also* focalization; perspective (in storytelling)
von Franz, Marie-Louise 107
Vonnegut, Kurt 4, 9, 159

walker 19, 166, 180
Walker, Daniel 97
Watson, Doctor 39, 45, 63–64, 175; *see also* Conan Doyle, Arthur; Holmes, Sherlock
Watson, Ian 153

We Can Build You 29, 142, 145–146, 156
Weinstone, Ann 104, 114
Wellman, Manly Wade 89
Wellman, Wade 89
Wells, H.G. 5, 86, 89
Werth, Paul 74
Westfahl, Gary 128
"What the Dead Men Say" 144, 145, 180
White, Allon 9
White, Hayden 89, 153
Whittle, David B. 122, 161
Wilde, Oscar 5
Winnicott, D.W. 178
Wolfe, Gary K. 6, 24, 27, 69, 79, 99, 107, 108, 114, 164, 174
Wolfe, Gene 60
Wolk, Anthony 135, 146, 147
Wollen, Peter 128
World War II 92, 149–151
wormhole 17
Wright, Frank Lloyd 128

xenophobia 107

Yossef, Abraham 97, 178

Zipes, Jack 6, 57, 69, 83, 176
Zukin, Sharon 3